48 TOP NOTCH TRACK PLANS

MODEL RAILROAD HANDBOOK NO. 39

FROM  MAGAZINE

Selected by Bob Hayden

KALMBACH BOOKS

Cover design: Lawrence Luser
Editorial Intern: Jennifer Kamke Black

The material in this book has previously appeared as articles in Model
Railroader magazine. The articles are reproduced here in their entirety.

11 10 09 08 07   7 8 9 10 11

Library of Congress-in-Publication Data

48 top notch track plans / from Model railroader magazine.
        p. cm. -- (Model railroad handbook no. 39)
     ISBN 978-0-89024-190-5
      1. Railroads--Models. I. Title: Forty-eight top notch track
plans. II. Series.
TF197.A135 1993
625.1'9--dc20   93-30051
                    CIP

Doodling by the squares

A master track planner shows you the basics of sketching a good track plan

BY JOHN ARMSTRONG

HOW do you take that first step toward designing a railroad that will make the best use of your layout area? You never have as much space as you'd really like, of course, so finding the arrangement that comfortably fits the most railroading into your garage, basement, spare room, or attic can be worth considerable thought and squirming. What you need is a quick and sketchy planning method that's orderly and accurate enough to avoid major disappointments when the time comes to break out the ruler and compass and attempt a scale drawing of the final plan. That's what "by the squares" track plan doodling is all about.

THE SQUARE

The key to this doodling method is the "square," a unit of measurement that allows you to represent the area available with a freehand grid upon which you can doodle your ideas. The basic track-planning square is defined and illustrated in fig. 1.

Note that the size of a square is determined by the sharpness of curve you have selected (tentatively in many cases at this stage) as your minimum mainline radius.

Figure 1 also shows how model railroad curves can be classified as sharp, conventional, or broad. The spacing between curved parallel tracks is the minimum necessary to prevent sideswiping. Allow a bit more if you are planning on running really long equipment on really tight curves. The square allows enough margin to avoid rubbing the corner steps off cars as they approach the walls, and locomotives are prevented from coming too close to the layout's edge for the comfort of the faint-hearted brass owner.

WHERE THE SQUARES HELP

If you have only enough room for a coffee-table-size railroad in N gauge or must make do with a 4 x 8-foot conventional-curve railroad in HO, then you are pretty well limited to a figure 8 or an oval and there is little that planning by the squares can do to help. In either case you have only a 2-square by 4-square grid in which to plan.

In any larger space, whether the increased number of squares is achieved by going to a smaller scale, pushing out the horizons, or adopting a tighter radius (as by going into traction or narrow gauge),

translating your space into a framework of squares within which to let your imagination run free may well prove worthwhile. It could help you hit upon a good arrangement that might not otherwise be obvious. It might let you quickly try out enough other possibilities to give you confidence that no radically better scheme has been overlooked.

A MODEL ROOM

Let's look at how the method works by taking a fairly common space situation, an 11 x 16-foot, completely walled room as shown in fig. 2, and beating a couple of radically different sets of model railroading desires against it. Many situations aren't this firmly defined, incidentally, and have only two or three boundaries set by immovable and impenetrable walls, with other limits being a matter of family political considerations. The "one end of the basement" situation is a good example. Here the squares may really come into their own

TYPICAL SQUARE SIZES		N	HO	O
SHARP CURVES Suitable for four-axle diesels, 40-foot freight cars	Min. radius	10"	18"	33"
	2X track center spacing	2 x 1¼"	2 x 2"	2 x 4"
	Square size	12½"	22"	41"
CONVENTIONAL CURVES All diesels, 2-8-2s, and shorty passenger cars operate well and don't look too repulsive	Min. radius	13"	24"	43½"
	2X track center spacing	2 x 1¼"	2 x 2"	2 x 4"
	Square size	15½"	28"	51½"
BROAD CURVES Will handle all equipment with normal modifications and good, if not great, appearance	Min. radius	16½"	30"	54"
	2X track center spacing	2 x 1¼"	2 x 2"	2 x 4"
	Square size	19"	34"	62"

Fig. 1

Track-center spacing x 2
Basic square size
Minimum radius

FIG. 2 THE SPACE...

FIG. 3 ...AS IT LOOKS IN TERMS OF HO BROAD-RADIUS SQUARES

16'

42"

30"

30"

76"

11'

DOUBLE-HUNG WINDOWS — OCCASIONAL ACCESS DESIRABLE BUT NOT ESSENTIAL

DOOR — MAY BE REHUNG TO SWING OUTWARD IF NECESSARY

30" 24"

$$\text{LENGTH} = \frac{16 \times 12}{34} = 5.65 \text{ SQUARES} - \text{CALL IT } 5\frac{1}{2}$$

$$\text{WIDTH} = \frac{11 \times 12}{34} = 3.9 \text{ SQUARES} - \text{CALL IT } 4$$

W

W

DOORWAY — A LITTLE LESS THAN ONE SQUARE WIDE AND A LITTLE MORE THAN ½ SQUARE FROM THE CORNER

as they "make perfectly clear to any right-thinking person" just what wonderful possibilities open up if only another foot or two is made available. I offer no guarantees on the outcome of such discussions, of course!

For easier comparison of principles involved, our examples will be in HO.

BROAD CURVES AND TRAINS TO MATCH

First, let's imagine designing a railroad to fit this space for a friend who wants to run passenger cars behind long-overhang steam locomotives. He wants his equipment to run freely and look good while rounding broad-radius curves. He wants scenic realism, so trackage along the walls with backdrop murals extending the apparent size of the modest empire is pretty much a foregone conclusion. Our friend sees little likelihood of having to move, so we don't have to include features to accommodate relocation.

For broad curves in HO a square is 34" on a side, and our space works out to 3.9 x 5.65 squares, as shown in fig. 3. For practical doodling we round off these figures in a conservative (usually downward) direction to the nearest half or third of a square, leaving us with a 4 x 5½-square grid with a doorway in the lower right corner.

Since we're going to eyeball-in curves on the basis of what we know will go into a square, rather than use a compass on a nicely drawn grid, the size and squareness of our sketch is unimportant; a felt-tip pen on a paper napkin at the greasy spoon becomes a perfectly adequate combination for trying out a sudden inspiration.

WALKING IN AND AROUND

We approach the track-planning process with several goals in mind. First of all, for any layout beyond large-table size, a prime consideration is access to all the trackwork (turnouts particularly) so you can lay and

maintain the right-of-way in reasonable comfort.

Medium and larger layouts are a lot more enjoyable and satisfying if they're of a "walk-in" design with no-stoop aisleways leading to all operationally important and scenically attractive parts of the railroad. With walkaround cabs (controls which let you follow a train along its route) now widely available, it's also highly desirable that a track plan allow you to move along with a train from its origin to destination without having to double back or duck under the benchwork en route. Though these goals aren't always attainable, particularly in smaller pikes where they're also not quite so important, they should always be among the most sought-after features of the "ultimate" track plan. Success isn't likely to just happen — the goals must be kept in mind from the start, and the more arrangements you can try, the better the chance that something ideal will turn up.

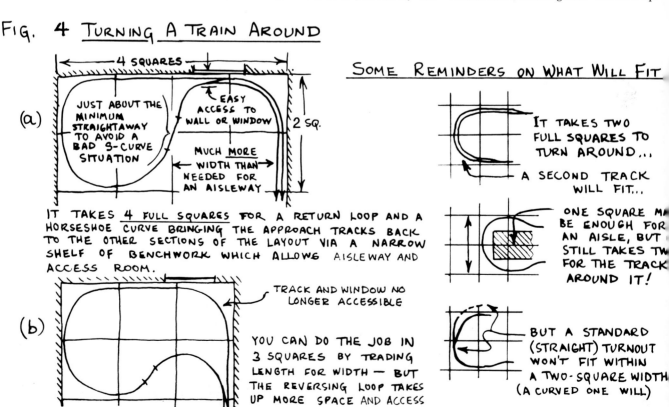

FIG. 4 TURNING A TRAIN AROUND

4 SQUARES

(a) JUST ABOUT THE MINIMUM STRAIGHTAWAY TO AVOID A BAD S-CURVE SITUATION

EASY ACCESS TO WALL OR WINDOW

2 SQ.

MUCH MORE WIDTH THAN NEEDED FOR AN AISLEWAY

IT TAKES 4 FULL SQUARES FOR A RETURN LOOP AND A HORSESHOE CURVE BRINGING THE APPROACH TRACKS BACK TO THE OTHER SECTIONS OF THE LAYOUT VIA A NARROW SHELF OF BENCHWORK WHICH ALLOWS AISLEWAY AND ACCESS ROOM.

(b)

TRACK AND WINDOW NO LONGER ACCESSIBLE

YOU CAN DO THE JOB IN 3 SQUARES BY TRADING LENGTH FOR WIDTH — BUT THE REVERSING LOOP TAKES UP MORE SPACE AND ACCESS SUFFERS.

SOME REMINDERS ON WHAT WILL FIT

IT TAKES TWO FULL SQUARES TO TURN AROUND...

A SECOND TRACK WILL FIT...

ONE SQUARE MAY BE ENOUGH FOR AN AISLE, BUT STILL TAKES TWO FOR THE TRACK AROUND IT!

BUT A STANDARD (STRAIGHT) TURNOUT WON'T FIT WITHIN A TWO-SQUARE WIDTH (A CURVED ONE WILL)

G. 5 WHAT CAN YOU DO IN 4×5½?

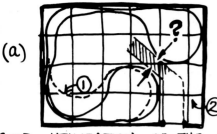

(a)

DOGBONE – AISLEWAY FOR WALK-IN MAY BE A BIT TIGHT BUT ALTER-NATE ALIGNMENT AT ① WILL EASE IT, IF NECES-SARY, WITHOUT TOO MUCH DAMAGE.

GOOD UTILIZATION OF THE PRIME SPACE AT ② MAY BE DIFFICULT IN A PASSENGER-ORIENTED RAILROAD.

(b)

OUT & BACK

AN OUT-AND-BACK PLAN WOULD ALLOW AMPLE ACCESS, BUT THE SHORT MAINLINE RUN BETWEEN TRAIN-TURNING OPERATIONS IS NOT COMPATIBLE WITH TRACK-PLAN PRIORITIES OPERATIONS.

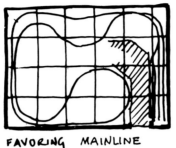

FAVORING MAINLINE

(c)

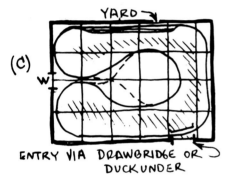

ENTRY VIA DRAWBRIDGE OR DUCKUNDER

ALONG-THE-WALL

ACCEPTING A DUCKUNDER ENTREE TO A HORSESHOE-SHAPED AISLEWAY WITHIN AN ALONG-THE-WALL PLAN CAN RESULT IN A LONGER MAIN LINE, A MAXIMUM-LENGTH YARD LOCATION, AND CONTINUOUS-RUN OR LOOP-TO-LOOP OPTIONS.

FOR ACCESS TO WINDOW AT LEFT, ENTIRE PLAN SHOULD BE FLIPPED, LEFT-TO-RIGHT.

FIG. 6 SAME SPACE, MORE SQUARES...

"SHARP" CURVES (18" MIN. MAINLINE RADIUS) = 22" SQUARES

W

ONE SQUARE

TYPICAL MINIMUM AISLEWAY

DOORWAY – 1½ SQUARES WIDE AND ABOUT ONE SQUARE FROM THE CORNER

LENGTH = $\frac{16 \times 12}{22}$ = 8.7 SQUARES — CALL IT 8½.

WIDTH = $\frac{11 \times 12}{22}$ = 6 SQUARES, EXACTLY

One of the most frequently needed track configurations for the walk-in pike is the return loop. It's also something that will stubbornly take up a certain amount of space no matter how clever or determined you are. So, a first step in the by-the-squares planning process is observing the number and arrangement of squares required to do the trick. Fig. 4 shows some basic return-loop configurations as well as the minimum area, in squares, that should be allowed for them.

MAINTAINING THOSE AISLES

So, coming down to cases in our 4 x 5½-square space, we can try a bent dogbone with an opening near the doorway, as shown in fig. 5. This gives us that highly desirable walk-in plan, provided those end bends leave enough room for a minimum-width aisleway leading to the interior. Notice that the aisle squeezes down to about one of our broad-radius squares, or about 22″ wide. This width would not be adequate for a long passageway but is okay as a short bottleneck leading to a wider operating area, particularly for a railroad which will usually be operated by its owner alone or with only one or two others.

It's hard to tell exactly how much leeway we do have in this particular situation. Certainly the aisle would be tight, and only a single track of the full mainline radius would be practical at the end-loop locations — too bad, since end loops are ideal places for passing tracks. Should the aisle prove too skinny when the plan is drawn to scale, a modest modification to the lower loop (moving it to the left as per fig. 4b) would ease the jam, so this can be considered a low-risk plan for further development.

The limited possibilities for efficient use of the leg-shaped space at the lower right of the plan pose a more serious question as to the overall merit of this plan. It would make a good diesel locomotive terminal, but our generous curves are aimed at big steam power. As a stub passenger terminal, it has possibilities, but probably for short trains only. So, we try again.

The out-and-back plan of fig. 5 has no access-aisle problems, but it is again incompatible with the basic desire to run long mainline trains in a pattern of fairly dense traffic. Try as you will, there is no way to come up with a combination of a stub terminal and an out-and-back operation feeding into a continuous-run main line that isn't essentially the plan of fig. 5 that we've already rejected.

STOOPING TO CONQUER

An alternative is some form of the doughnut, wherein a single duckunder (or drawbridge opening) gives entry to a suitably contorted "hole" with access to the entire main line. This is usually a second choice in comparison to a walk-in arrangement, but it's far superior to some of the "gopher prairie" pikes of yesteryear where train running meant considerable time spent scurrying about under the railroad between scattered pop-up openings.

Trying the doughnut approach in our example leads to a plan which preserves the large-radius main line, allows maximum yard length, is compatible with continuous or loop-to-loop operation, and in general looks like the best compromise for this situation. If the railroad is built fairly high —

and it can be since we have only a short reach in to any of the trackage — the occasional forays out for coffee, forgotten tools, and the telephone needn't be too crippling.

Sometimes a walk-in design may not be the best overall solution. In this case, examining alternatives via the sloppy squares has provided some confidence that stooping once to conquer is the best answer.

MOBILITY AND SHORT CARS

Now for our second example. Consider designing a railroad to fit the same room for a friend who figures he will have to move in the not-too-distant future and wants to be able to take his railroad with him. He favors complex dispatching of numerous trains over a single-track main line with frequent passing tracks. Short trains of limber equipment (old-time, narrow gauge, or freight-only diesel, perhaps) are accepted as part of the price to be paid.

Under these ground rules we can consider sharp curve standards and our square shrinks to 22" on a side. Our space now balloons to 6 x 8½+ squares, as shown in fig. 6, but a couple of important considerations now reveal themselves. Notice that access areas now take up more squares, since the squares are now smaller, so any aisleway that will allow two people to pass each other easily is at least a full square wide (a square-and-a-half, 31", would be far more comfortable) and the doorway is about a square-and-a-half wide.

For this second railroad we'll consider an "island" arrangement, since it offers advantages for a pike that might be relocated. The likelihood of finding a new home that has an area enough like the previous habitat of an around-the-wall layout for it to fit in readily is not at all good, but a freestanding railroad can be reassembled in almost any space that's at least as large as its predecessor and of the same general shape. If additional length or width becomes available, there is not much problem in expanding the layout to match, but taking tucks in a plan that already fills its space to the limits is usually out of the question. So, in trying out ideas for the situation we'll allow room between the railroad and the wall on at least two sides.

A rectangular platform with a one-square-wide aisle surrounding it would mean a two-square reach to the center. That's still 44" with our sharp-radius curves — far too long a reach! The area needs to be "ventilated" with notches or an internal aisleway to the central area. A doughnut with a duckunder to a central operating slot is an alternative, but unattractive in this situation where you'd be ducking back and forth between trackage and scenes on the inside and outside edges of the railroad.

If we run a single "fjord" into the interior, as shown in fig. 7, we have a horseshoe. We don't have space enough for a free-standing horseshoe that you could walk all around, but you can still follow a train on its entire run, provided you design a point-to-point, out-and-back, or loop-to-loop plan. An oval would run you into the wall every time. By stacking a second loop in the upper right-hand corner we could convert our out-and-back plan to a loop-to-loop scheme with a resulting increased emphasis on running a lot of trains over the main line with less terminal switching.

The once-around scheme on the

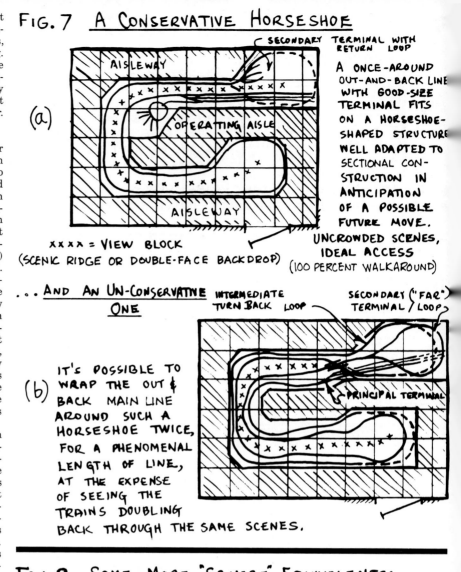

FIG. 7 A CONSERVATIVE HORSESHOE

(a)

SECONDARY TERMINAL WITH RETURN LOOP

AISLEWAY

OPERATING AISLE

AISLEWAY

A ONCE-AROUND OUT-AND-BACK LINE WITH GOOD-SIZE TERMINAL FITS ON A HORSESHOE-SHAPED STRUCTURE WELL ADAPTED TO SECTIONAL CONSTRUCTION IN ANTICIPATION OF A POSSIBLE FUTURE MOVE. UNCROWDED SCENES, IDEAL ACCESS (100 PERCENT WALKAROUND)

XXXX = VIEW BLOCK
(SCENIC RIDGE OR DOUBLE-FACE BACKDROP)

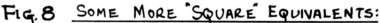

... AND AN UN-CONSERVATIVE ONE

INTERMEDIATE TURN BACK LOOP

SECONDARY ("FAR") TERMINAL / LOOP

(b) IT'S POSSIBLE TO WRAP THE OUT & BACK MAIN LINE AROUND SUCH A HORSESHOE TWICE, FOR A PHENOMENAL LENGTH OF LINE, AT THE EXPENSE OF SEEING THE TRAINS DOUBLING BACK THROUGH THE SAME SCENES.

PRINCIPAL TERMINAL

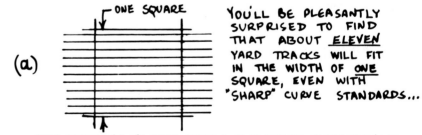

FIG. 8 SOME MORE "SQUARE" EQUIVALENTS:

ONE SQUARE

(a)

YOU'LL BE PLEASANTLY SURPRISED TO FIND THAT ABOUT ELEVEN YARD TRACKS WILL FIT IN THE WIDTH OF ONE SQUARE, EVEN WITH "SHARP" CURVE STANDARDS...

BUT DISMAYED TO FIND THAT A FIVE-TRACK SHARP-TURNOUT LADDER IS TWO WHOLE SQUARES LONG!

(NO. 4½ TURNOUTS SHOWN)

2 SQUARES

(b) AN ENGINE TERMINAL WITH TURNTABLE & STALL LENGTHS APPROPRIATE FOR LOCOMOTIVES MATCHING THE CURVE STANDARDS TAKES ABOUT 1¼ x ¾ TO 1¼ SQUARES (FOR 4 TO 12 STALLS)

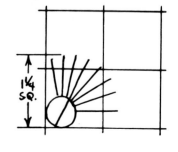

1¼ SQ.

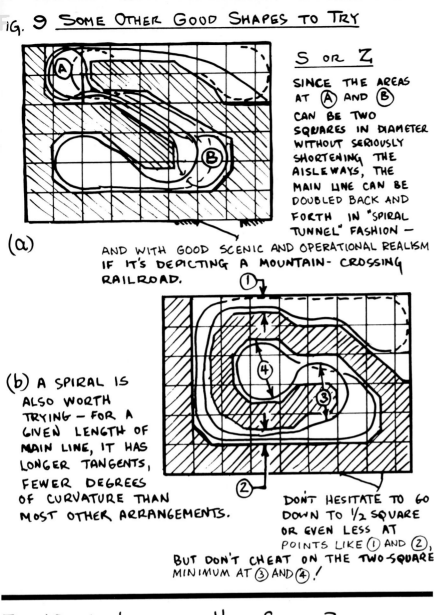

FIG. 9 SOME OTHER GOOD SHAPES TO TRY

(a)

S OR Z

SINCE THE AREAS AT Ⓐ AND Ⓑ CAN BE TWO SQUARES IN DIAMETER WITHOUT SERIOUSLY SHORTENING THE AISLEWAYS, THE MAIN LINE CAN BE DOUBLED BACK AND FORTH IN "SPIRAL TUNNEL" FASHION —

AND WITH GOOD SCENIC AND OPERATIONAL REALISM IF IT'S DEPICTING A MOUNTAIN-CROSSING RAILROAD.

(b) A SPIRAL IS ALSO WORTH TRYING — FOR A GIVEN LENGTH OF MAIN LINE, IT HAS LONGER TANGENTS, FEWER DEGREES OF CURVATURE THAN MOST OTHER ARRANGEMENTS.

DON'T HESITATE TO GO DOWN TO ½ SQUARE OR EVEN LESS AT POINTS LIKE ① AND ②, BUT DON'T CHEAT ON THE TWO-SQUARE MINIMUM AT ③ AND ④!

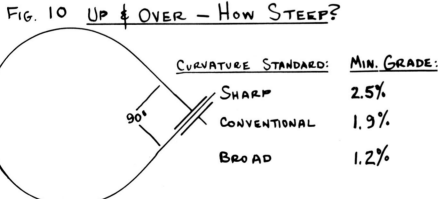

FIG. 10 UP & OVER — HOW STEEP?

90°

CURVATURE STANDARD:	MIN. GRADE:
SHARP	2.5%
CONVENTIONAL	1.9%
BROAD	1.2%

The disappointing number of yard tracks that can be reached by ladder in a given length is an age-old problem which emphasizes the importance of favoring designs that provide at least one straightaway, taking advantage of whatever "long side" the space may provide.

The twice-around horseshoe of fig. 7 looks feasible on this basis, with at least six or seven places where passing tracks can be located. With as many squares as this available, though, there are many, many alternatives. Figure 9 looks at a couple of arrangements that often have particularly desirable characteristics and usually should be given a try during preliminary planning stages for any pike — whether island or around-the-wall — in the size range starting with six squares on a side or thereabouts.

THE THIRD DIMENSION

So far we've shown lines crossing over each other without much consideration as to whether the resulting grades are likely to be practical or not. Figure 10 illustrates the most common situation where the amount of grade is likely to be critical. The shortest distance in which a track can cross over itself is determined by the minimum radius we're using, and since the minimum railhead-to-railhead clearance is determined by train height, a scale factor, the minimum grade for any scale is the same. The minimum grade is most likely to be a limitation on pikes built to sharp-curve standards; if the short trains typical of such an operation can't cope with 2.5 percent, the crossing point may have to be shifted to ease the slope.

The squares automatically compensate for the scale in which the railroad is to be built so far as the track itself is concerned. People and the aisleways required to accommodate them don't change correspondingly, of course, so it's important to realize that an aisleway may vary as much as from ⅓-square wide in O scale to 1½ or more squares in N scale. In railroads built to broad-curve standards or in the larger scales, the proportion of the area that can be devoted to railroad increases, but considering just how access can best be provided to the interior or turnback or reverse loops becomes more important. Keep in mind that you can only reach in about 30″.

The basic by-the-squares process will also work with the increasingly exotic multilevel concepts of layout design now gaining favor, though it's a cinch you'll want to resort to different colored lines to keep the mess intelligible. Somewhat more refined estimates of distances and grades will also be in order.

In due course, doodling should lead to satisfaction that you have probably settled upon the one or two best candidate schemes. If you've been reasonably honest with the squares, you are then ready to move ahead to the more laborious drafting of a for-real plan with the assurance that you'll be able to draw your way to a successful conclusion with very little chance of having to start over again halfway through. ◘

horseshoe is scenically ideal, for thanks to the view block, a train completes its run without visibly doubling back through the same territory. If we want to run a lot of trains, though, a twice-around like the one shown in fig. 7b will increase dispatching possibilities.

SECOND STAGE DOODLING

Figure 8 looks into the next step in track doodling: estimating the ways that essential secondary trackage — passing tracks, yards, engine terminals, and the like — can be fitted in once the general mainline arrangement has evolved. Here the news is generally good. If you've been sketching with a broad line, you're especially likely to find when it comes to drawing the track plan to scale that parallel trackage is somewhat more compact than expected and that wiggling the main lines around within the squares can get away from what may look in the sketches like too much crowded spaghetti.

Scenery profiles

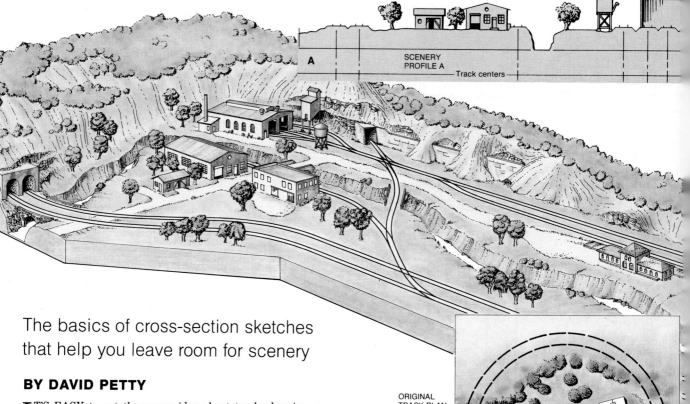

The basics of cross-section sketches that help you leave room for scenery

BY DAVID PETTY

IT'S EASY to get the wrong idea about track planning, especially if you hear veteran modelers speaking in reverent tones of "The Track Plan" as if the track were the only important consideration. There's much more to a model railroad than just track, and maybe we'd do better if we used the term "layout planning" rather than "track planning."

The simple fact is that many modelers just don't put enough thought into planning their scenery. Scenery seems to be regarded by some as a magic substance to be sprinkled on the layout after the track is laid, thus transforming the entire mess into a fantastic scene. The best scenery techniques in the world can't compensate for poor planning, and poor planning is usually the result of trying to cram too many tracks into the space available.

Many of us have learned this hard lesson through disappointing experience, and I'm afraid I'm no exception. Figure 1, an example taken from a layout I built many years ago, will demonstrate my point. I knew I wanted a hill at the end of the layout and along the back to hide the return loop mainline tracks. I also wanted a stream, a town tucked into a mountain valley, and engine facilities. It looked fine on paper, and it didn't look all that bad when I actually built it. It beat the heck out of bare plywood, but I was never really pleased with it either.

It took a long time to figure out why the scene did not satisfy, but when the revelation came it hit me like a ton of hot cinders — I hadn't left room for the scenery! Displeased as I was with the scene, I was even more displeased that my track plan had not pointed up the problems. Perhaps a more experienced eye would have detected them. The hillside behind the enginehouse was practically vertical and the stream was a steep-sided trench.

I decided that you have to draw the scenery onto a track plan with a fair amount of detail, and even then the plan can be deceiving. One deception results from using a single line to represent the tracks. Most of us are careful to allow for correct center-to-center track spacing and draw our curve radii accurately. What we tend to overlook, however, is that the track and right-of-way extend a considerable distance beyond the track center line. The rest of the world just doesn't butt up against the rails. The unfortunate truth is that a two-dimensional plan just doesn't show forcibly some of the problems you are likely to encounter in the third dimension.

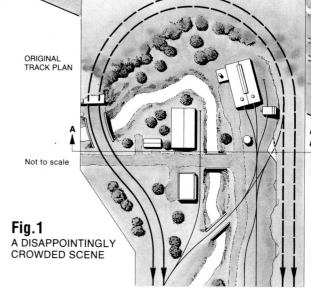

ORIGINAL
TRACK PLAN

Not to scale

Fig.1
A DISAPPOINTINGLY
CROWDED SCENE

DRAWING SCENERY PROFILES

Disappointments are easier to bear if they're discovered on paper and not in the plaster, paint, and ground foam of a finished scene. That's why I now draw scenery profiles. These require no more artistic ability than drawing a track plan and can be done rather quickly. They give you a very good idea of what the scenery will look like at a particular point on the layout. You can draw a profile of any area on the layout you want to, but the places where crowding is most likely to occur will be those places where elements are close together on the plan.

I draw my profiles on graph paper that is ruled five squares to the inch, and I almost always allow one square to represent 1" on the layout. Here's how I go about it, using the profile in fig. 1 as an example. If I had drawn this profile back when I was working on this layout, I could have saved myself some grief.

I begin by drawing a base line which will be at least as low as the lowest scenic feature, in this case, the stream bed. Next I locate all the track center lines along this base line and establish how high above it I want them to be.

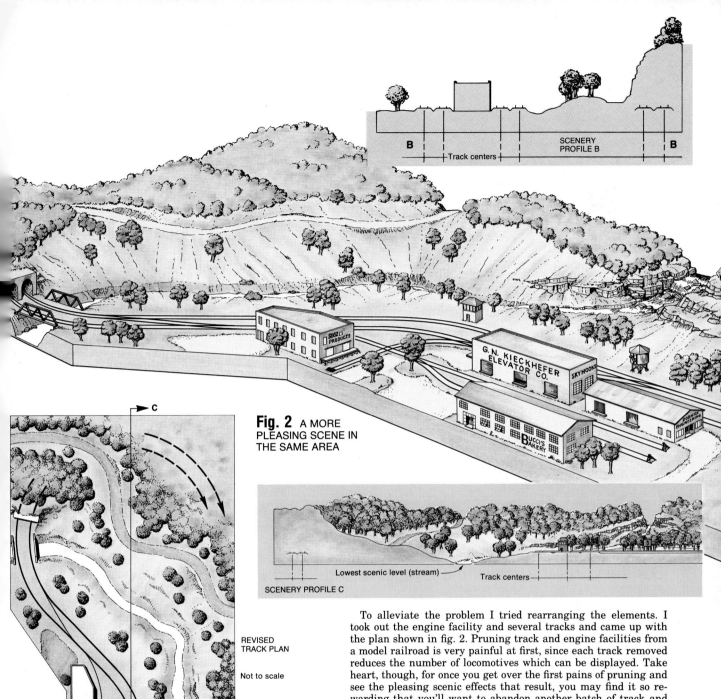

SCENERY
PROFILE B

Track centers

Fig. 2 A MORE
PLEASING SCENE IN
THE SAME AREA

Lowest scenic level (stream)   Track centers

SCENERY PROFILE C

REVISED
TRACK PLAN

Not to scale

In this example my hoped-for scenic effect was for a stream 2″ lower than the tracks with banks sloping down on each side, so I located the tracks two squares above the base line. I use cork roadbed in N scale modeling, and it measures 1¼″ across the bottom — in other scales, determine the actual measurement of the material you are using. I draw the roadbed on the profile, and for added visual effect I sketch the bevel and thickness of the cork and add ties and rail for each track.

Then I draw in the structures in scale at their locations, as well as the roads and driveways. Last I draw in the scenery contours, or at least see if they can be drawn in. The profile drawing shown at fig. 1 confirms what I had learned the hard way. I had not left enough room for the scenic effect I wanted.

To alleviate the problem I tried rearranging the elements. I took out the engine facility and several tracks and came up with the plan shown in fig. 2. Pruning track and engine facilities from a model railroad is very painful at first, since each track removed reduces the number of locomotives which can be displayed. Take heart, though, for once you get over the first pains of pruning and see the pleasing scenic effects that result, you may find it so rewarding that you'll want to abandon another batch of track and replace it with scenery.

In getting rid of the engine facilities and excess tracks, I had obtained more space for sizable hills, a stream, and a more interesting industrial area. To me this new track plan looked good, but if you'll recall, so had the plan I'd drawn earlier. Better play it safe and draw a profile or two to check it out. I drew a line through B because it was the most congested spot, drew a profile, and was happy with the results.

Next, I wanted to preview the effect a visitor would get when first stepping into the layout room, so I drew a cross-section at C. On this one I got carried away, making my first attempt ever at showing depth. The artist's rendering of my rough sketch is certainly an improvement, but even my original drawing proved to me that the scene had potential for the effect I wanted.

In looking back it is easy for me to see how a little time with a pencil, paper, and some thought could have saved me a lot of time, material, and frustration. Try profile drawings — they can give you a peek into the three-dimensional world of a finished model railroad. ✿

Come-and-go layout design

Our trains are the actors; the layout's a stage

BY JEFF MADDEN

A HIGH-STEPPING eastbound Northern, a string of hotshot reefers in tow, slows for the depot, responding to an orderboard signal. A set of orders is plucked from midair, and the caboose disappears, its reflection chasing it down the shining rails. Soon a whistle blast breaks the calm, and the westbound *Limited* appears around a low rise and glides into the station. The engineer eases his Pacific up to a water plug, and passengers and mail are shuffled on and off.

Thirty minutes later, a grimy 2-8-0 pulls in with an assortment of cars to be switched to local industries. An eastbound coal drag is being held at a signal just outside town until the passenger local departs — and the parade goes on. A similar sequence in our more modern era would see GP40s, Amtrak, trailer jets, and grain trains replacing the trains of yore, but the excitement and suspense would still hold.

This could easily be an excerpt from the action on a typical small railroad city on a Class 1 main line anywhere in our good ol' USA or Canada. Or it could be a design feature of your model empire.

ALL THE ROAD'S A STAGE

Frank Ellison described a model railroad as the stage and the trains as actors who enter and exit. The modern concept of walkalong layouts follows this theme, except that as we follow a train we are using a series of stages, not just one.

Many modelers I have met — especially those working in the smaller scales — have said they wanted to run long mainline trains but didn't want to construct large layouts. Yet these same modelers would like some sort of scheduled train sequence without the constant making up and breaking down of trains. In short, they would like to watch the trains as if they were a railfan watching from one location.

For these modelers I offer the "Come-and-Go" design concept. It just might be the answer for the modeler who has a fair amount of space for a layout, but wants something simple with only a single stretch of main line being on display — a stage if you will.

Figure 1 shows some possibilities for these mainline segments. These would be showpiece sections built mainly along one wall, with some open portions curving around corners to reach the staging areas, which would be out of view.

Option F in fig. 1 is sure to be a winner for Pennsy four-trackers, who are often frustrated with trying to design a layout that is both scenically and operationally realistic, yet doesn't require a gymnasium to put it in!

Staging options are shown in fig. 2. These areas are meant to be out of sight and unscenicked. They could be placed in a closet, wind around the furnace, duck under stairs, go on a shelf over the laundry tubs, or whatever.

Note that options A and B offer continuous running, whereas the others would require 0-5-0 switching, using your hand to redirect the trains after each operating session. (The British refer to this as "fiddling" — see Paul J. Dolkos' article on page 82 to learn more about layout concepts in Great Britain.)

These simple, dogbone-like designs

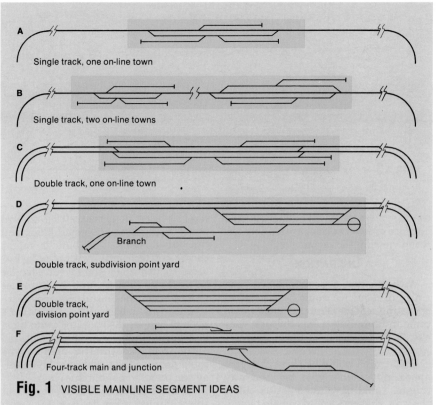

Fig. 1 VISIBLE MAINLINE SEGMENT IDEAS

A — Single track, one on-line town

B — Single track, two on-line towns

C — Double track, one on-line town

D — Double track, subdivision point yard — Branch

E — Double track, division point yard

F — Four-track main and junction

can be adapted to virtually any medium-size or larger room, as shown in fig. 3. In HO scale, there should probably be at least 15 to 20 feet of visible layout between the staging tracks or return loops.

Since return loops will double as staging yards, it will be important to use as large a radius as possible, so that your staging tracks will be long. In HO scale, a 30″ radius on the inside loop would be a preferred minimum. If tighter curves were necessary, perhaps some trains could be restricted to the sharper curves, others to the wider.

ADVANTAGES

Here's a list of good reasons for building a come-and-go layout:
- Easier track planning. You have none of the complexities and impossible scenicking situations often seen in bowls of spaghetti.
- Simpler benchwork. You could build it in take-apart, modular sections for the scenicked portion of the design. Staging areas could be portable, knockdown, or foldaway sections, or even be folded up or rolled out of the way when not in use.
- Limited scenery area. You can concentrate your efforts while saving time and money.
- Unscenicked portions can be run into areas that need not be finished off — a laundry or furnace room.

- Grades can be eliminated, which would make operation more trouble-free. Of course, gradual mainline grades can always be added for effect or to justify helper districts.
- A winding branch or secondary main can be added, thereby making your modeled town or towns serve as junction points.
- No duckunders. You'll probably need pop-ups in staging loops though.

- Control can be central, walkaround, or both.
- Cheaper prefab track and turnouts can be used in unscenicked areas. With a simpler track configuration on the scenicked portion, handlaying track would be easier than on a larger layout.
- Full signaling would be much simpler than on a layout with track strung out all over the basement or train room.
- Ideal opportunity for installing a

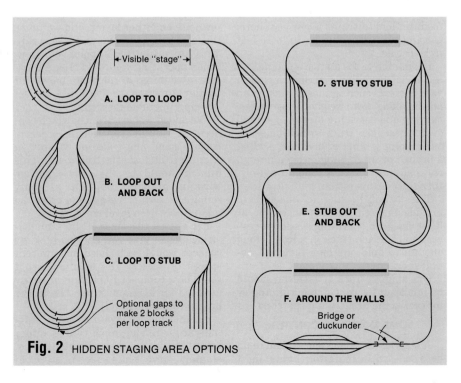

← Visible "stage" →

A. LOOP TO LOOP

B. LOOP OUT AND BACK

C. LOOP TO STUB

Optional gaps to make 2 blocks per loop track

D. STUB TO STUB

E. STUB OUT AND BACK

F. AROUND THE WALLS

Bridge or duckunder

Fig. 2 HIDDEN STAGING AREA OPTIONS

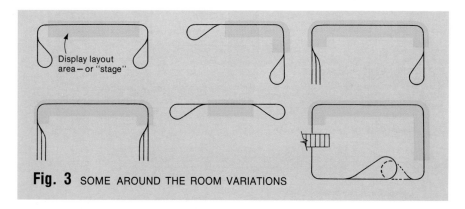

Fig. 3 SOME AROUND THE ROOM VARIATIONS

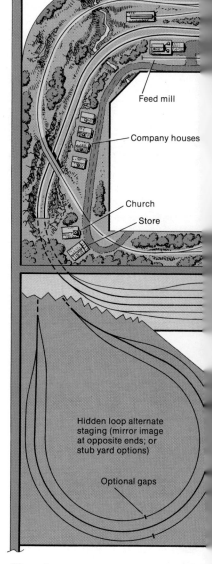

Feed mill

Company houses

Church

Store

Hidden loop alternate staging (mirror image at opposite ends; or stub yard options)

Optional gaps

Fig. 4 COME-AND-GO TRACK PLANS

sound system, since an audience would be more or less captive, as in a theater, when viewing the layout.

OPERATION

With this type of design, dispatching trains in sequence would be the typical operating scheme. The challenge would come in funneling trains through your one locale, much as a tower operator would do.

Most trains would be through trains appearing only briefly, but the way freight would have to be gotten out of the way. Freights would be held temporarily away from the station area while waiting for passenger trains to clear. Slower-class trains would have to wait in the hole while hotshots passed them on the opposite main, and so on.

Towns offer numerous operational possibilities, and most likely at least one should be included on the visible stretch. These would provide many industrial switching opportunities, depending on design.

Another option is for the town to be an interchange point or a junction with a short branch. Since running long or medium-length trains is our goal here, passing sidings should be 10 to 15 feet in HO scale.

In addition to the station stopping and industrial switching, you could include a yard to create such options as making up and breaking down freights, icing reefers, turning and servicing locomotives, and even passenger train switching, such as dropping a diner or mail car. Adding a branch or interchange with a foreign railroad to the yard location could further spice up operation.

The goal of the staging concept is to provide enough holding space for at least one good operating session of several hours. Each track in a loop is long enough to hold one long train or several short ones.

One staging track at each end should be left open for continuous running or to receive the first train dispatched.

SOME NOTES ON CONTROL

A staging area detection system could be used, with indicator lights most likely placed at a centralized control panel, along with the usual block and turnout controls. The builder might choose carrier control with plug-in features located along the layout edge, or he might go with conventional throttles grouped near the central control panel.

Since this is basically a dispatcher's style of layout, the operator could have a separate CTC-style board located away from the throttle area, or he could just use the traditional layout diagram panel to handle this chore.

So, there you have it, a layout concept you might use if you desire a stage with actors (trains) coming and going — railfan style, if you please. Now let's look at a couple of complete designs.

THE GAULEY RIVER RR

I have developed two come-and-go track plans, as shown in fig. 4. Both are based on semimodular construction, with portability and flexibility being the prime goals. For example, the Gauley Junction sections could be constructed and scenicked in an apartment. Later they could be pieced into a layout.

Gauley Junction is the only major townsite on either layout and would be the focal point, to be viewed from a railfan's or dispatcher's point of view. When operating you could create intricate switching or passing moves at Gauley Junction, or you could just let 'em rip, timetable-fashion.

I've added a short branch, which connects at Gauley Junction in order to permit some non-mainline variety in operation and scenic treatment. This branch would be the only trackage with any grade. It could just as easily remain at zero elevation and cross the main line with a level crossing.

I've shown two sizes of the same basic design to give you an idea how my concept would be utilized for different spaces or scales. The smaller layout could be a compact HO layout or easily adapted for a larger scale. The larger design could work well for N or HO.

On the smaller layout separate staging yards are shown. Of course, either layout could use any combination of staging yard types — loop, stub, or through. The larger layout shows a through staging yard serving as both ends of the railroad wrapped into one location, with continuous running as an option. The only drawback is the inconvenience of a lift bridge.

On the smaller layout about six normal-size trains could be set up for one operating session. That's usually plenty for any home layout.

One to four operators seems about right for these layouts. A lone wolf using a tethered throttle can easily step back from a single main panel to view the trains in the staging area. Just as easily, two or more operators can divide the duties and run several trains at once.

Perhaps this brainstorm of mine will give you some ideas for a home layout that can have the appearance of an empire, provide plenty of mainline operation, and yet be simple to construct, wire, and maintain. ✿

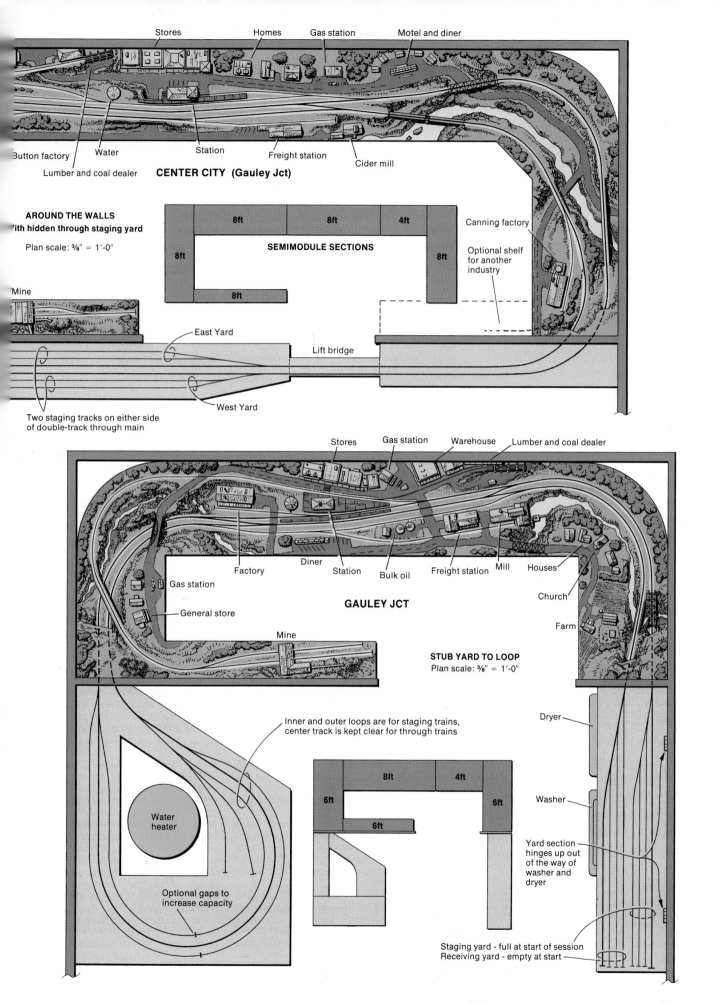

CENTER CITY (Gauley Jct)

Stores • Homes • Gas station • Motel and diner

Button factory • Water • Lumber and coal dealer • Station • Freight station • Cider mill

AROUND THE WALLS
with hidden through staging yard

Plan scale: ⅜″ = 1′-0″

SEMIMODULE SECTIONS

8ft • 8ft • 4ft • 8ft • 8ft • 8ft

Canning factory

Optional shelf for another industry

Mine

East Yard

Lift bridge

West Yard

Two staging tracks on either side of double-track through main

GAULEY JCT

Stores • Gas station • Warehouse • Lumber and coal dealer

Factory • Diner • Station • Bulk oil • Freight station • Mill • Houses

Gas station • General store • Church • Farm

Mine

STUB YARD TO LOOP

Plan scale: ⅜″ = 1′-0″

Inner and outer loops are for staging trains, center track is kept clear for through trains

Water heater

Optional gaps to increase capacity

8ft • 4ft • 6ft • 6ft • 6ft

Dryer

Washer

Yard section hinges up out of the way of washer and dryer

Staging yard - full at start of session
Receiving yard - empty at start

Railroading for city-lovers

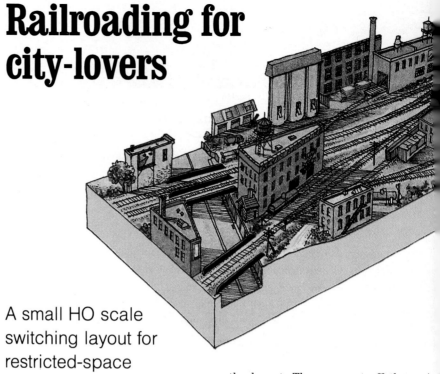

A small HO scale switching layout for restricted-space operation

BY LARRY FORGARD

IT'S funny how often certain words evoke a mood or create fantastic scenarios in our mind. Two words which model railroaders respond to are "basement" and "spare room." Both bring about immediate flights of imagination: scenes with gaping canyons, mountains to the ceiling, and beautiful stretches of right-of-way gently snaking through a spacious, bowling-alley sized room. The dreams are there, but usually the room is not.

For those of you who live in apartments or condos, or for those who have only small rooms available, or even for those who want to build a layout for mall shows, this HO scale layout (though you could build it in N or Z) may be just the thing. It's lightweight, has operating possibilities, and is scenically interesting — and it measures only 2 x 7 feet. It will be a challenge to build but small enough to complete. Think of the detail that can be added to an urban scene like this! An added benefit of closeup detailing is that the illusion of distance will automatically be obtained.

If you intend to make this layout portable, I'd recommend using lightweight materials: Homasote, plastic foam, and thin layers of plaster or Hydrocal. I'd also suggest that you make the buildings removable.

When it comes to operation, like many larger layouts, this one is designed to move rolling stock from some storage space or yard area to local industries. Rolling stock may be introduced at any point where tracks run to the edge of the layout. One idea would be to bring cars in on the two long tracks at the front of

the layout. These are set off the main line so that many cars can be sorted or stored without interfering with switching maneuvers. These tracks could also serve as an interchange point. In addition, one or two switchers can be stored and fueled at the small fuel facility near the turnouts. The fuel tank also serves as an industry for spotting tank cars.

The junction is an interesting scenic point since it creates the illusion that the main line is passing through this city to destinations somewhere beyond. If additional modules are added at some time in the future, this layout could still be the hub of switching activity, even though the main line is already built in.

The perspective illustration provides some structure ideas. I had no particular kits in mind when I designed the layout, so the choice of structures is up to you and your imagaination. The idea is to create the crowded inner-city look; an appropriate city background would enhance this feeling.

Interior lighting of buildings and street-lights would be another worthwhile addition since railroads do run around the clock. These effects should be considered early in the game so lighting can be provided for while building the structures.

One of the more scenic features on any layout, especially of this size, is the introduction of various levels. Figure 1 shows how this is done using the cookie-cutter method. The cross-section sketches, figs. 2 and 3, help show how the four levels are interconnected with ramps and scenic elements. When the scenery is completed, the slight differences in elevation will really look good.

I'm confident that this layout will be a lot of fun to build. It's a visually interesting scene that is reasonable in size so it will fit restricted spaces. On top of that, it also offers all sorts of possibilities for operational enjoyment. ⌀

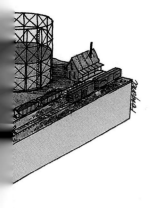

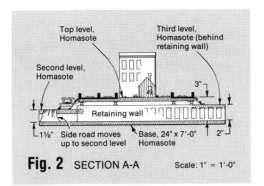

Top level, Homasote

Third level, Homasote (behind retaining wall)

Second level, Homasote

3″

1½″ Side road moves up to second level

Base, 24″ x 7′-0″ Homasote

2″

Retaining wall

Fig. 2 SECTION A-A   Scale: 1″ = 1′-0″

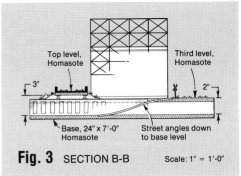

Top level, Homasote

Third level, Homasote

3″

2″

Base, 24″ x 7′-0″ Homasote

Street angles down to base level

Fig. 3 SECTION B-B   Scale: 1″ = 1′-0″

Fig. 1 TRACK PLAN AND SUBROADBED

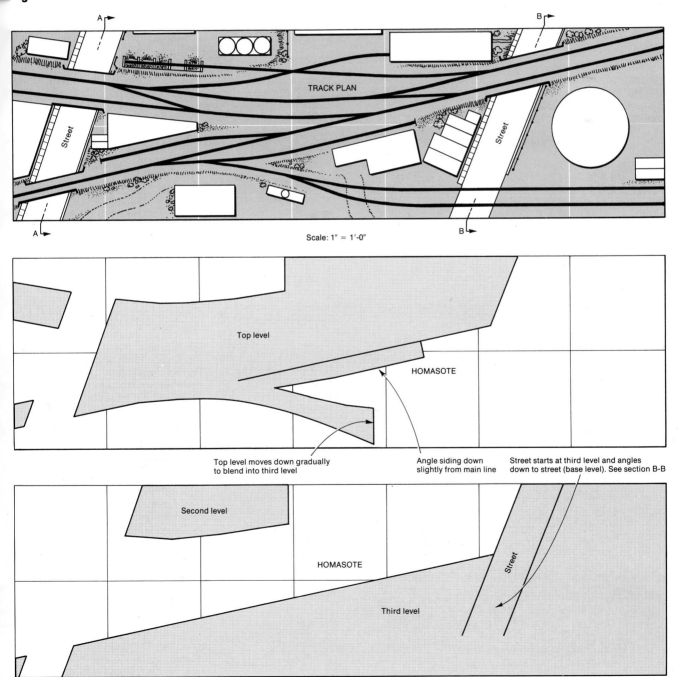

A

B

TRACK PLAN

Street

Street

A

B

Scale: 1″ = 1′-0″

Top level

HOMASOTE

Top level moves down gradually to blend into third level

Angle siding down slightly from main line

Street starts at third level and angles down to street (base level). See section B-B

Second level

HOMASOTE

Third level

Street

The Lost River District Ry.

A 3 x 7-foot N scale layout is Part 1 of the Big Dream

BY KENNETH L. ANTHONY

I HAVE a problem shared with lots other model railroaders — no space start my big, dream railroad, even in scale. My solution was to design a 3 x foot N layout that can be operated all itself, yet will be compatible with th bigger system. Best of all, I won't have tear anything up to make the connectic

The main theme of that big, dream la out will be a Santa Fe main line set the middle 1950s and running across th Texas Coastal Plain in the Houston/Ga veston area. Featured will be full-leng passenger trains running on a wye o of a big-city stub terminal and bein switched en route at a junction statior

I wanted my small compromise layo to be something that could eventually h incorporated into the larger scheme. would have to be small enough for me move easily by myself, and that mear tight curves if it was to have a self-co tained oval of track. There went the 10 car passenger trains with 85-foot equip ment. Also, with such tight curves, th small layout couldn't be part of the mai line — it soon became clear that I wa looking at a freight-only branch.

The prototype came to my rescue. Th Santa Fe has an interesting line, th Conroe District, which is strikingly di ferent from anything most people asso ciate with the Santa Fe. As shown in fig 1, the Conroe District is a secondar main line that cuts off from the Secon District main at Somerville and head east to the Beaumont area, carryin

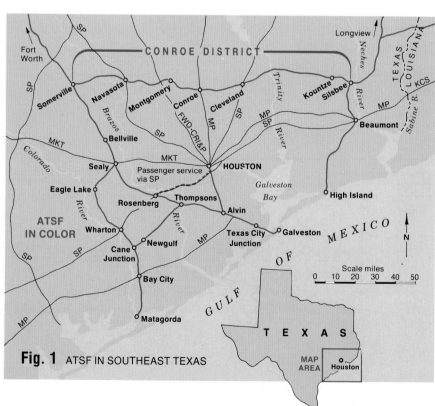

Fig. 1 ATSF IN SOUTHEAST TEXAS

rains through the Piney Woods of East Texas, including the famed Big Thicket. Culturally, the area served is the beginning of the "Deep South."

I had toyed for years with the notion of an East Texas layout, but the bug had never bitten hard enough to make me want to commit all of my layout space and effort to it. Building it as a little layout would be just fine — and it would take only a million or so trees instead of a billion. The dense Piney Woods would also give me a place to hide trains that supposedly have moved on down the line.

LAYOUT FEATURES

The little layout I ended up designing is called the Lost River District; my larger system will be called the Santa Vaca & Santa Fe Ry. Figure 2 shows how the two will fit together schematically.

The centerpiece of the Lost River District layout is the courthouse-square town of Johnston, Texas, county seat of Wayne County and named in memory of the late Corpus Christi modeler, Roland Johnston. Fictitious Wayne County is named after the composite Texas hero created by John Wayne. Texas has so many counties — 254 in fact — that we ought to be able to sneak in an extra one and fool even Texans.

My theory for names of free-lanced railroad locations, incidentally, is that they should sound right for the region being modeled, but should not be the names of real towns. Nobody should be able to say, "I've been to Johnston, Texas, and it's not the way you modeled it."

Considering this is such a small layout, I am using a lavish amount of space to model the downtown area — dating back to about 1910 — as well as some more recent strip development out along the highway.

Johnston industries with some special East Texas flavor are the Creotex yard which treats wood ties, poles, and pilings with that tarry black stuff, and the Dixie Darlin' peanut butter and salad dressing plant. Johnston also has a farm store and a bulk oil dealer.

This is a two-sided layout. A dense line of trees hides the layover tracks and separates them from Johnston. A row of

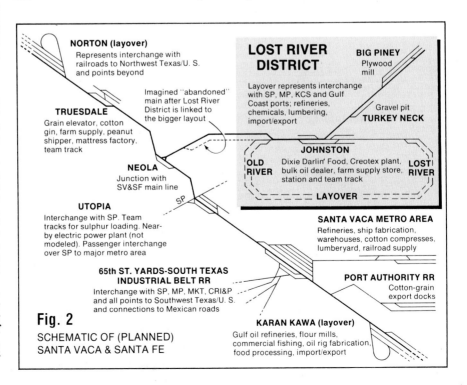

Fig. 2

SCHEMATIC OF (PLANNED) SANTA VACA & SANTA FE

NORTON (layover)
Represents interchange with railroads to Northwest Texas/U. S. and points beyond

Imagined "abandoned" main after Lost River District is linked to the bigger layout

TRUESDALE
Grain elevator, cotton gin, farm supply, peanut shipper, mattress factory, team track

NEOLA
Junction with SV&SF main line

UTOPIA
Interchange with SP. Team tracks for sulphur loading. Nearby electric power plant (not modeled). Passenger interchange over SP to major metro area

65th ST. YARDS-SOUTH TEXAS INDUSTRIAL BELT RR
Interchange with SP, MP, MKT, CRI&P and all points to Southwest Texas/U. S. and connections to Mexican roads

LOST RIVER DISTRICT

BIG PINEY
Plywood mill

Layover represents interchange with SP, MP, KCS and Gulf Coast ports; refineries, chemicals, lumbering, import/export

Gravel pit
TURKEY NECK

JOHNSTON
Dixie Darlin' Food, Creotex plant, bulk oil dealer, farm supply store, station and team track

OLD RIVER   **LOST RIVER**

LAYOVER

SANTA VACA METRO AREA
Refineries, ship fabrication, warehouses, cotton compresses, lumberyard, railroad supply

PORT AUTHORITY RR
Cotton-grain export docks

KARAN KAWA (layover)
Gulf oil refineries, flour mills, commercial fishing, oil rig fabrication, food processing, import/export

Fig. 3. The author is already building his N scale railroad. He likes to mock up structures to get a sense of how they'll look together. The rows of temporary trees are green-painted shirt cardboard.

mill building flats beyond those tracks serves as a backdrop for Big Piney, a 7"-wide terminal on the far side.

I could have made Big Piney a sawmill, and that would have fitted in just fine in the East Texas scene. So many modelers build sawmills, though, that I wanted to make it something else. Big Piney is a plywood plant.

That 700-foot-long row of mill buildings suggests Big Piney is a major shipper — and it is, the traffic in and out being 8 to 10 almost-unit trains a day. I say "almost" because the Big Piney train also handles a car or two a day for the gravel pit at Turkey Neck.

CONVERTIBLE OPERATION

When the Lost River layout is operated all by itself, the layover tracks represent points in each direction beyond Johnston. Trains entering Johnston running clockwise are presumed to be coming from Old River and beyond. Trains running counterclockwise are presumed to be coming from Lost River, which corresponds somewhat to Beaumont on the prototype.

I found the names Old River and Lost River on an interstate highway bridge halfway between Houston and Beaumont. When you're traveling east, the sign reads "Old and Lost River." The sign for westbound drivers reads "Lo and Old River." It seems the conflue of the two waterways is right under t bridge and the signs tell you which riv you're crossing first.

Lost River sounded appropriate for t name of a hidden layover — a neve never land that doesn't quite exist. the same time, Lost River sounds lil the name of a town built on a lazy sout ern river that later changed its channe A place like that eventually might d velop into a refining and shipping poin

When you're crossing that bridge yo can't quite tell where the Old River pa ends and the Lost River part begins. Th same is true for my layover tracks.

Obviously, the mainline run on th Lost River District is not long, but sever types of operating events can be staged:

● Through trains running in opposi directions can meet at Johnston.

● Locals can switch at Johnston, keep ing an eye on the clock to clear the mai for through trains.

● A Big Piney Turn could run from Old River through Johnston and out th branch to Big Piney.

How do the trains get turned whe there's no reverse loop on the layout Barring giant hand action, there's n way to change the direction a locomotiv is pointed. But the layout is set after th Santa Fe has entirely dieselized. We ca just run the Geeps around their train and run the engines backwards some o the time.

LINKING WITH THE BIG LAYOUT

The track running off the edge of the self-contained layout will become the connection with the bigger layout once it is built.

What justification is there for one track being the main line this year, and another track, already built, becoming the main line a few years from now?

Once the big layout is built I'm going to imagine that offstage on the old line is a bridge and approaches that have been torn out, perhaps in conjunction with building the first automobile expressway in East Texas — that would be appropriate to the mid-50s.

The old line has been abandoned beyond the torn-out bridge, and a new line has been opened. The old line is now used to store old cars that are used only seasonally, or we can imagine that it has become a spur serving one lone industry still remaining on the stub of the old line.

For now the unconnected "new line" can act as a receiving industry. One interesting possibility would be setting out the construction supplies and work-train equipment eventually needed to build the new line.

Needing a name for this new route, I looked in the *Official Guide* under "New" and "Neo," and came up with "Neola." There's a Neola, Iowa; a Neola, Kansas; and a Neola, Saskatchewan; but no Neola, Texas. Sounds just right.

As fig. 3 shows, I already have a good start on building the Lost River District. Those big dreams are nice, but to be actually building something while waiting makes them even nicer. ⍟

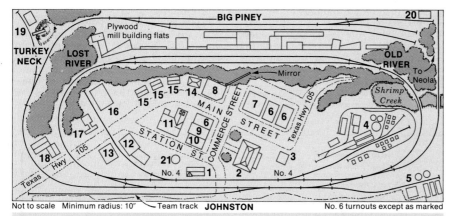

Structure key

1. Johnston Station. Scratchbuilt from MR plans (November 1979, page 84)
2. Wayne County Courthouse. Kitbashed from three Arnold Apartment Houses, no. 0697
3. Bail Bondsman. Scratchbuilt from wood
4. Creotex. Creosote treating yard
5. Bulk oil dealer. Scratchbuilt from Sealy, Tex., prototype
6. Masonry downtown store buildings. Mainly Heljan Courthouse Square
7. Movie house. Heljan no. 609
8. King Furniture Co. Based on MR plans (October 1972, page 68) Heljan no. 603
9. First State Bank. Scratchbuilt from MR plans (May 1974, page 34)
10. Woolworth's. Heljan no. 604

11. First Baptist Church. Scratchbuilt
12. Richardson's Grocery. 1950's suburban style. To fit
13. Farm supply store
14. Major-brand service station
15. Various homes
16. Dixie Darlin' Foods. Magnuson Mercury Shoe Factory, M512. Additions from other kits
17. Drive-in Hamburger Stand. Scratchbuilt from Corpus Christi, Tex., prototype
18. Independent gas station with beer joint in rear
19. Parker Brothers gravel pit with small concrete batch plant
20. One-room agent's office. Scratchbuilt from wood from *Santa Fe Modeler* plans (July/August 1980, page 18)
21. 100-foot-tall city water tower

The Third Street Industrial District

Track plan for an HO switching layout

BY BILL BAUMANN

T HE THIRD St. Industrial District is a small (2 x 10 feet) HO scale layout designed with two goals in mind: switching operation now, and expansion later.

The "District" was formed by a group of industries that banded together, took over some track, and purchased a secondhand engine to do their switching. Cars bound for District industries are brought in by a transfer run from the downtown yard of the Burlington Northern — *your* favorite railroad would do just as well.

The transfer ties up on the siding along the BN main, and its motive power lays over on the siding in front of the grounded caboose that serves as the District's yard office while the switching road's crew makes the setouts and pickups. Then the transfer returns to its home terminal with outbound cars from the District.

The urban scenery, street trackage, grades, and the BN main line running across the layout all make the District interesting to build and operate. Life can be made more interesting

for the District's switch crew by using a fast clock and scheduling some imaginary BN trains, so the switcher will have to clear the main from time to time.

The industries suggested on the plan are intended to provide destinations for most types of freight cars, but others could be substituted to suit your own tastes. The same is true of other structures on the layout. Putting a small coal dock next to the District's yard office instead of the oil tank would set the railroad in the steam era.

While the grade down Third and Commerce Streets is steep, just over 6 percent, and the S-curve leading to Mildue Malting is sharp (20″ radius), a small engine moving a few cars at a time should have no trouble. All sidings where cars will be spotted are level.

The district would be easy to expand. There's room for a turnout under the bridge over Commerce Street. Track could extend from there to reach additional industries, making an L-shaped layout. The main line could be extended in either or both directions to make the Third St. Industrial District part of a larger layout. ☼

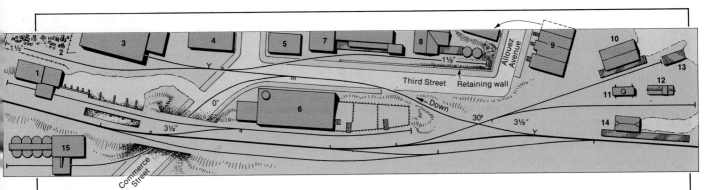

Scale of plan: ¾″ = 1'-0"

Main line	
Other	
No. 4	
No. 5	
No. 6	
Wye	

KEY TO STRUCTURES

1 Conglomerate Aggregate (scratchbuilt) — sand, gravel, cement, coal
2 Rust-Bangor scrap yard (scratchbuilt) — enclosed in chain link fence
3 Chilsom Refrigerated Warehouse (scratchbuilt)
4 The Grain Exchange (Magnuson)
5 Bank of Victoria Falls (Magnuson)
6 Gristle Packing Co. (Heljan slaughterhouse)
7 Phlaud Furniture Co. (scratchbuilt)
8 ISP Co. (scratchbuilt) — Industrial Strength Paint

9 Victoria St. townhouses (Magnuson, one front and one side wall used across the street)
10 Freight house (scratchbuilt)
11 Fuel oil tank for fueling switch engine
12 Third St. district yard office (Athearn caboose w/o trucks)
13 End loading ramp (scratchbuilt)
14 Highlands Station (Magnuson)
15 Mildue Malting Co. (Suncoast grain elevator)

Buzzard'

An N scale layout to fit on a door

BY JIM KELLY

Smooth contours with Sculptamold

1″-thick foam insulation board

Dunes and hills (optional) can be built up with foam

Hollow-core interior door

Water — paint surface of door black, then brush on one or two coats of acrylic gloss medium

Furniture factory
Heljan no. 672

Cold storage warehouse
Heljan no. 674

Track plan scale: 1$\frac{1}{2}$″ = 1'-0″

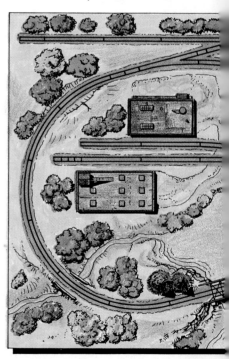

HERE'S A PLAN for any of you who'd like to build a first layout in N scale. You won't need much room, as N scale trains are small — a diesel locomotive $\frac{1}{160}$ of full size is only about 4″ long — yet these little trains run quite reliably. Lots of locomotives, cars, and other products are currently available, and more are on the horizon.

N scalers like to point out that this is a scale in which you can have a lot of layout in a small space, with plenty of room for scenery. This track plan bears them out. It all fits on a hollow-core door only 28″ wide. These are available at building supply stores everywhere. The standard length is 6′-8″, but the widths vary, starting at 12″ and stepping up 2″ at a time to 36″. Such a door will cost you about $20. If you call around, you may even find a damaged one for much less.

Atlas N scale sectional track is readily available and easy to work with, so that's what we're recommending here. On a small layout like Buzzard's Cove, manual turnouts (switches) work just fine and save you the job of wiring remote-control switch machines. If you should ever wish, you could add the electric switch machines later.

The railroad runs along the shore so you need a way to establish some land. This can be done easily with a sheet of extruded foam insulation, also available at building supply stores. A 2 x 8-foot sheet 1″ thick will do nicely. Just tack it on temporarily with a few drops of white glue until you've test-fit the track together and know exactly where you want to cut the foam.

Mark the edges of the track, then cut the foam with a sharp knife — a steak knife with a serrated edge works fine — and cement it on permanently. I recommend using a latex-based contact cement that won't attack the foam. You can use this same cement to attach cork roadbed.

This is a layout for the modeler who likes big bridges and lots of water. I think of it as being located along the East Coast somewhere, but you could just as easily scenick it for a river set in the Midwest or a lake in the mountains. The structure kits listed here are only suggestions. Feel free to substitute anything you want.

Your hobby dealer can help with recommendations on a locomotive, rolling stock, power pack and so on.

Good luck and we hope you enjoy building Buzzard's Cove. ♻

Cove

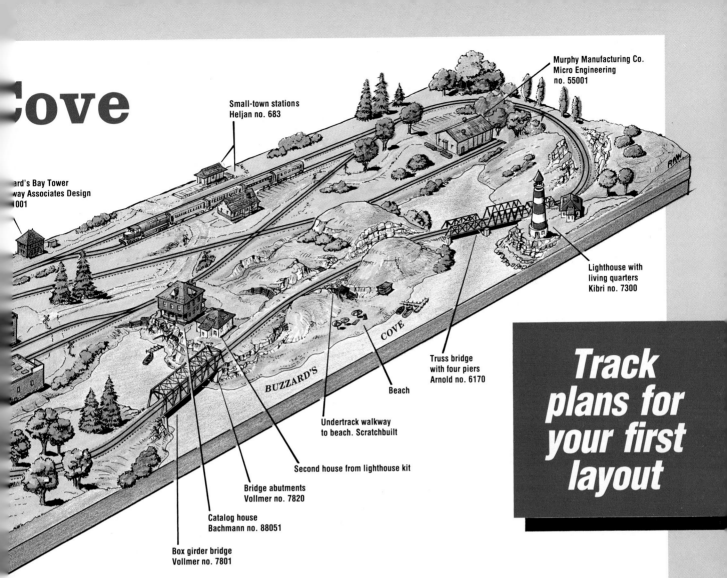

Small-town stations
Heljan no. 683

Murphy Manufacturing Co.
Micro Engineering
no. 55001

...ard's Bay Tower
...way Associates Design
...001

Lighthouse with
living quarters
Kibri no. 7300

Truss bridge
with four piers
Arnold no. 6170

Beach

BUZZARD'S COVE

Undertrack walkway
to beach. Scratchbuilt

Second house from lighthouse kit

Bridge abutments
Vollmer no. 7820

Catalog house
Bachmann no. 88051

Box girder bridge
Vollmer no. 7801

Track plans for your first layout

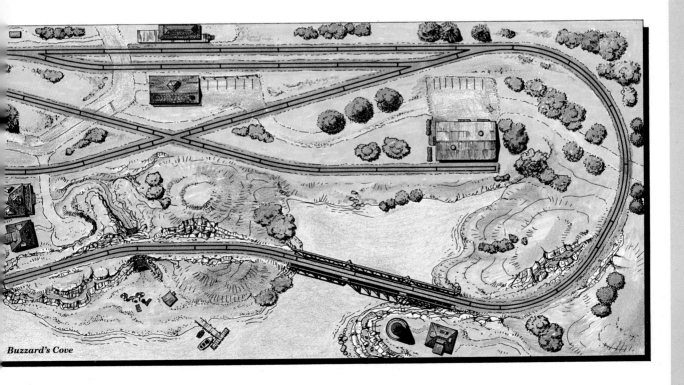

Buzzard's Cove

The Morgan Valley RR

This 4 x 6-foot track plan could become your first HO model railroad

BY RICK HENDERSON

Who SAYS you can't have a layout that's interesting to operate in 4 x 6 feet? The HO scale Morgan Valley RR offers a variety of operating possibilities not normally found in such a limited space. It's an ideal layout for beginners, yet can hold the interest of more experienced modelers as well. The design allows for easy expansion, though even as it is the MV can keep you busy for a long time. It may not be large, but as you'll see it can offer as much to do as a much bigger model railroad.

TRACKS AND TRAINS

The plan in fig. 1 is designed for Atlas Tool Co. sectional track, and you'll find a list of everything you'll need right there. The turnouts ("switches") are Custom-Line Mark IIs. These are more dependable in operation than the Atlas Snap Switch because they're more gently curved.

The two wye turnouts and some 15"-radius curves leave more space for industries in the center of the layout, so the three sidings reaching into this area can serve several good-size buildings. The Morgan Valley is meant to be a branch line using small engines and 40-foot cars, so the 15"-radius industrial tracks won't be a problem.

One engine and about 12 cars would be enough for this layout. Since the emphasis will be on switching, the engine and cars need working couplers at both ends. I recommend Kadee Magne-Matic couplers. Their small extra cost will buy a large amount of operating satisfaction. The five Kadee delayed-action uncoupling magnets shown on the track plan will service all the industries. In other locations you can uncouple with a handheld tool, such as the Rix Products no. 14 magnetic uncoupler.

If you'll be running a single engine, all the wiring you need do is replace any pair of regular rail joiners with a pair of Atlas terminal joiners and connect them to your power pack. Be sure not to use any plastic rail joiners on the layout. If you'd like to be able to run two locomotives, use the optional wiring scheme shown in fig. 2, along with plastic insulating joiners and terminal joiners as shown in fig. 1.

This second wiring scheme uses the plastic joiners to divide the railroad into five insulated sections or "blocks." Each block is fed power through its own single terminal joiner, with the "C" or "common" terminal joiner completing the circuit for all five. Switches on the Atlas Connectors let you turn each block on or off independently of the others, so you can park one engine while you run the other.

Another electrical option would be to add a handheld walkaround throttle to your power pack. A Model Rectifier Corp. no. 55 Cab Control can be connected to your power pack with a 6- or 7-foot cable. That would let you move around the layout while you run a train, to follow the action and throw the turnouts manually. Many people prefer to operate this way because they find that it's more like the way a switching crew works on a real railroad.

SWITCHING AND RUNNING

Look carefully at the track plan and you'll see how operating the MV can hold your interest. You'll see that the engine can't simply back into every siding to drop off or pick up cars. Of the nine industrial locations on the plan, five are on spurs leading off in one direction, and four are on spurs going the other way. The short passing track with turnouts at both ends lets the engine run around any car for correct positioning or "spotting" from either direction. This variety is interesting and, like a real railroad, requires you to think before you start to work.

Wait, there's more. Most industries on the MV share a siding with other businesses. If there is a car sitting at Hegert Wholesale when you have a delivery for Getty Oil, you'll have to make several extra moves. You must first move the car at Hegert's, spot the tanker at Getty, and then return the car to Hegert's. Again, just like real railroading.

Now, with just a little imagination, we will make the MV operate as if it were five times its actual size. Follow along with this example and concentrate on just one industrial siding at a time.

Starting at the passing siding, uncouple the engine from your train and pick up a car at the Amhurst loading dock. Next, deliver a boxcar to Bill's Hardware. Return to the passing siding, pick up your train, and make a lap or two around the mainline loop. Then stop at the passing siding again, imagining that it's really the "next" siding or town down the line, and make a delivery to the Forman Foundry.

Pick up your train and make another lap. Arriving at the next town (in fact, the same passing siding), drop your train and service the Evergreen Furniture and Daggett Electrical siding. Pick up your train and continue to the next town, one or more laps away, then drop off a car at Community Lumber.

As you're making the next lap or two consider how you will complete switching at your last stop. You may make several laps before you're ready, then you have a tank car to deliver to Getty Oil and need to pick up a flatcar from

Independent Iron Works, and there is a boxcar sitting at Hegert Wholesale.

It's simple really, but enough of a job to be very entertaining. See if you can figure out how to do it, leaving the train at the passing siding while you do the work on the spurs. Remember, it's okay to move Hegert's boxcar out of the way — just don't forget to replace it before you return to the train and finish your run.

If you were counting you've seen that the Morgan Valley operated as if it had five stations with as many separate industrial sidings and miles of track along the way. After operating for a time, you'll find those switching problems in MODEL RAILROADER easier to solve.

CONSTRUCTION HINTS

The Morgan Valley RR can be in operation in a very short time as construction is quite easy. In a few nights or a weekend you'll be running trains. Figure 3 shows one way to build the layout table or "benchwork." The book *How to Build Model Railroad Benchwork*, published by MR's publisher, the Kalmbach Publishing Co., explains benchwork in detail and offers many useful ideas.

Homasote, a paper wallboard, makes a good top surface because it's soft enough to make driving track nails easy, yet firm enough to hold them tightly. Glue the Homasote to the plywood with an evenly spread coat of yellow carpenter's glue. Clamp or weight the Homasote to keep it flat while the glue dries.

You can go ahead and lay the track right on top of the Homasote. Fit all the sections in place and install any insulating

Scale of plan:

Unmarked track se[...] full 18"-radius curve[...] straights. Turnouts [...] Custom-Line Mark [...]

Block wiring (optional) symbols. See fig. 2

Terminal feeders

Plastic rail joiners

Kadee u[...] coupling[...]

	TRACK PIECES REQUIRED (Atlas nickel-silver track)	
150	9" straight	12
151	15"-radius curve	5
152	18"-radius curve	15
172	25-degree crossing	1
260	wye turnout	2
261	no. 4 left-hand turnout	2
262	no. 4 right-hand turnout	4
263	no. 6 left-hand turnout	1
822	6" straight	3
823	3" straight	5
834	½ 18"-radius curve	1
835	⅓ 18"-radius curve	2
842	terminal rail joiners	1
847	track assortment	2
2540	track nails (or use no. 18 x ½" flathead nails)	

Fig. 1
MORGAN VALLEY RR TRACK PLAN

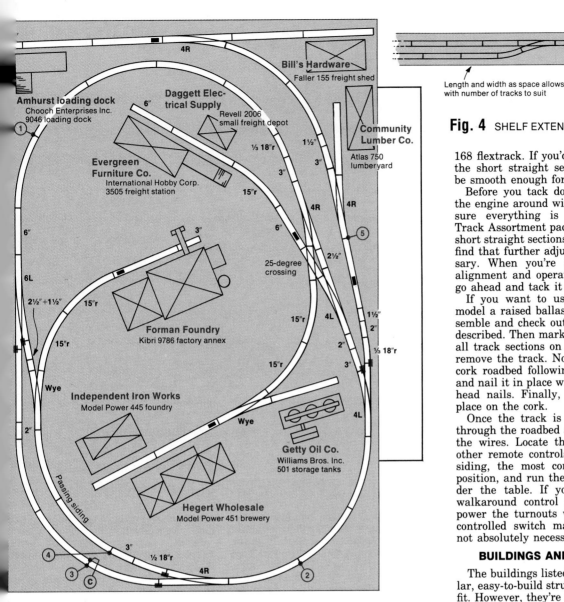

Amhurst loading dock
Chooch Enterprises Inc.
9046 loading dock

Daggett Electrical Supply

Revell 2006 small freight depot

Bill's Hardware
Faller 155 freight shed

Community Lumber Co.
Atlas 750 lumberyard

Evergreen Furniture Co.
International Hobby Corp. 3505 freight station

Forman Foundry
Kibri 9786 factory annex

25-degree crossing

Independent Iron Works
Model Power 445 foundry

Getty Oil Co.
Williams Bros. Inc. 501 storage tanks

Hegert Wholesale
Model Power 451 brewery

Wye

passing siding

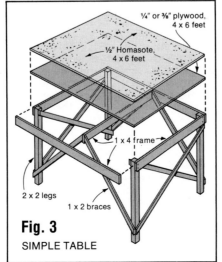

Length and width as space allows, with number of tracks to suit

Fig. 4 SHELF EXTENSION

168 flextrack. If you'd rather stick with the short straight sections, they'll still be smooth enough for good operation.

Before you tack down the track, run the engine around with a few cars to be sure everything is okay. The Atlas Track Assortment packs have some very short straight sections you can use if you find that further adjustments are necessary. When you're satisfied with the alignment and operation of your track, go ahead and tack it to the Homasote.

If you want to use cork roadbed to model a raised ballast roadbed, first assemble and check out the layout as I've described. Then mark the center lines of all track sections on the Homasote and remove the track. Now you can lay the cork roadbed following the center lines and nail it in place with no. 18 x ½" flathead nails. Finally, tack the track in place on the cork.

Once the track is secure, drill holes through the roadbed and tabletop for all the wires. Locate the power pack and other remote controls near the passing siding, the most convenient operating position, and run the wires to them under the table. If you won't be using walkaround control you may want to power the turnouts with Atlas remote-controlled switch machines, but that's not absolutely necessary.

BUILDINGS AND EXPANSION

The buildings listed in fig. 1 are popular, easy-to-build structure kits that will fit. However, they're shown only as suggestions, and you should feel free to use any other buildings that you like. If you're ready for more challenging construction, you'll find many craft structure kits, using wood and other materials, that will be perfectly at home on the Morgan Valley RR. Scenic elements such as roads and vegetation to give the trains and buildings a realistic setting I'll leave to your imagination.

The siding that serves Bill's Hardware and the Amhurst loading dock is perfect for expanding the layout when you're ready. One simple way to do that is to add the shelf and storage yard shown in fig. 4. This yard can be used to add operating variety by serving as a staging yard for two or more trains.

You'd put trains on these tracks ready to arrive on the main railroad as if from a distant terminal. After running laps and switching as described before, run the engine around the whole train at the passing siding and work your way back to the staging yard. If you can make the shelf wider to hold more staging tracks, you'll be able to have that many more different trains ready to operate.

I know you'll enjoy building and operating your own Morgan Valley RR. ✿

or terminal joiners you need as you go. Try to make all rail joints straight, even, and tight. You may have to leave some slight gaps to fit everything as shown. This is normal with sectional track, but try to split the difference over a couple of sections to keep the gaps as small as possible.

A particular trouble spot in this plan will be the 2" and 3" sections between the two no. 4 left-hand turnouts on the right side of the plan. You could make a smoother transition between these turnouts by using a short length of Atlas no.

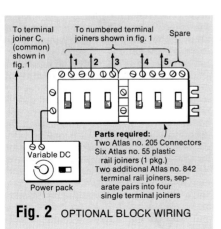

To terminal joiner C, (common) shown in fig. 1

To numbered terminal joiners shown in fig. 1

Spare

1 2 3 4 5

Variable DC

Power pack

Parts required:
Two Atlas no. 205 Connectors
Six Atlas no. 55 plastic rail joiners (1 pkg.)
Two additional Atlas no. 842 terminal rail joiners, separate pairs into four single terminal joiners

Fig. 2 OPTIONAL BLOCK WIRING

¼" or ⅜" plywood, 4 x 6 feet

½" Homasote, 4 x 6 feet

1 x 4 frame

2 x 2 legs

1 x 2 braces

Fig. 3
SIMPLE TABLE

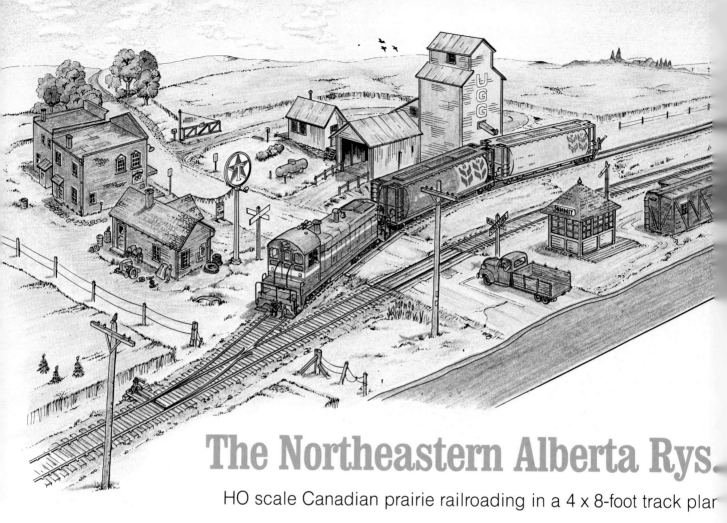

The Northeastern Alberta Rys.

HO scale Canadian prairie railroading in a 4 x 8-foot track plan

BY GREG PANAS

ONE ADVANTAGE of a center backdrop over three-dimensional scenery as a scene divider on a small layout is its adaptability to even the flattest topography. A backdrop makes it possible to depict flatland prototypes on "island" or tabletop layouts while concealing the toylike mainline oval. Granted, there is still the challenge of camouflaging the "tunnels" where tracks pierce the backdrop, but this can be taken care of by judicious placement of foliage, structures, or other features.

The accompanying track plan shows how this idea improves an otherwise ordinary 4 x 8-foot HO layout. Called the Northeastern Alberta Rys. (NEAR), it is set in the rolling farmland east of Edmonton, the capital of its namesake province. The NEAR makes its living forwarding that region's mostly agricultural freight traffic to the outside world via the Canadian National's line from Edmonton to Lloydminster, Alta. I envision the NEAR as having been chartered before the First World War, when convenient, reliable rail transportation was a necessity for western Canada's small, isolated communities.

The plan provides ample room for scenery without severely penalizing operation. At Mann Lake, the layout's operational center, there is a short passing track and a good-sized frame depot serving as both local station and railroad

general offices. On the opposite side of the backdrop, a small passenger shelter and company-stores shed mark Royalite, a village that largely owes its existence to the United Grain Growers elevators. In addition, a spur leaves the main line at this point to connect with a drop-leaf fiddle yard, which I'll discuss in detail later in this article.

The plan is drawn for Atlas no. 4 Custom-Line turnouts, and it could use Atlas code 100 flextrack as well. This is a small layout, so the mainline curve radius is 18", but I splurged and gave the fiddle yard lead a generous 30"-radius curve. The tracks run at angles to the benchwork edges for a better visual effect, a technique I also applied to the roads and even to the backdrop.

The scenery should suggest gently rolling farmland dotted with clumps of white poplar and evergreens, so that groups of these trees can disguise the openings that let tracks through the backdrop. I'd try using the fake-fur method of modeling tall prairie grass that Eric Bronsky described in the March 1985 issue of MR. For an illusion of greater depth on each side of the backdrop, the fur's texture and coloring could be evened out slightly towards the rear of each scene.

Structures on the NEAR should be small so as not to detract from the look of open prairie terrain, and simple frame buildings should predominate. I've suggested some buildings which are all, except for the Campbell elevator and grain

bin, readily available plastic kits and mostly used straight from the box.

Detail makes any layout look better, and one advantage of a small layout is that you can go all out on detail with a lot less work than on a larger system. Mann Lake and Royalite should look as though they've been around awhile, with realistic clutter, litter, and advertising signs. Plant flowers in the ditches and tall weeds wherever appropriate, and load the roads and parking lots with as many vehicles for your chosen era as you can lay your hands on. Firsthand observation of the real world will give you more ideas than you'll be able to use.

Earlier I mentioned the fiddle yard. Without it, operation on the NEAR would be hampered by the lack of a runaround at Royalite and by the lack of someplace for a train to go other than around the oval. The fiddle yard helps solve both problems.

The fiddle yard is simply a 6" x 36" shelf attached drop-leaf style to the end of the layout, with a length of track to connect to the spur from the Royalite junction. It represents the interchange with the Canadian National, the connection with the outside world "beyond the layout."

You'd begin a typical day's operation on the NEAR by assembling a train in the fiddle yard by hand, with the locomotive pointed towards the layout. Then you'd run the train through the junction and onto the main.

After running a fixed number of laps around the oval at scale speeds, you'd stop the train at Mann Lake, having reached the modeled "end of the line." You'd switch the two industries here and run the engine around by way of the short passing track. If there are more than just a few cars in the train, it could take a couple of trips through the siding to get the locomotive and caboose on opposite ends of the consist and ready to go back where they came from. If you're sharp you'll remember to keep any cars bound for Royalite blocked next to the engine for the trip back.

When ready to return you'd start the train out and run half the number of laps around the oval that you used to reach Mann Lake; the train could then arrive in Royalite. After you switch the elevators, you'd take the train out again for a similar number of laps before taking the junction turnout and ending the run back in the fiddle yard.

Locomotives and cars on the NEAR should be representative of a prairie branch line. For the steam era, a few 40-foot boxcars, mostly lettered for the CN, would be the backbone of the freight roster, with an assortment of miscellaneous tank, flat, and perhaps refrigerator cars for variety. A small Mogul or Ten-Wheeler could provide the power.

For a present-day NEAR you'd want a small fleet of government-owned cylindrical grain cars. Tips for converting these from Model Power hoppers were featured in the December 1982 Paint Shop. An Athearn EMD switcher, maybe modified with Juneco parts to resemble a GM Diesel (of Canada) SW1200RS, would do nicely to stretch the slack.

The NEAR's sharp curves put it in the freight-only category for most modelers, but for the steam era a short combine at the end of the train might offer mail, express, and passenger service. Then the switching at Mann Lake could be made more interesting by the need to leave the combine spotted at the station for an appropriate loading/unloading interval, thus limiting use of the main for run-around moves.

It's simple and small, but the Northeastern Alberta Rys. has a lot of potential for success. What you can do on a layout this size is limited, but within those limits you can enjoy doing everything to as high a standard as you'd like. Even a small layout can offer many ways to have fun. ₒ̃

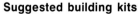

Suggested building kits

Mann Lake
  Lumber Co., Atlas no. 750
  Station, Tyco no. 7761
Royalite
  Gas station, IHC no. 4108
  Passenger shelter, Atlas no. 701 (use without elevated tower supports)
  Storage shed, Heljan no. 9033
  Stores, Heljan no. 810
  United Grain Growers elevators, Campbell no. 384 with no. 449 annex

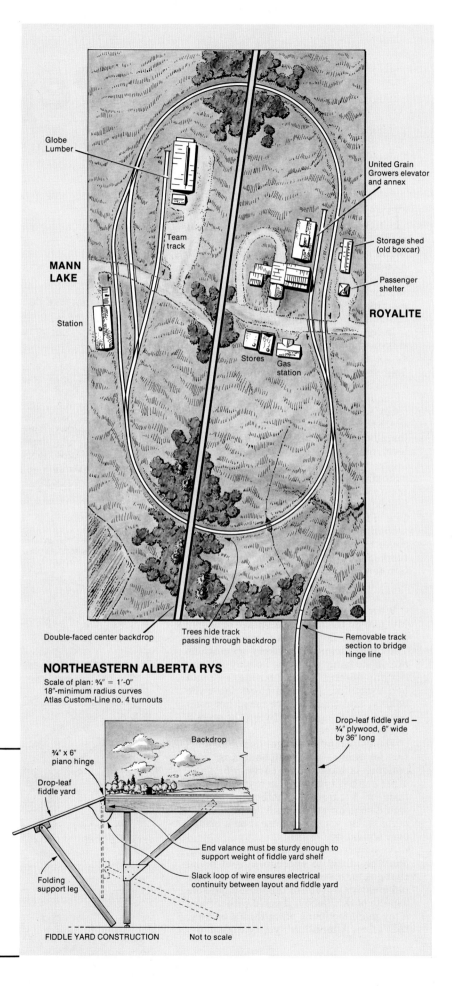

Globe Lumber

Team track

MANN LAKE

Station

United Grain Growers elevator and annex

Storage shed (old boxcar)

Passenger shelter

ROYALITE

Stores

Gas station

Double-faced center backdrop

Trees hide track passing through backdrop

Removable track section to bridge hinge line

NORTHEASTERN ALBERTA RYS

Scale of plan: ¾" = 1'-0"
18"-minimum radius curves
Atlas Custom-Line no. 4 turnouts

Drop-leaf fiddle yard — ¾" plywood, 6" wide by 36" long

Backdrop

¾" x 6" piano hinge

Drop-leaf fiddle yard

Folding support leg

End valance must be sturdy enough to support weight of fiddle yard shelf

Slack loop of wire ensures electrical continuity between layout and fiddle yard

FIDDLE YARD CONSTRUCTION   Not to scale

The Peppermin

An HO layout that uses train set track

BY JIM HEDIGER

THE PEPPERMINT CENTRAL is an HO scale railroad designed for new model railroaders. HO is the most popular model railroad scale. It's 1/87 of full size, so a 50-foot boxcar is about 7″ long. Without too much crowding this 4 x 8-foot layout can include a mainline loop for continuous running, a passing siding, and three industrial spurs in a small-town setting.

In common with many starting layouts, this one fits on a table that's made from a single sheet of plywood supported with 1 x 4 framework. This provides sufficient strength to use a "cookie cutter" technique for the stream, Coffee Creek. Use a saber saw to cut out the waterway and notch the framework. When the pieces are installed, the creek bed is below track level, providing a reason for the bridges.

The plan calls for mostly 18″-radius curved track, the size that comes in most train sets. A larger 22″ radius on the passing siding lets it fit outside the 18″ curve. One of the industry tracks is made with a section of flexible track — track you can curve by hand to fit. Two of the industry tracks may be switched by a train running counterclockwise, while one is a switchback that must be worked from the opposite direction.

With the wide choice of easy building kits now on the market, a village of nearly any era can be built in a few evenings. The candy factory and bakery suggestions are in keeping with the holiday season, but any number of other businesses could be substituted. A row of stores faces the bakery, and there's space for either residences or more stores between the angled street and Coffee Creek.

The two grade crossings offer opportunities for some easy scratchbuilding. One crossing is built into a curve, while the other one has to be fitted across the angled rails of a turnout. Another possibility would be to lower the roadway into an underpass. Or, you could raise it on a bridge over the siding.

As a newcomer to model railroading, don't be afraid to experiment and make changes to this or any track plan. Individual creativity is one of the most enjoyable aspects of this hobby. If you'd rather have a toy manufacturing plant than a bakery, that's fine. After all, it's your railroad! ✿

TRACK COMPONENTS NEEDED		
Atlas		
150	9″ straights,	22
152	18″ curves,	12
168	36″ flexible track,	1
822	6″ straights,	1
823	3″ straights,	4
835	1/3 18″ curves,	2
836	22″ curves,	8
847	track assortment,	1
860	left-hand Snap-Switch,	3
861	right-hand Snap-Switch,	2
2540	track nails,	1 pkg.
Midwest		
J3013	cork roadbed,	16

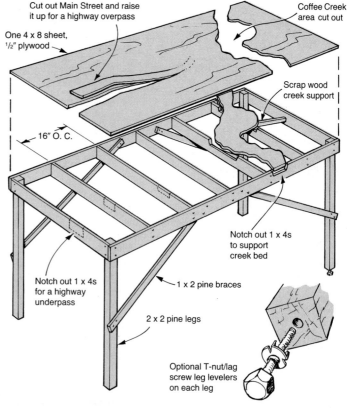

Cut out Main Street and raise it up for a highway overpass

Coffee Creek area cut out

One 4 x 8 sheet, 1/2″ plywood

Scrap wood creek support

16″ O. C.

Notch out 1 x 4s to support creek bed

Notch out 1 x 4s for a highway underpass

1 x 2 pine braces

2 x 2 pine legs

Optional T-nut/lag screw leg levelers on each leg

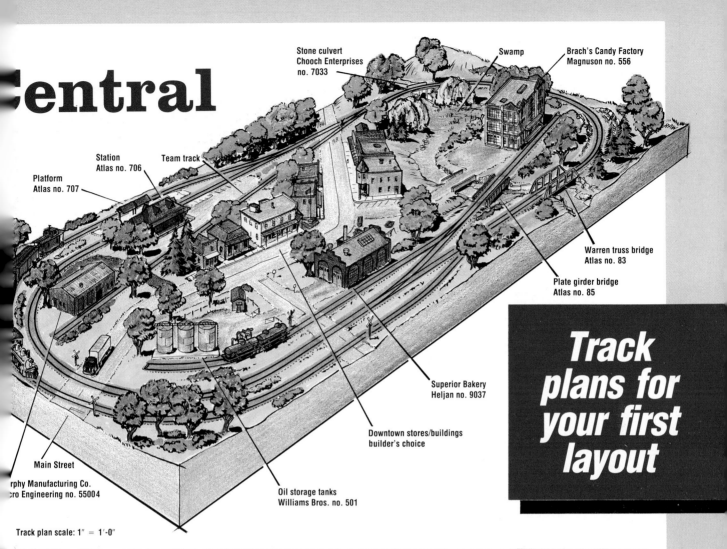

Central

Stone culvert
Chooch Enterprises
no. 7033

Swamp

Brach's Candy Factory
Magnuson no. 556

Station
Atlas no. 706

Team track

Platform
Atlas no. 707

Warren truss bridge
Atlas no. 83

Plate girder bridge
Atlas no. 85

Superior Bakery
Heljan no. 9037

Downtown stores/buildings
builder's choice

Main Street

rphy Manufacturing Co.
cro Engineering no. 55004

Oil storage tanks
Williams Bros. no. 501

Track plans for your first layout

Track plan scale: 1″ = 1′-0″

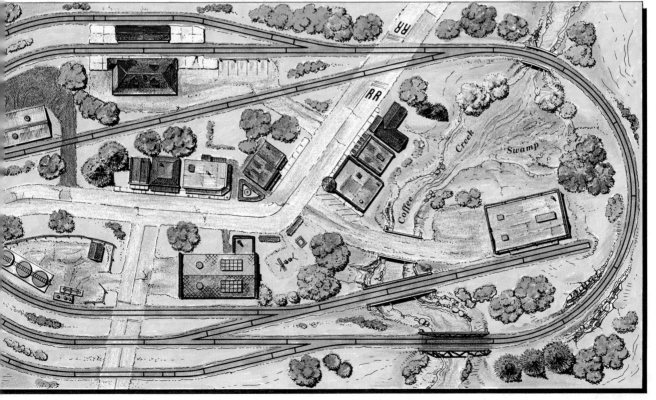

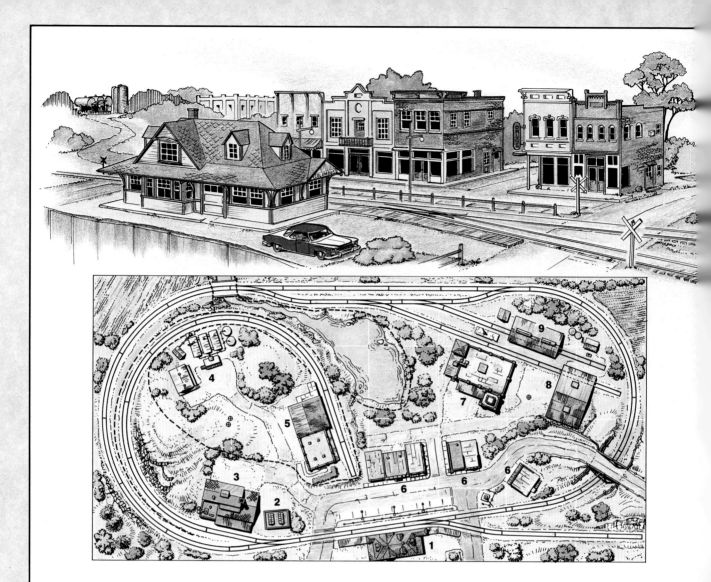

The HO scale Columbus

BY JIM HEDIGER

Most new HO modelers build an oval track plan on a 4 x 8-foot table. It's easy to build the flat-top benchwork from a single sheet of plywood, some 1 x 4 framing, and 2 x 4 legs, and all the components from the train set can be used. That's the idea of the Columbus Junction, with a few wrinkles to make it seem larger.

First, nearly everything is angled a bit to help minimize the boundaries of the plywood sheet. Only one side of the

loop, where the passing siding is located, follows the edge. By using an 18"-radius curve at one end and a 22"-radius at the other, the diagonal track between them appears to be heading where it's needed, not where the board requires.

Four spur tracks angle away from the main track in different directions. One is an interchange track, where cars may be transferred to or from another railroad. A long curving spur

loops around one end to bring a track into the center of town. The remaining spurs include a small engine service area and give the feeling of a yard.

Adding some rolling terrain will also break up the loop effect. A small creek and pond mark the low spot. From there, the base terrain rises a little and levels out toward the factory area. The ground continues to rise in the opposite direction, so the track winds up in a cut and runs beneath the overpass.

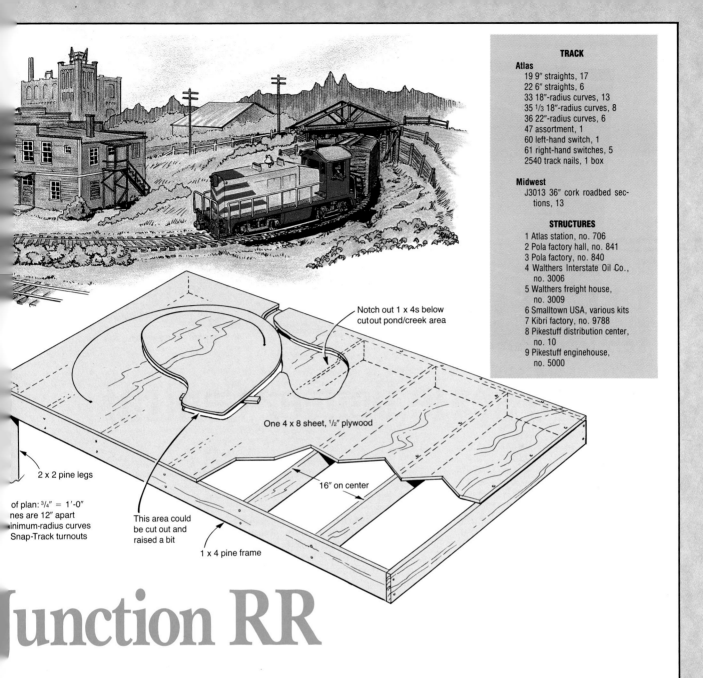

TRACK

Atlas
19 9" straights, 17
22 6" straights, 6
33 18"-radius curves, 13
35 ⅓ 18"-radius curves, 8
36 22"-radius curves, 6
47 assortment, 1
60 left-hand switch, 1
61 right-hand switches, 5
2540 track nails, 1 box

Midwest
J3013 36" cork roadbed sections, 13

STRUCTURES
1 Atlas station, no. 706
2 Pola factory hall, no. 841
3 Pola factory, no. 840
4 Walthers Interstate Oil Co.,
no. 3006
5 Walthers freight house,
no. 3009
6 Smalltown USA, various kits
7 Kibri factory, no. 9788
8 Pikestuff distribution center,
no. 10
9 Pikestuff enginehouse,
no. 5000

Notch out 1 x 4s below
cutout pond/creek area

One 4 x 8 sheet, ½" plywood

2 x 2 pine legs

of plan: ¾" = 1'-0"
nes are 12" apart
inimum-radius curves
Snap-Track turnouts

This area could
be cut out and
raised a bit

16" on center

1 x 4 pine frame

Junction RR

Curving roads, driveways, and structures also draw attention. A road lined with small businesses is fun to build, and everyone identifies with "Main Street." Naturally, the railroad station is right downtown. Starting the road into town from an overpass also provides an opportunity to step the businesses down the hill for more interest.

The major industries provide a sense of history. The former freight house (now a beverage distributor), the factory near the station, and the plant next to the pond represent the older, brick-built businesses. Modern steel buildings simulate the newest additions. The oil dealer provides a link between industry and agriculture.

A bit of "cookie cutter" construction may be used to vary the levels in the layout. The creek and pond should be cut out and lowered beneath track level. Making another cut outside; the long spur would allow the downtown industrial area to be raised (or lowered).

If the Columbus Junction will be your first layout, I recommend reading All Aboard, The Practical Guide to HO Railroading a Kalmbach book. It tells you everything you need to know to get the CJ up and running.

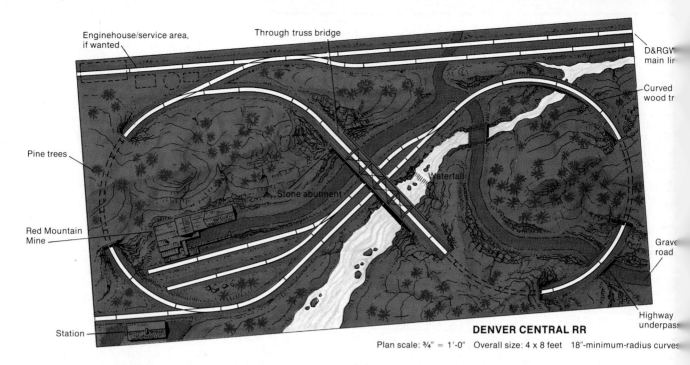

Enginehouse/service area, if wanted

Through truss bridge

D&RGW main lir

Curved wood tr

Pine trees

Waterfall

Stone abutment

Red Mountain Mine

Grave road

Station

Highway underpass

DENVER CENTRAL RR

Plan scale: ¾″ = 1′-0″   Overall size: 4 x 8 feet   18″-minimum-radius curves

The HO scale Denver Central

BY JIM KELLY

Those of you who did well in geography know that half of Colorado is flat and the other half is anything but. Modelers, especially beginners, love mountains and bridges, so for this medium-difficulty pike we chose to represent the "anything but" portion.

Also, we chose to use the good, old figure-eight track configuration. As a general rule, figure-eights aren't a good choice for small layouts - they look artificial and offer limited possibilities for spurs. For a mountain layout, though, we thought it would work well because of the scenic possibilities it offers looking right down the middle of the layout. The view of the train running along the river, then crossing through that Cen-

tral Valley bridge should work out great.

Some of you may be leery of the grades on this layout. No problem. You can cut in a couple of 90-degree crossings where the track crosses over itself and built it flat if you prefer. Lots of nice tunnel portals are available, so we'll leave the choices up to you.

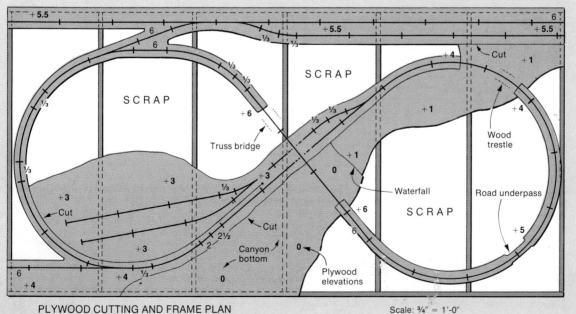

SCRAP

SCRAP

Truss bridge

Cut

Wood trestle

Waterfall

Road underpass

Cut

Cut

SCRAP

Canyon bottom

Plywood elevations

PLYWOOD CUTTING AND FRAME PLAN

Scale: ¾″ = 1′-0″

ATLAS
TRACK REQUIRED
Straight
26 - no. 150 9″-straight
5 - no. 822 6″-straight

18″-radius curved
16 - no. 833 full section
4 - no. 835 ⅓ section
1 - no. 860 left-hand switch
5 - no. 861 right-hand switc
1 - no. 847 track assortment
1 - no. 2540 track nails
Midwest cork roadbed, no. J3
21 - 3-foot sections

STRUCTURES
Campbell no. 429 Red
    Mountain Mine
Campbell no. 303 70-foot
    curved wood trestle
IHC no. 4101 station
Central Valley no. 1902
    150-foot through truss brid
AIM no. 104 random stone
    bridge abutments

Those of you who finish the layout and want to add more could build a neat western town between the bridge and the mine. Some sort of engine-service facility over on the Denver & Rio Grande might also be nice. In addition, you might add a circle of N scale track to haul ore from the hill behind the Red Mountain Mine on an HOn2 1/2 line. Perhaps you could work in another industry or two, though you don't want the layout to start looking like a bowl of spaghetti, i.e., the Chef Boyardee Central!

For anyone who might attempt the Denver Central as your first layout, let me recommend All Aboard: The Practical Guide to HO Railroading, published by Kalmbach. This will have all the information on benchwork, scenery, etc., that you would need.

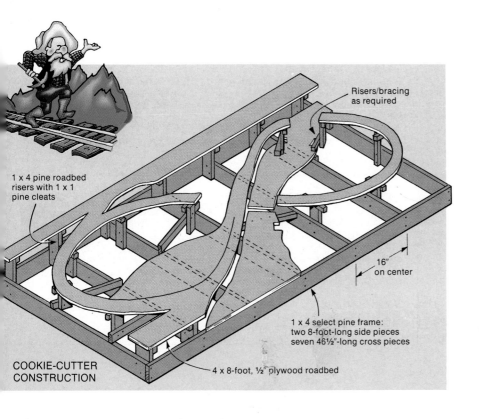

Risers/bracing as required

1 x 4 pine roadbed risers with 1 x 1 pine cleats

16" on center

1 x 4 select pine frame: two 8-foot-long side pieces seven 46½"-long cross pieces

4 x 8-foot, ½" plywood roadbed

COOKIE-CUTTER CONSTRUCTION

Bashing a 4x8

With a little cutting a basic 4 x 8 layout can be arranged into an interesting form

BY RUSSELL D. SCHOOF

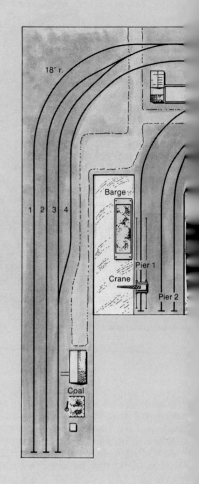

BY FAR the most popular layout size in HO scale over the years has been 4 x 8 feet. The reasons for that popularity are well known: it's relatively compact, the materials are easily obtained, and construction of the benchwork is simple and quick. One can go from a pile of lumber to running trains in almost no time at all.

Conversely, the drawbacks of a 4 x 8 layout are also well known: the shape doesn't provide much space for scale model railroading; it's too short and too wide, and the track has to curve back upon itself if a run of any length is to be gained. The resulting closed loop in most 4 x 8-foot track plans doesn't look realistic, the operation is generally repetitive and dull, and the scenery and structures don't fit well in between all those curves. Moreover, most 4 x 8 plans require access to all sides of the layout, thus consuming a disproportionate amount of floor space for a limited layout area.

It would be nice if one could have the ease of construction of a 4 x 8 without some of its drawbacks. With careful planning and a little ingenuity, it can be done. Here are some suggestions on how to attack the problem. I should note that these rearrangements are suited to HO scale switching layouts. Once you cut up and rearrange the pieces of a 4 x 8 sheet, you lose the capability of a continuous-run loop.

DESIGNING THE LAYOUT

Space for a layout is usually the primary limiting factor in layout design and an important reason for choosing a 4 x 8-foot size in the first place. As I said before, many 4 x 8 table layouts take up a lot of floor space because access to all sides is necessary for construction, operation, and maintenance. See fig. 1a. Floor space can be saved if the layout can be placed against one or two walls, but to do

that, it's necessary to use a track plan that can be operated from only one or two sides of the layout. To counteract this condition the shape of the layout must be changed so that everything is within reasonable reach. A reach of 3 feet is a practical maximum.

The way the change in shape is carried out is the key to keeping construction simple. I suggest that it be done by cutting small shelves out of the 4 x 8-foot sheet and tacking them on in other places. See figs. 1b and 1c. With careful cutting and fitting you can get good access with minimal disturbance of the basic construction. The small extensions can be supported by a cantilever or a single leg and require only a few extra pieces of material.

The track arrangement and the layout shape are interrelated. The shelf extensions can provide space for a longer run without the need for a circle. More prototypical track arrangements can be used, in turn giving more prototypical operation. Another benefit is that the scenery and structures can be placed more realistically.

I think that the key to good track planning is to work within the limitations of

the available space. Many modelers t_ squeeze too much railroad into a g_ area. To me, a small layout is much _ interesting if it is a plausible represe_ tion of a small area, rather than an_ probable representation of a large on_

The two sample track plans show_ figs. 2 and 3 illustrate what I think _ be accomplished toward this end.

Fig. 1

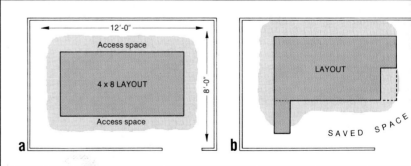

a

b   SAVED SPACE

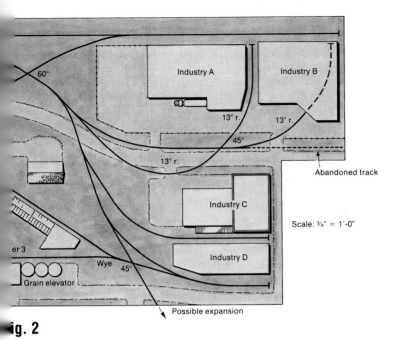

60°

Industry A

Industry B

13" r.

13" r.

45°

13" r.

Abandoned track

Industry C

Scale: ¾" = 1'-0"

er 3

Industry D

Wye   45°

Grain elevator

Possible expansion

Fig. 2

WESTPORT TERMINAL

THE TABLE for the Westport Terminal RR is made by cutting a single x 2-foot piece out of one corner and adding it to an adjacent corner as a shelf. See Figs. 1b and 2. The shelf provides enough room for a small yard and a runaround track. The two storage tracks have about 20-car capacity. The WTRR represents a section of a large railroad with a yard serving a busy wharf and industrial area. A yard office and minimal engine service facilities are provided for locomotive and crew comfort. Connection with the main railroad (simulated) is made via the main track to the front edge of the layout. In theory it leads to the WTRR's off-layout classification yard.

The two docks in the wharf area are equipped to handle all types of cargo. Two cranes and a grain elevator take care of loading and unloading ships and barges. The docks receive boxcars, flats,

reefers, gondolas with various loads, and hoppers for movement of bulk loads. Cars are moved in blocks to deliver and pick up cargo carried by the vessels. The double track on Pier 2 allows through-car loading of house cars, or bulk handling of flat and gondola cars by the crane on Pier 1. A warehouse and an office complete the dockside facilities. Loaded and empty box-cars are spotted at the warehouse for handling inbound and outbound merchandise. The grain elevator is served by boxcars and covered hoppers.

The industrial area has four large industries. The switching lead to the two largest industries runs along the shoulder of a street, and the spurs curve alongside industry A and into industry B. The extension of the lead track is modeled abandoned (rails removed and weed grown over the ties) in order to keep local switching activity on the layout. Industries C and D are served by a single spur branching off the main. This sometimes makes it necessary to move already spotted cars when a new car is to be spotted or pulled. The switchback lead to Pier 3 should be kept clear for frequent switching moves.

All turnouts are no. 4, and the crossings are standard 45- and 60-degree sizes. The curves are 15" radius, except for the two industrial spurs, which are 13" radius, and Track 1, which is 18" radius. The motive power should be small, such as a Keystone 44-tonner, a Roundhouse boxcab diesel, or an 0-4-0 or 0-6-0 steam engine. Due to the sharp curves it would be best to use 40-foot freight cars rather than longer contemporary stock.

The scenery can be relatively simple, although there is tremendous opportunity

for detailing. This area is just the place for old, sooty, multistory brick factories and warehouses. The layout is designed to accommodate structures that are large and to give a good sense of realistic proportion between the structures and rolling stock. Commercial kits such as Heljan's slaughterhouse, brewery, and bottling plant, and Magnuson structures can be used with some modification.

I see plenty of opportunity for operation on the WTRR. A typical session begins with inbound cars (left by the morning transfer run) sitting on Track 3. Track 1, the holding track for outbound cars, has been emptied by a previous transfer run.

The local crew starts blocking the inbound cars for delivery to Piers 1 and 2, Pier 3, and the industries. Piers 1 and 2 are switched first. Cars pulled from the piers are moved to Track 1 for later movement outbound on a transfer run. Inbound cars are then spotted at the piers. Cars that, for lack of space, cannot be spotted are dropped on Track 2 to await the next run. When the work at Piers 1 and 2 is finished, the process is repeated for Pier 3.

After the wharf work is finished the crew starts on the industrial area. The four industrial spurs have trailing-point turnouts, so cars to be set out are left on Track 3 and the engine run around them on 4. Track 4 is then used as the lead for switching the industries. When the work is completed, the outbound cars are again spotted on Track 1.

It should now be afternoon, by fast-clock time, and the piers can be switched again, if necessary. That completes the day's work, and the locomotive is returned to the service track for the night. The next day's cycle will begin with the engine pulling the cars from Track 1 and moving them to Track 3, simulating the arrival of new cars from the transfer run.

Other operating schemes can be devised. A second transfer run could be added to increase traffic movement. With suitable wiring, a second control and engine could be added to switch the piers while the first one is used to work the industries. Expansion is possible off the main track, at the abandoned industrial lead, or at both places. The simple addition of an off-scene staging yard for a real transfer run would add a great deal to the operation.

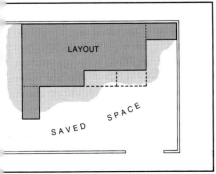

LAYOUT

SAVED   SPACE

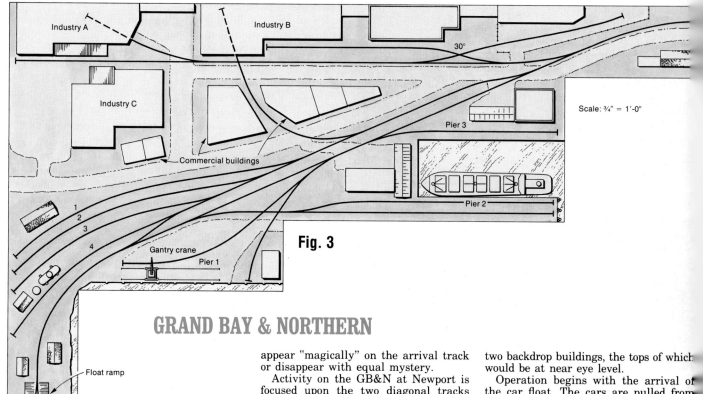

Scale: ¾″ = 1′-0″

Fig. 3

Industry A

Industry B

30°

Pier 3

Industry C

Commercial buildings

Pier 2

1
2
3
4

Gantry crane
Pier 1

Float ramp

Car float

GRAND BAY & NORTHERN

F OR THE Grand Bay & Northern I propose two other 1 x 2-foot bites out of the 4 x 8-foot table to provide a pair of shelves. See figs. 1c and 3. This arrangement will give you enough space to place a long track on a diagonal, with a yard with secondary tracks branching off to both the left and the right. The railroad can be operated from the front, and there is access along the one long side for maintenance. During construction, access from the back of the layout is desirable, if not absolutely essential.

The GB&N layout represents a part of a large railroad that is operationally isolated from the main railroad by a river, with the only connection via a car float (eight-car capacity). The layout is complete in itself, with a movable car-float module serving as the offstage connection. [For a prototype example of this arrangement, see page 62 of John Armstrong's *Track Planning for Realistic Operation* (Kalmbach)]. In theory, when all the manufacturing and industrial space in the original port area was occupied, Newport was established to handle the expanding marine traffic. The low-cost land and reliable service attracted industry and created additional traffic for the railroad.

The particularly attractive feature of this track plan is that all train movements take place within view, including those of the movable car float. No cars

appear "magically" on the arrival track or disappear with equal mystery.

Activity on the GB&N at Newport is focused upon the two diagonal tracks which serve as switching leads and run-around tracks. There is a lot of activity at the wharf and the car float.

At the left side of the layout are the yard, engine facilities, and the lead to the car-float ramp. The yard serves for classification of incoming cars and temporary storage of cars for movement out onto the float. Its capacity is about 18 40-foot cars. Minimal engine facilities are located on Track 4, which doubles as a holding track for idler flatcars (about three) used to switch the float. The lead to the car float also serves as a tail to the runaround track and the lead to Piers 2 and 3.

The wharves occupy most of the front of the layout. Pier 1 has a crane and bulk-handling facilities. Piers 2 and 3 handle general cargo operations. Cars are moved on and off in blocks as vessels are loaded and unloaded.

The entire rear area is industrial. Spurs branch off to the industries from a lead that goes along a street. An additional spur off the yard lead cuts through a block of commercial buildings and enters factory B at near right angle.

The two large industries against the backdrop (A and B), and a third (C), stand free. The large buildings provide for multiple spurs to a single industry — common enough in the prototype world, but often overlooked on model railroads.

I envision the scenic treatment as similar to that of the Westport Terminal. Structures from Rio Grande Models, Lyttler & Lyttler, and many other manufacturers would fit nicely in the commercial area. The very large industry along the backdrop could be scratchbuilt or kitbashed along the lines of Edward Steinberg's Mahjek Furniture Company in the October 1979 MR. I suggest using low structures in the front and gradually increasing the average height up to the

two backdrop buildings, the tops of which would be at near eye level.

Operation begins with the arrival of the car float. The cars are pulled from the float (with idler flatcars between locomotive and cars) and put into the yard. Outgoing cars are pulled from the yard and loaded on the float, which then departs. Incoming cars are classified for three separate switching jobs: Pier 1, Piers 2 and 3, and the industries. Each is switched in turn.

The apparently simple operating scheme is deceptive. Several trips by the car float during each operating session would be needed to handle the heavy traffic generated. The cycle times of the float loading and unloading wouldn't correspond exactly, posing scheduling and switching problems. Temporary storage of cars would use up some of the otherwise ample yard space, and dock tracks might be full. Some judicious maneuvering would be necessary to avoid a complete jam-up.

One locomotive is ample for this layout, but if you like operating challenges, it could be wired with a second control and another locomotive used. Standard wiring would be relatively complex with many short blocks. One of the command control systems would eliminate the confusion of controlling many short blocks. The 15″-radius curve on the industrial spur is the limiting factor on locomotive size. If large locomotives are employed, you can use a few idler cars (any type) to reach into Industry B.

OTHER IDEAS

These layouts are but two of an almost unlimited number of possible variations. Other types of railroading than the dock railroads I've described can be modeled. You might try a small town on a main line, a shortline terminal, or a single large industrial complex. Scenery can be as simple or as complex as you want to make it, within the limitations of the tabletop form. A lot of good model railroading can be accomplished in a small area. ◖

The Hazzard County Short Line

An HO scale 4 x 8 in Duke country

BY ED SUMNER

THE HAZZARD COUNTY SHORT LINE is a railroad for the modeler with little space and even less time. The HCSL can be pretty much completed in a fairly leisurely month's work and requires few expensive items (i.e., one or two locomotives, a few freight cars, and a passenger car, some plastic buildings, track, and scenic materials).

The layout has scenery both above and below track level, but not to excess. The low areas are not too low, and the mountain is not too high. This makes it ideal for the model railroader who is ready to leave the flat-top layout stage. The trackwork along the extreme front of the river is about 1″ lower than the track north of it. The separation between the two parallel tracks begins at the turnout at the west end of the layout and returns to the same level at Hazzard Station.

The mountain is actually little more than an oversized hill, designed to suggest some distance between the town of Hazzard and the mine at the other end of the county. Of course, somewhere on the hill you'll want to have a house that represents the Duke boys' diggin's.

OPERATION

Operation on the HCSL begins early in the morning at Hazzard Station, where the line's lone road engine (either a small steam engine or a first-generation Geep) retrieves the freight cars on the interchange track directly behind the passenger station. The engineer sets out the cars in front of the station, continues down the track past the wye, and then heads back into the industrial area at Hazzard.

Here the crew picks up the cars at the co-op and textile mill (the night shifts loaded them) and brings them to the station where they are connected to the cars spotted there earlier. The entire train then heads west onto the main, through the tunnel and on to the Hazzard County Mine, a small two-carload operation on the southwestern slope of the mountain.

To switch the mine the engineer leaves the small train just to the portal side of the grade crossing to avoid blocking the road. When switching is completed, the train then returns via the inner loop and pulls into the outer track of the passing siding. It spots the cars and returns to the interchange track where a local freight from a connecting road has left some cars to be set out at the Hazzard industries. By the time the crew finishes this task, it's time for the morning break at the local watering hole.

Other HCSL operations include the twice-daily mixed train that takes miners to and from the mine, and the setting out of other cars for the local freight of the connecting railroad. As a short connecting line, this is the job that the HCSL was designed to do.

Rolling stock will be mostly boxcars, hopper cars, and an occasional tank car of heating oil or a flat of lumber. One passenger car for the mixed train ought to suffice.

I have designed the HCSL to be inexpensive as well as space-saving. Hopefully, these will be incentives enough to make you want to build the HCSL. Of course, that's in addition to the fact that it's a neat little layout. ◊

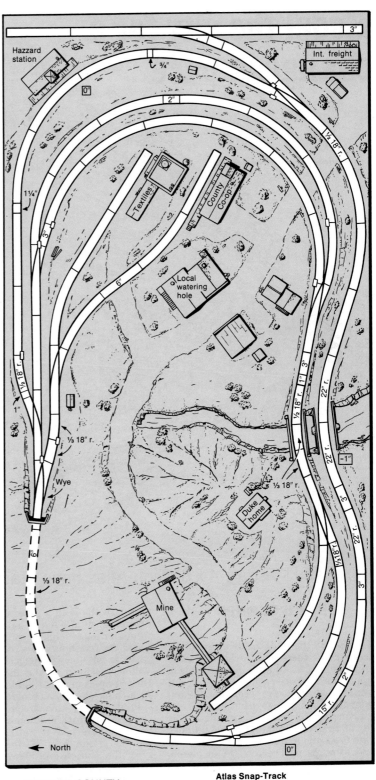

HAZZARD COUNTY SHORT LINE

Scale: 1″ = 12″

Atlas Snap-Track

Turnouts	Straight - 13	Curved
Right-hand - 5	Partial straight	18″ curved - 33
Left-hand - 3	6″ - 2	22″ curved - 3
Wye - 1	3″ - 5	15″ curved - 1
	2″ - 2	⅓ 18″ curved - 6
	1¼″ - 1	½ 18″ curved - 3
	1″ - 1	
	¾″ - 1	

Model the city for a change of pace

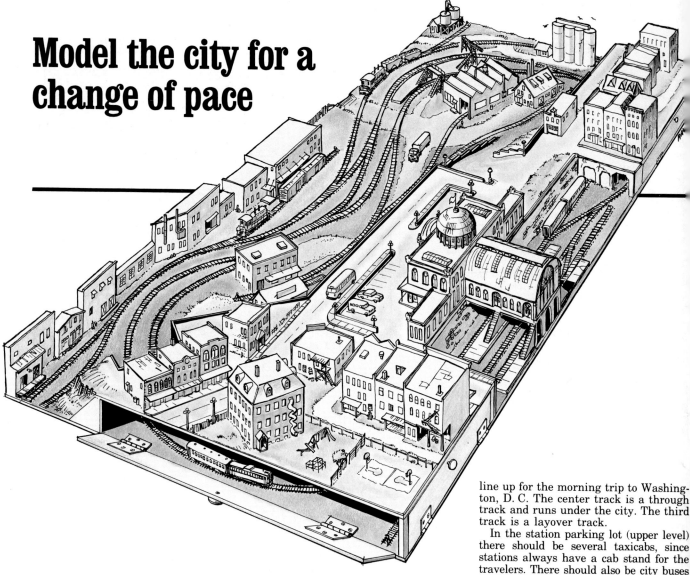

An HO scale 4 x 8 using Atlas Snap Track

BY ED SUMNER

IT SEEMS that with model railroaders, wherever there are tracks, there are also mountains. Admittedly, this type of scenery is impressive and beautiful, but frankly, when you've seen one mountainous layout, you've seem 'em all.

Living in Baltimore, Md., a major port city and rail terminal (but no mountains), I get to see the inner city almost daily. On several occasions I've thought to myself, why not design a track plan which allows for the type of operations seen near a city, rather than the wide-open spaces? That's what this is.

PASSENGER TRAFFIC

I'd suggest building the urban side of the layout on a box-like structure of re-taining walls with a piece of ⅛″ Masonite on top. Access to the hidden tracks is through hinged flaps as per the drawing. Cover the retaining walls with stone wall paper or plastic sheet (such as made by Vollmer) and go heavy on the weathering. Dirty it up as much as you like; there's no such thing as too much here.

In designing this track plan I borrowed a lot from Baltimore. On the urban side you have a station not unlike the real Penn Station. Like its proto-type, the station sits above the tracks, which must be reached by stairways coming down from the waiting room. The station building itself may have to be scratchbuilt, since I know of no manufacturer who makes a structure of this type. I have arranged the track similar to that of Penn Station, with the closest track being where RDC commuter trains

line up for the morning trip to Washington, D. C. The center track is a through track and runs under the city. The third track is a layover track.

In the station parking lot (upper level) there should be several taxicabs, since stations always have a cab stand for the travelers. There should also be city buses on the streets leading into or near the station. Cars and people on the sidewalks are the order of the day too, along with street-lamps, mailboxes, trash cans, fire alarm boxes, and an occasional phone booth.

You can make your own choice of buildings. I suggest the Con-Cor Court-house Square, Magnuson Victoria Falls Townhouses, Life-Like Belvedere Hotel, or any other buildings which look like inner-city buildings. City streets are a dull gray color, and the lines in the street are white and faded. The streets are also full of potholes, ruts and cracks, oil spots, and other weathering.

At the south end of the layout are rows of city buildings, residential and commercial. At the north end of the lay-out there is a school building and an asphalt playground behind it. This is typical of many of our urban centers. So are filthy alleys and weatherbeaten old structures. If you really want to model the in-ner city, board up some of the buildings and print graffiti all over the sides of the buildings, or maybe break a window or

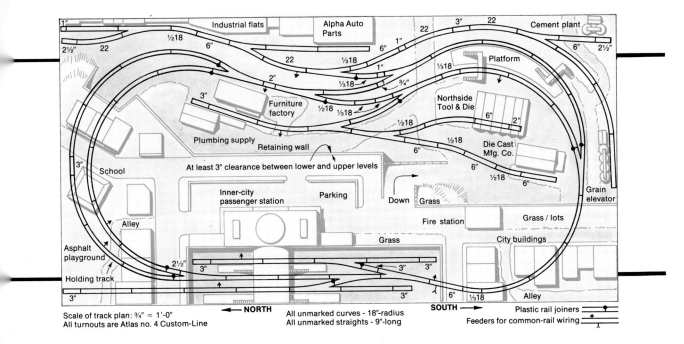

All turnouts are Atlas no. 4 Custom-Line

Scale of track plan: ¾" = 1'-0"

← NORTH   All unmarked curves - 18"-radius   SOUTH →
               All unmarked straights - 9"-long

Plastic rail joiners
Feeders for common-rail wiring

two. Grates over basement windows at street level are also commonly used to prevent break-ins.

FREIGHT TRAFFIC

There is another side to this layout: freight operations. It's on this side of the layout, opposite the passenger station, through which the railroad's real lifeblood flows. There are lots of kits on the market that you can use for industries over here, and these are prime candidates for kit-bashing and heavy weathering.

There are two industrial areas to be switched by two small switchers, perhaps SW1500 types or a road engine small enough to fit. They deliver cars a cut at a time and set them out at their proper industry, removing the cars already in place. Judicious use of the passing siding at the southeast corner of the layout is needed to shuffle loaded cars out and empties in, and all of this without fouling the main . . . which brings us to our next topic.

OPERATION

You say that a 4 x 8 doesn't have much operation? Well, I beg to differ. This one does, if you're careful. There's not a lot of track here, so you need to use what you have wisely. I envision a typical operating session to start like this. . . .

6 a.m. The RDCs are humming on the siding, preparing to take their loads of passengers to work. They are scheduled to leave at 6:15, if all goes well.

Over at the freight yard, the first switcher comes in with one car each for Die Cast Manufacturing and Northside Tool & Die. The engineer has 10 minutes to get from the yard to the industries without fouling the main for a southbound passenger train.

Carefully, he edges the throttle up to yard speed. The aging Geep growls a bit, and the engineer mutters a curse under his breath, recalling the problems he had with his last shipment to Northside. Can you imagine that? Complaining to the main office because he was late by a lousy 5 minutes! Edging onto the main, the skilled engineer brings the train to a halt while the brakeman uncouples for a run-around. Checking his watch, he finds that he's still 6 minutes to the good. Maybe he'll get it in on time this morning.

6:05 a.m. The southbound *Silver Streak* pulls into the station on its way to Florida. There are only five cars in this train because it's summer and not too many people want to go to Florida right now. (The train's abbreviated consist comes in handy when you hide it on the storage track underneath the school, which is where it just came from.)

6:10 a.m. Its 5-minute stop complete, the train hustles southbound, past the grungy industries and into a second tunnel (the holding track that it came from a moment ago).

The switcher has just eased into the industrial area now, and the hogger thanks the Lord that this morning he made it. It isn't always that easy with the old Geep. The maintenance boys do their best, but this baby is old with a capital O, and the company says it's too expensive to get something better.

6:15 a.m. The engineer of the commuter run slides the throttle forward ever so slowly. The *Silver Streak* is long gone by now, but with the lousy track between here and the Capitol, well, he can't pick up too much speed without his

passengers losing their breakfast from being tossed side to side like a ship in rough seas. Once through the tunnel at the south end of the station, he'll stop at the various stops between Metropolis and the Capitol.

(When the commuter train has finished its run and has pulled into the tunnel on the holding track behind the *Silver Streak*, you open the hatch and remove the Florida-bound train. Place a couple of the passenger cars on the long spur and use a switcher to move them into the station area.)

6:25 a.m. The switcher from the yard is just bringing in cars for a northbound commuter run. It'll be ready to go by 7 or so. (Continue periodically placing cars on this track until you have a fair-sized commuter train, but no more than six cars and an A and B unit.)

Over in the industrial area the second switcher is ready with a short cut for the cement plant and the grain elevator and also for a pickup at Alpha Auto Parts. The first switcher can make a pickup at the plumbing supply warehouse: a boxcar full of toilets.

Or can he? Well, he can if the evening run yesterday took out that flat of lumber for the furniture factory, and that depended upon whether or not they got it unloaded before 5 o'clock last night. If they didn't, he'll have to move the flat, pick up the boxcar load of toilets, and put the flat back so that the day shift can finish unloading it when they come in. All of that switching around will make him late. It could foul up the main for the 7:15 northbound commuter run . . . but then that's railroading in the big city.

TRY SOMETHING DIFFERENT

I think you get the picture. There's a lot more to this layout than you might think, especially if you use the clock and a card-order system. Urban modeling is easy and fun, it doesn't require a whole lot of skill at making scenery, and it's a great change of pace from the country. Try your hand at it sometime; you might find that you like it! ✍

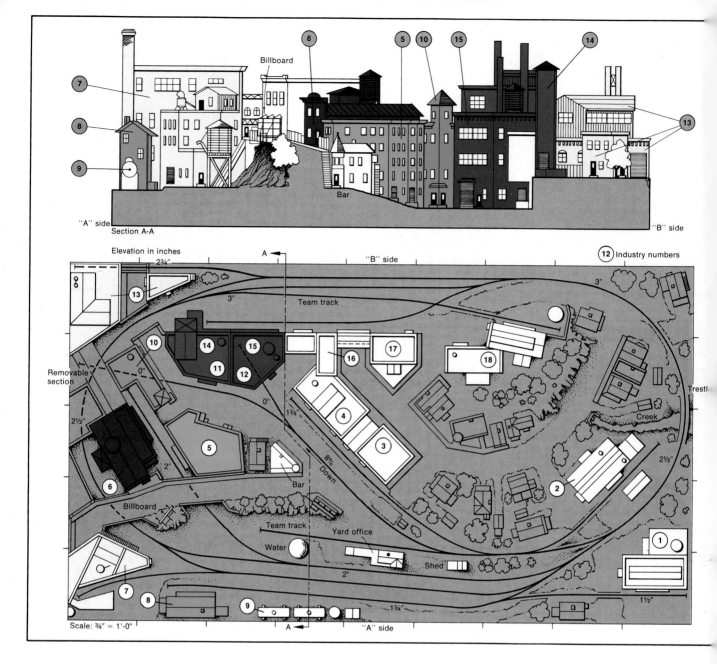

Billboard

6 5 10 15 14

7

8

9

13

Bar

"A" side
Section A-A
"A" side   "B" side

Elevation in inches   A◄   "B" side   12 Industry numbers
2¾"
13
3"   Team track   3"
10   17
14   15   16
11   12   18
0"
0"
1¾"
2½"   4
5   8%   3
2"   Down
6
Billboard
Bar
Team track
2½"
Water   Yard office
2
Shed
7   1¾"   1½"
8   2"
9
Scale: ¾" = 1'-0"   A◄   "A" side

Trestl
Creek

The BTR RR.

An unconventional approach to layout design

BY ART CURREN

THIS track plan for a 5 x 9-foot HO layout is about as nontypical as a track plan can be if you judge it by normal track planning criteria.

BTR stands for Break The Rules since that is what I did in designing this plan. Most track plans are either of someone's already built railroad and reflect his or her desires, or they are plans that have been very laboriously thought out and are practically foolproof in design so that anyone can adopt them without fear of making a mistake.

Track planners try to include as many features as they can so the builders will enjoy operating the layouts. The BTR has none of these "standard" features: no

yards, no engine facilities, and no stations. The BTR interchanges with itself, has an 8 percent grade, subradius curves, and very little scenery. And to cap it all off, it is just a simple oval on which the trains go round and round.

Why break all those track planning rules? Well, I wanted to design a small layout that would be fun to operate, and I also wanted to include lots of structures. To have room for lots of buildings, some other features had to go. I began by eliminating a lot of "standard" features. The first things to go were the yards and the engine-servicing area that usually take up huge amounts of space. I also decided not to include other railroad structures like depots, interlocking towers, etc. Stop and think of how many nonrailroad structures are found along rights-of-way in relation to ac-

tual railroad structures. Usually the ratio is very top heavy in favor of nonrailroad structures. So, I think the BTR is very prototypical.

You do have to pay close attention to details along the right-of-way to give the layout a railroady look without the aid of typical railroad structures.

Another compromise I feel is necessary when designing a small layout is to eliminate the aspect of time when it gets in the way. The same with distance. There is no way you can convey realistically any form of length in a 5 x 9-foot space. What we have on the BTR is a run from one crowded industrial area through the edge of a residential area and into another industrial area. Wouldn't most prototype railroads like to have that kind of concentrated — and profitable — operation?

By having the tracks on different levels in industrial areas and the streets twisting winding in all directions, we are able to ate the illusion of greater depth and disce and make these areas of the layout k very realistic.

Revenue-producing industries are the key he BTR, and they dominate the layout. managed to squeeze 18 BTR customers this small space. I've also provided some ef from the industrial areas by including ree-laced residential area between the ustrial areas on each side of the plan. e buildings on the creek end of the layout low, and they get progressively higher as u head toward the left and center of the out. The buildings on the left end should tall enough so that at normal viewing ight they will form a view block so that e A cannot be seen from side B and vice rsa. The best way to accomplish this is to rt with a layout height that is just a little low eye level.

Modeling this many structures using mmercial kits will not be as difficult or as pensive as you might think. Note that any of the buildings can be seen only from e side, so the rear walls can be left off and ed as the front or back of another build-g. If you don't use a wall here, you can use there.

You can get trains running quickly if you e flextrack and commercially available rnouts. Once the trains are running, you n work on the structures whenever you ave some free time. I suggest you use Code 0 rail to convey the look of the light rail sually used by the prototype in industrial reas.

Slight grade separation, such as lowering e sidings to industries 8 and 9, is very pro-typical, as is the steep grade down to dustries 10, 11, and 12. A grade this steep 8 percent) can be negotiated by most loco-otives with one or two cars. It is not the teepness of the grade that causes most roblems on a model railroad, but rather the ertical transition from level to grade. This the critical area. This transition must be ery smooth so couplers and pilots do not nag or short on the rails.

My old layout had an 8 percent grade ith a 12"-radius curve at the bottom and I ad no problems with it. The vertical transi-ion was accomplished by using 3/16" panel-ng for roadbed in this area. The paneling an be flexed into gentle transitions natu-ally. I screwed and adjusted the slopes by ightening or loosening the screws as I ran a ocomotive and car up and down, until there vere no snags or shorts.

Although I did not plan the BTR to be an xpandable layout, a foot more of space at he wall end would allow you to actually route the tracks in the direction that the buildings along the tracks suggest. The tracks would cross behind industries 6 and 10 and then continue along the walls. If the trestle at the right side of the layout were eliminated, the layout could be expanded in that direction, if space were available.

The BTR RR could be imagined to be a lesser line of anything from Conrail or the Family Lines (or their predecessors) to the Burlington Northern or the Southern Pacific. You might also want to change the name to the F & P, for Fun & Pleasure - that's what this layout offers n a 5 x 9 foot space.

A terminal solution
Too little space? Try this HO scale engine facility from a 4 x 8

BY RUSSELL SCHOOF

Limited space - the all-too-common buga-boo of model railroading. Twenty years ago my solution to this problem was a small engine terminal - and nothing more. All of the action involved in servicing engines made the layout fun to operate, but I was always bothered by the fact that there was nowhere for the engines to come from or go to. The imaginary comings and goings to which I was forced to resort soon lost their appeal, and in less than a year I lost interest in the layout.

Since then, layout design principles have evolved appreciably. One of the more notable advances has been the increased use of hidden staging tracks to represent the world beyond the layout. However, that concept is difficult to apply to small layouts: hiding whole trains takes a lot of room.

But what if one wanted to hide only the engines? Why, a little space would do quite nicely. With that idea in mind, I decided to see whether I could overcome the shortcomings of that long-gone first layout. The HO scale track plan you see here is the result.

This is definitely a layout for the modeler who likes engines, but who has little space

in which to run them. The plan represents an engine terminal at a division point on a large railroad. It has facilities for routine maintenance of, and minor repairs to, both steam and diesel engines; major work is performed elsewhere. The terminal is able to handle a high volume of traffic, providing a steady parade of motive power for the observer.

The layout, built from a single 4 x 8 sheet of plywood, is divided into two parts, both operationally and physically. The terminal proper occupies the larger area, and the action that takes place there is in full view. The staging tracks that represent the rest of the railroad are hidden from view along the back (under a removable street and behind a retaining wall) and down one side (behind a "front-drop"). That puts out of sight the not-so-prototypical activity of stashing engines on short spurs for later recall.

I show the tracks at the rear of the layout hidden by a long retaining wall topped by a street. Buildings in low relief against a sky backdrop run along the street to form the horizon. The street is made in hinged or lift-out sections to give

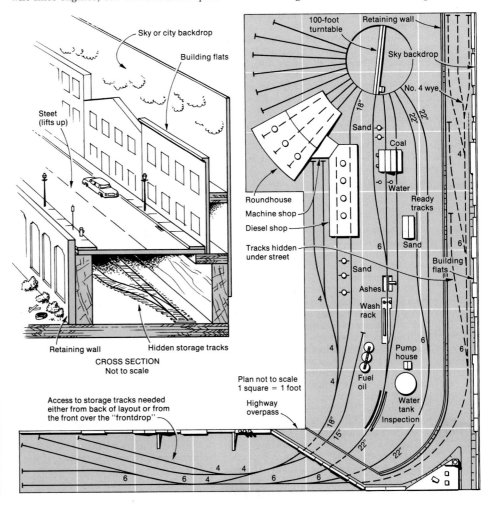

access to the tracks below. A simpler scene could be created by putting a scenic backdrop in place of the retaining wall, but it might be a bit high to reach over in case of trouble. That problem could be circumvented by leaving room to get around behind the layout.

Engines move between the two areas by passing under a highway overpass that covers holes in the separating backdrop. Thus, a realistic scene is achieved: engines arrive from the hidden yard for service and storage, and fresh engines are dispatched off scene to that same functional yard to assume their duties.

SERVICE AND STORAGE

The steam facilities are designed to accommodate small to medium-size engines, the limiting factors being the 100-foot turntable, no. 6 turnouts, and 22"-radius curves. Incoming engines are inspected, have their running gear cleaned at the wash rack, and drop their ashes in the ashpit. Then they go to one of two service tracks for water, coal, and sand. Finally, they head onto the turntable for turning and delivery to the roundhouse or a storage track. Outboard engines await their call on two ready tracks, one for each direction.

A single track for cars to serve the coaling dock, sandhouse, and ashpit rounds out the facility. Its connection to the turntable allows access from either end.

Diesels have a two-track shop, with fueling and sanding facilities out front. One track runs through to the turntable for turning. Two outside storage tracks hold two or three units each, depending on type. A spur holds tank cars that bring in fuel oil. Sand is piped from the sand house.

The layout could be made steam-only by eliminating the diesel facilities. A rip track, maintenance-of-way car storage, or some other maintenance-related track could be laid in its place. A diesel-only terminal could

be modeled simply by having the diesels take over the steam area with unneeded facilities either abandoned or town down. Or, the diesel area might be expanded at the expense of all or part of the now-defunct steam era.

The hidden tracks can store five or six steam engines and a half-dozen diesels. The capacity will vary with the size of the engines used. There is also room for a few hoppers, gondolas, and tankers for fuel, sand, and ash service. Most turnouts are no. 6 to accommodate the steamers. (Using short-wheelbase engines would make no. 4 turnouts practical, increasing the storage capacity.) The space advantage of engine-only operation is evident here - imagine how much space would be needed to store a dozen trains!

OPERATION

The operating-scheme for this layout could range from simple to extremely complex. At one end of the scale, a simple rotation of engines between the terminal and the storage tracks would provide a steady stream to keep one or two operators busy. Variety would be introduced by occasional trips to the shop for maintenance, plus some switching of the fuel, sand, and ash facilities.

At the complex end of the scale, the possibilities seem almost without limit. The two imaginary divisions (or subdivisions) served by the yard could be laid out on paper and schedules devised for train movements over them. The engine terminal, then, would be operated so as to meet the motive power demands generated by that schedule. Engines would be assigned to trains according to their tonnage and speed ratings over the divisions. Random or unscheduled events (e.g., extra trains or sections, snowplows, breakdowns, late arrivals, engines out of service) could be introduced by way of cards drawn from a pack or some other similar device.

Operation on this plane elevates the ope ator from hostler to motive-power foremaassigning engines to trains and controllir the flow through the terminal to see that tl trains can move as scheduled. Three oper tors could be employed: the foreman to co trol the operation and two hostlers to ru the engines.

Wiring to run so many engines would ne essarily be extensive since many sho blocks would be needed. Limiting the nur ber of engines in motion at any one time two would help keep things from getting tc far out of hand, though. To simplify things bit more, the hidden trackage could t divided into two large blocks - one on eithe side of the highway bridge - for cab-selectio purposes. Power would be fed to the spur through contacts on their switch machine (and through a diode to prevent over-rur ning). Conversely, any wiring for multiple unit storage on a single track would ad complication.

A lot of effort (and probably grief) could b saved - through at some expense - by th use of a command control system.

Scenery, like operation, could be eithe simple or complex. One could achieve th look of an engine terminal with only a fev structures and an appropriate commercia backdrop. However, a trip to the nearest pro totype engine facility quickly reveals th details that give the place its true atmos phere - clutter. Reproducing that clutter or the layout would be a challenge worthy o great effort.

A layout such as this would be appropri ately placed near eye level, to give a good view of the action. The engines' running gear would be plainly visible, and the scenery along the back would be viewed through the jumble of railroad structures, as though one were actually standing in the terminal.

There you have it. A combination of a realistic scene and interesting, prototypical operation. And, I think, a lot of fun.

4 x 8 + 1

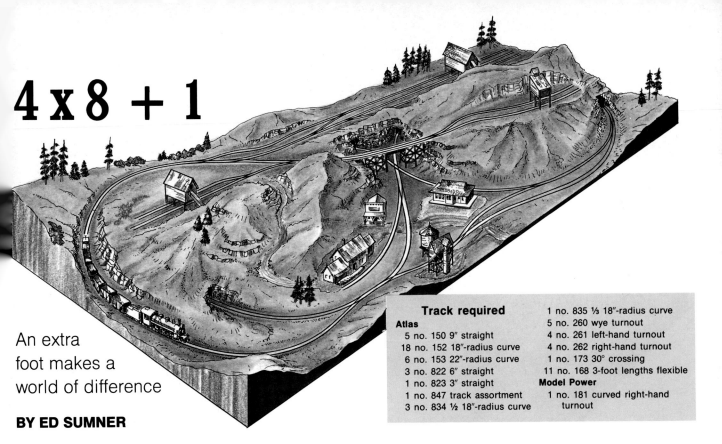

An extra foot makes a world of difference

BY ED SUMNER

Track required	
Atlas	1 no. 835 ⅓ 18″-radius curve
5 no. 150 9″ straight	5 no. 260 wye turnout
18 no. 152 18″-radius curve	4 no. 261 left-hand turnout
6 no. 153 22″-radius curve	4 no. 262 right-hand turnout
3 no. 822 6″ straight	1 no. 173 30° crossing
1 no. 823 3″ straight	11 no. 168 3-foot lengths flexible
1 no. 847 track assortment	**Model Power**
3 no. 834 ½ 18″-radius curve	1 no. 181 curved right-hand turnout

THE standard size for small HO railroads is the good-old 4 x 8, basically because that's the standard size plywood comes in. Lots of modelers get their start by buying a sheet of plywood and tacking their loop of train-set track to it. You can do a lot in 4 x 8, but you can do so much more with even just another foot of length. And after all, if you have room for a 4 x 8, the chances are excellent that you have room for the 4 x 8 + 1 presented here.

If you want you can still start with a single piece of plywood. It may be hard to find in your area, but plywood is also offered in 4 x 10 sheets. Another possibility would be to buy a 4 x 8 sheet and a 2 x 4 sheet. Cut the 2 x 4 in two and join half of it to the 4 x 8. You'll have enough plywood left to make a control panel and some other odds and ends.

LOOKING AT THE PLAN

The plan is simple. It's a figure 8 with a branch line winding its way up the side of a mountain. Most of the action will take place on the branch. I have it serving three separate mines. If your thing is logging, this layout would also make for a good logging pike.

The main line isn't much as far as variety is concerned, but with a little ingenuity this pike could be made interesting for two-train operation. First, forget the notion of simply running one train around and around. While a switcher works the mines a second train could be switching the mining supply warehouse and dropping off a cut of hoppers on the reversing section to be picked up by the branchline switcher. When the job is done run the mainline train into the tunnel nearest the branch and cut the power, using the hidden block as a holding track.

Another operating possibility for this layout is mixed passenger/freight trains or local gas-electric or RDC service. By tacking a shorty coach or combine onto the end of a branchline train, the miners have transportation to their work and back.

Small steam locomotives would look great on this layout. It would make a perfect home for an MDC Shay, a Rivarossi Heisler, or perhaps a brass 2-8-0 or 2-8-2. The railroad could also be built as a narrow gauge line, or even electrified for an interurban operation with steeplecabs and combines.

Mines are interesting structures to begin with, and on a small layout like this you can add detail to your heart's content. In a year or two this small layout could shine like a jewel. ⛭

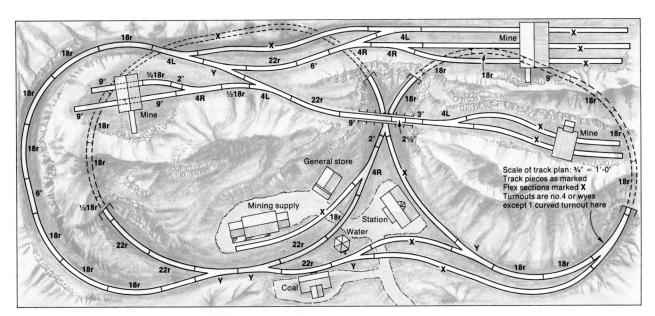

The Laurel Highland RR

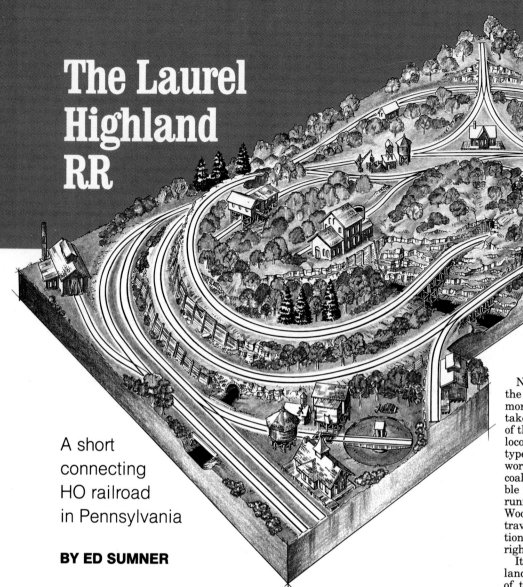

A short connecting HO railroad in Pennsylvania

BY ED SUMNER

THIS TRACK PLAN for an HO scale layout is similar to the arrangement I used for my own pike. The topography of the Laurel Highland RR, as I've named it, resembles the mountain areas of eastern Pennsylvania. Beginning at an upper level, the main line works its way down to an interchange with a Class 1 railroad. Among other features the Laurel Highland has a brewing operation in Highland, Pa., where a master brewer uses natural springwater in his brewing process. Since Pennsylvania has coal mining, I threw in three coal mines to provide the railroad with more revenue. Logging camps could be exchanged for the mines because there were sizable logging operations in that state as recently as 50 years ago.

This plan can be set in any number of periods, but the one that comes to my mind is 1920 to 1940, the days when billboard-side private reefer cars were still being used. In addition to hopper cars full of coal, you would see boxcars carrying bagged grain, flatcars loaded with mine timbers or machinery, gondolas carting away mine refuse, and a special boxcar or two of explosives for the mines. There would also be a short old passenger car for transporting the brewery and mine workers.

BENCHWORK AND TRACK

The benchwork is a box grid constructed of 1 x 4 lumber with 2 x 2 legs braced with 1 x 2 pieces. For the track base use ½"-thick plywood supported by 1 x 2 and 1 x 4 risers. The zero elevation portions of the plywood at Laurel are screwed directly to the top of the 1 x 4 grid. Only the track elevations for other risers are given. Fit intermediate risers to suit the grade. Note that the plywood for one leg of the wye (piece A) and for the supports for mines numbered 2 and 3 (pieces B and C) are cut from scraps and spliced to the main section. Pieces D and E as well as the streambed are cut from an extra ½" x 24" x 48" piece of plywood. Notch five of the grid members (one end, one side, and three intermediate 1 x 4 pieces) about ¾" deep to accommodate the stream.

Both Roco and Model Power make code 100 rail curved switches with 18" and 22" radii. Other curved switches are available with different radii, and the track arrangement would have to be adjusted to suit. Wye switches come in different sizes too. The ones shown are no. 4s.

OPERATION

Now here's the part I like best ab the layout — operation. Early in morning, 'long around sunrise, the cr takes the motive power and backs it of the Laurel enginehouse. I envision locomotive to be a Shay or other gea type, but a 2-8-0, 4-6-0, or 2-6-0 wo work just as well. After fueling up w coal and water it's turned on the turn ble for the trip up the hill. To extend running time, trains take the left track Woods and return to Laurel Junctio traverse the tracks between Laurel Jun tion and Woods again, and then take t right track at the Woods switch.

It's a long and hard climb to Hig land, with the train winding up the s of the mountain, passing through tu nels, and then crossing the stream th furnishes water for the brewery. On t upgrade run the engineer can look to h right and see the brewery sitting maje tically on the mountainside, support by a stone retaining wall.

Speeds are restricted to 20 scale m across the bridge on the high line. D spite its stone footings, the bridge ha washed out several times, and it groa and protests every time it's crossed.

Coming past Highland Mine No. 1 the crest of the grade, the train heads f the left leg of the wye, slowing to 5 m so a crew member can jump off and get the station for the schedule of pickup The train is turned on the wye, which ha one leg on an old timber trestle. One these days, before a stray spark sets afire, the management is going to replac it with a steel bridge — one of these day

The first stop is at Highland Mine N 3 for a pair of loaded hoppers. Next Mine No. 2 and another loaded hoppe After a stop for a reefer full of Highlan Laddie Beer at the brewery, two mor loads of coal are retrieved from Mine N 1. After running the locomotive aroun the train so the six cars are behind, th crew heads down the hill. These move may sound simple, but it will take som fancy maneuvering to accomplish the job

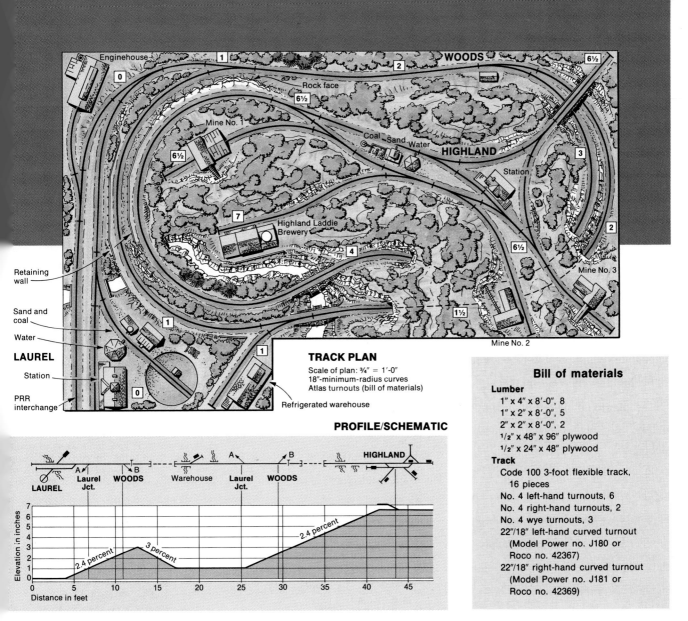

TRACK PLAN

Scale of plan: ¾″ = 1'-0″
18″-minimum-radius curves
Atlas turnouts (bill of materials)

Bill of materials

Lumber
1″ x 4″ x 8'-0″, 8
1″ x 2″ x 8'-0″, 5
2″ x 2″ x 8'-0″, 2
½″ x 48″ x 96″ plywood
½″ x 24″ x 48″ plywood

Track
Code 100 3-foot flexible track,
    16 pieces
No. 4 left-hand turnouts, 6
No. 4 right-hand turnouts, 2
No. 4 wye turnouts, 3
22″/18″ left-hand curved turnout
    (Model Power no. J180 or
    Roco no. 42367)
22″/18″ right-hand curved turnout
    (Model Power no. J181 or
    Roco no. 42369)

PROFILE/SCHEMATIC

On the return trip the reefer from the Highland Laddie Beer Co. is dropped at the refrigerated warehouse. The four full hopper cars are set onto the Pennsylvania RR interchange at Laurel and exchanged for empties bound for the mines. Every morning and night there is an extra run with an old coach to Highland and back to take the workers at the brewery and mines to and from work.

I think you'll find the Laurel Highland RR interesting both visually and operationally. If you made some changes in the topography, the LH could easily be set in some other areas of the country. Colorado comes to mind first, although Oregon or West Virginia or several other locales might also be considered. With any such change the mines could be producing silver, lead, iron, or other substances in place of coal. The Laurel Highland could also be a narrow gauge line following the practices of any of the Colorado lines, the East Broad Top of Pennsylvania, or the East Tennessee & Western North Carolina RR. Use your imagination, and make this a unique, evocative model railroad. ✿

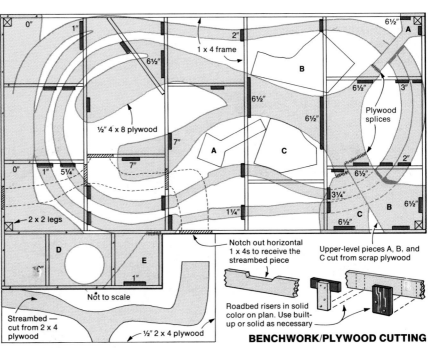

BENCHWORK/PLYWOOD CUTTING

Red Mountain Ry.

An HOn3 Colorado layout in a small space

BY BILL BAUMANN

INSPIRATION FOR the Red Mountain Ry. came from a trip to Colorado a number of years back. That trip included a drive from Ouray over Red Mountain Pass to Silverton and Durango, as well as a ride on the Denver & Rio Grande Western narrow gauge from Durango to Silverton.

The fictional Red Mountain Ry. depicts a line beginning at a connection with the D&RGW at Silverton and winding its way northward into the mountains, ending at the community of Red Mountain. While there were a few narrow gauge railroads that once ran out of Silverton into the mountains beyond, the Red Mountain Ry. is not intended as an adaptation of any specific road. The layout reflects my observations of the narrow gauge railroading and the topography I saw during my trip. The area adjacent to the tunnel, two bridges, and depot at Muley Gap Junction is based on an HO scale model diorama built by MR author John Olson (Stop Gap Falls) about 10 years ago.

The HOn3 layout I've designed represents the Northern Division of the RMR from Muley Gap Junction, through Bendaire, to Red Mountain. The Southern Division to Silverton is represented by two holding tracks behind the backdrop that ends under Red Mountain.

There is no engine escape crossover at the end of the holding tracks since trains are never turned here. The assumption is that the terrain between Silverton and Muley Gap was so rugged that a series of switchbacks was necessary to make the connection. Muley Gap is located on the end of the last switchback tail. In theory, a train arriving on the Southern Division (from the holding yard tracks) has negotiated the switchbacks and arrives in Muley Gap Junction running backwards, with the caboose arriving first and the locomotive (running backwards) pushing the train.

There are turntables at both ends of the division. After a train arrives at Red Mountain the locomotive is turned and run around the train, and the caboose i͏s transferred to the rear. The locomotive i͏s then ready to lead the train back dow͏n the 3 percent ruling grade. At Muley Ga͏p the same manuever is accomplished s͏o the equipment will head into the holdin͏g tracks engine first. At a future operatin͏g session the train is in the proper arrange͏ment to be backed, caboose first, into Mu͏ley Gap, simulating a new train.

The passing tracks are short (capacity four freight cars and one short caboose) but the typical narrow gauge trains are intended to be only a few cars long. With the exception of one wye at Red Moun͏tain, all turnouts are no. 4.

SCENERY AND STRUCTURES

While the 6 x 8-foot layout is compact. there is quite a large expanse of vertical scenery simulating the rugged Rocky Mountains. I've indicated a partial backdrop, and you can use commercial printed materials here if you don't want to paint your own mountains. Since the backdrop does not extend out the entire length of the wide leg of the layout, I suggest the

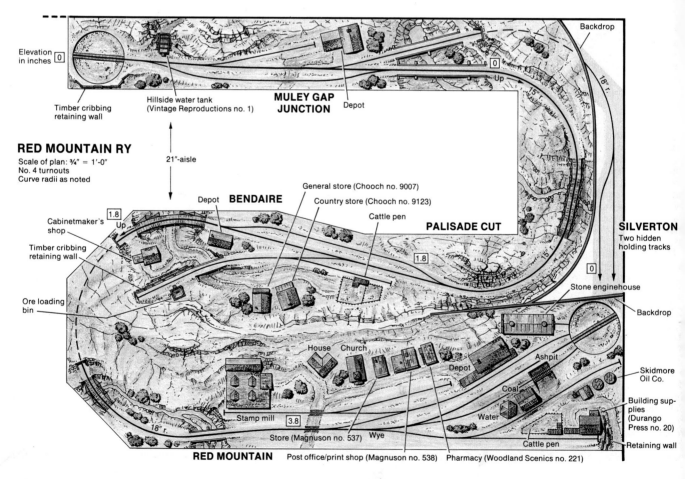

Elevation in inches [0]

Timber cribbing retaining wall

Hillside water tank (Vintage Reproductions no. 1)

MULEY GAP JUNCTION — Depot

Backdrop

Up

18" r.

15" r.

RED MOUNTAIN RY
Scale of plan: ¾" = 1'-0"
No. 4 turnouts
Curve radii as noted

21"-aisle

Depot — **BENDAIRE**

General store (Chooch no. 9007)

Country store (Chooch no. 9123)

Cattle pen

[1.8]

PALISADE CUT

[1.8]

SILVERTON
Two hidden holding tracks

Cabinetmaker's shop

Timber cribbing retaining wall

[1.8] Up

15" r.

[0]

Stone enginehouse

Backdrop

Ore loading bin

House   Church

Ashpit

Skidmore Oil Co.

Depot

Coal

Building supplies (Durango Press no. 20)

Stamp mill   [3.8]

Water

18" r.

Store (Magnuson no. 537)   Wye

Cattle pen

Retaining wall

RED MOUNTAIN   Post office/print shop (Magnuson no. 538)   Pharmacy (Woodland Scenics no. 221)

MOTIVE POWER AND ROLLING STOCK

The motive power and rolling stock needs are minimal for this layout. Adequate operation can be achieved with a single locomotive and a handful of freight cars, though slightly larger rosters would be desirable. In HOn3 Roundhouse (Model Die Casting) has 2-8-0, 0-6-0, and geared Climax locomotive kits. Precision Scale offers brass two-truck Shay 2-8-2 and 4-6-0 locomotives. Durango Press, Funaro & Camerlengo, Grandt Line, Precision Scale Co., Rail Line, Trains of Texas, and Ye Olde Huff-N-Puff have freight cars.

Since the layout is small, attention can be paid to detailing. A series of highly detailed small scenes, combined with slow-moving narrow gauge trains, will make the mainline length seem much longer than it is.

It would be very easy to expand the overall dimensions of the track plan. Modelers in other scales should be sure to maintain the 21″ aisle width. An N scale RMR layout would be 50″ x 53″, an S scale layout 8'-6″ x 12'-0″, and an O scale version 10'-4″ x 16'-0″. The Southern Division to Silverton could also be modeled by extending the line out from the holding track lead or the ends of the holding tracks. ⌀

top of the mountain ridge between Bendaire and Red Mountain be at eye level to scenically divide these areas. If the 21″-wide aisle is widened, the scenery at Muley Gap can be carried farther down below the track level to make the area look more rugged. An outside backdrop could be added to Muley Gap, too.

The structures are typical Colorado narrow gauge country types, mainly dealing with mining, cattle, and the necessities of the populace involved in these trades. Several building kits are suggested in the track plan structure notes. Most of the others will have to be scratchbuilt.

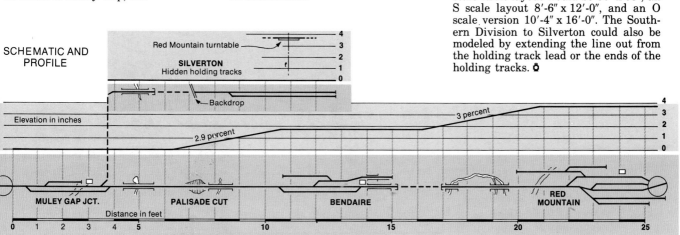

SCHEMATIC AND PROFILE

Red Mountain turntable

SILVERTON
Hidden holding tracks

Backdrop

Elevation in inches

3 percent

2.9 percent

MULEY GAP JCT.　　PALISADE CUT　　BENDAIRE　　RED MOUNTAIN

Distance in feet

From N to Z

A dual-scale layout that will look as big as all-outdoors

BY CHARLES F. GARTRELL

"WHAT! MORE THAN one scale on a layout? It's just not done!"

Okay, okay, I can hear my fellow model railroaders now. Just hold on and let me explain what this is all about. Not long ago a friend of mine got the itch to get back into modeling. Astounded by the scenes he had seen in magazines and books, John naively asked, "Can two or more scales be mixed to reinforce the illusion of scenic depth?"

"Yes," I replied. "For example, you can place an N scale building against a backdrop behind HO scale buildings."

"But," said John, "those are static models, what about using the actual trains?"

Now here was a challenge: How could we use two or more trains of different scales to convey the impression of distance? Furthermore, which scales would work well together?

SOME ANALYSIS

Let's examine the scale question first, restricting the discussion to the primary commercial scales as shown in fig. 1.

Not only are the scales themselves important here, but also the relative proportions between scales. It seemed to me a 20 to 30 percent differential between two scales would be about right. Two of the scale combinations have this relative ratio: O/S and N/Z. The next question naturally was, Which combination would be most suitable? For an answer, let's turn to nature and figure out what we see in a scene.

At a distance of 5 to 20 miles, objects on the horizon are basically indistinct. If a quarter is held at arm's length, most of those objects will be hidden behind it (see fig. 2). The edges of the quarter form an angle of about 2 degrees with the eye. Now a literal scaling of distance is out of the question — that 10-mile-away horizon would be 1100 feet away in O scale. On the other hand, if we use

the 2-degree angle to convey apparent size, then the vanishing point of an O scale foreground object could be located at a more reasonable 10 to 12 feet. Furthermore, the distance between an O scale locomotive and its S scale counterpart would be about 3 feet if this convergence angle were maintained.

All the same, the O/S combination is not very workable. It takes quite a basement indeed to accommodate scenes 10 feet deep. True, some of this depth could be reduced by using any number of visual tricks; nonetheless, the practicality of curve radii and so forth would require a considerable scenic depth.

Coming to the rescue is the more promising N/Z combination. Using the 2-degree angle, the scene depth can be reduced to about 3 feet and the minimum separation between scales to about 9"

SCALE	RATIO	Proportion of next larger scale
O	1:48	– –
S	1:64	75%
HO	1:87.1	73%
N	1:160	54%
Z	1:220	73%

Fig. 1 SCALE RELATIONSHIPS

Fig. 2 VIEWING DISTANT OBJECTS

Most distant objects are indistinct and (unless huge) will be blocked out by a quarter held at arm's length

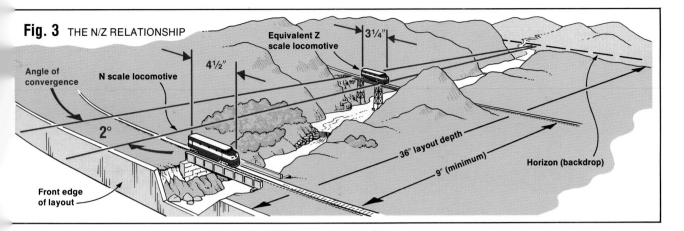

Fig. 3 THE N/Z RELATIONSHIP

Equivalent Z scale locomotive — 3¼"

Angle of convergence

N scale locomotive — 4½"

2°

36" layout depth

9" (minimum)

Horizon (backdrop)

Front edge of layout

see fig. 3). This combination is all the more convenient because John once did some modeling in N.

Before discussing the pike design, some other observations are pertinent:

• Scenic forms know no scale, though texture does in a rough sense.

• Parallel lines, such as rails, can be used to draw the eye in any direction and to indicate convergence into the horizon.

• Water in any form is great at grabbing a viewer's attention.

• Curvilinear shapes can be used to convey a sense of spaciousness.

• To look their best, curves viewed from the outside need to be of a broader radius than those viewed from the inside.

THE DUAL-SCALE LAYOUT

Our layout design, as shown in fig. 4,

is a railfan's pike designed to show off the trains. Let's follow a train over the route to see what happens. Our train, modeled in N scale, enters from the tunnel portal at the left and moves across the front of the layout. It crosses the river, then curves around a hill, enters a tunnel, and stops on the hidden return loop. After an appropriate interval we see our train again, emerging from a deep cut at a higher elevation. Identical in all respects though now in Z scale, it crosses the river on a suitably impressive bridge. Having crossed to the other side of the valley, it follows the river on a high rocky cliff before crossing it again and disappearing behind a hill in the distance.

Adding to the forced-perspective view is a dummy mine spur tapering from N to Z gauge as it recedes toward the background.

The owner of this pike wants it simple, so I've left out any hidden staging yards. In fact, there are no operating turnouts at all. Thus, the only way to make the transition possible and provide for hidden staging — a real must in this pike — is to have stacked loops hidden in the hills, leading us to classic dog-bone track configurations, one for each scale. Each bone is about 1¾ scale miles long, making timing and train speeds comparable on each.

This is a model railroad reduced to its core — just the sight of trains moving goods and people through nature's scenic splendor. I'd love to see it, preferably in fall colors. Maybe one day John will build it, sit back in his easy chair, and watch a miniature version of the magic of railroading. ⚲

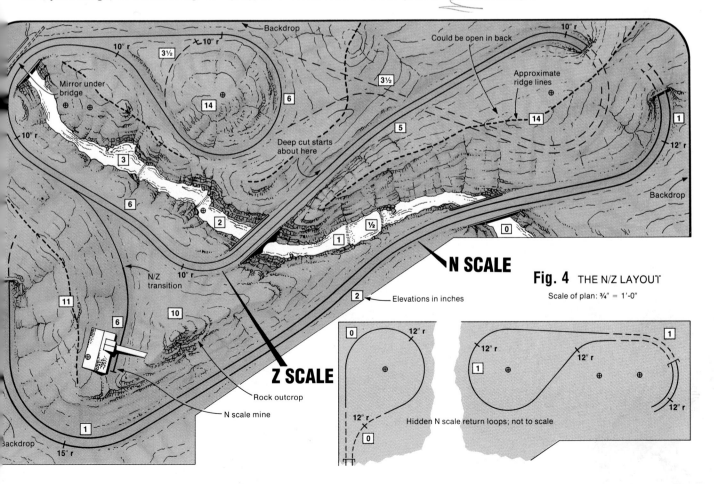

Fig. 4 THE N/Z LAYOUT

Scale of plan: ¾" = 1'-0"

N SCALE

Z SCALE

Elevations in inches

Backdrop

Could be open in back

Approximate ridge lines

Mirror under bridge

Deep cut starts about here

N/Z transition

Rock outcrop

N scale mine

Hidden N scale return loops; not to scale

The Bedford Valley RR

BY GORDON ODEGARD

ACCORDING TO ITS CCH (concocted corporate history) the Bedford Valley RR was founded in 1890 when a vein of zinc ore was discovered in the hills above Lac du Flambeau by down-but-not-quite-out prospector/entrepreneur Claude Zinderneuf. Quick to spot a profit when it hit him between the eyes, Zinderneuf began construction of a railroad from the mine to Bedford. Though, as yet, there was no railroad in town, Zinderneuf knew that when the news of his find reached the right corporate ears, railroads would come from all directions to offer their services.

No sooner were the right ears reached than both the Mid Central & Gulf and the Tonawonda & North Eastern railroads began laying track toward Bedford. Hoping to be able to "serve" Zinderneuf by carrying his zinc from Bedford to market, (that was the public version — the board-room version was quite another thing, including words such as "takeover" and "grab"),

the two railroads raced feverishly to get to the town first.

As it turned out, Zinderneuf got his BV to Bedford ahead of both companies (much to their chagrin). Thus the BVRR not only got its ore outlet, but even more important in the long run, it became a bridge line between the two other railroads, putting Claude in a position to do some real horse-trading.

Unfortunately, Zinderneuf's zinc vein ran dry early in the 1920s. But lest you feel too badly for Claude, he had already earned (and probably lost) his millions and sold the railroad. Besides, in the 30 years since its founding, industries had sprung up along the railroad's properties, and ore traffic had become secondary to a broad base of commercial and agricultural products shipped by the railroad.

And that's where the BV stands today — a small, but profitable, bridge-route railroad with modern power to haul a variety of materials and serve a mix of industries.

The BVRR offers the builder the opportunity to enjoy most of the projects and develop the mechanical and artistic skills that are a part of model railroading. Included are carpentry (benchwork), tracklaying, electrical wiring, scenery, some kitbashing, and even some basic electronics. Since not all of these areas are described in great detail here, I recommend three Kalmbach books that will be of great help: The ABCs of Model Railroading, How to Build Model Railroad Benchwork, and How to Build Realistic Model Railroad Scenery. Other Kalmbach books carry detailed information on more specific areas, such as car and structure construction, layout operation, and electronics.

As I've designed the HO scale layout, it represents a railroad located almost any-

where in the area east of the Mississippi River and a short distance to the west. It has hills with green shrubbery and a fair number of deciduous trees. Of course, with some modifications to the scenery, the BVRR could easily be made to look like a western or southwestern railroad. This would mean browner foliage, warm earth colors, and mountainous rockwork. For a railroad of the southwestern United States the architecture of the structures could be modified to include some mission-style structures.

The Bedford Valley RR, complete with modern GP40 hood units as motive power, is set anytime from 1965 to the present.

DESIGN

To eliminate the confining parameters of the common 4 x 8-foot model railroad, I've suggested using two pieces of 1/2" plywood cut and rearranged to get a free-flowing form. See the artwork on page 50. The advantage of the free form is the latitude that can be exercised in placing

structures and industries. Without the free form the track plan would tend to be a symmetrical oval paralleling the edges of a rectangle.

One plywood piece has a corner cut off and repositioned, and the other piece is cut into four sections. Three of these latter sections are used as extenders for the track base, while the remaining 30" x 96" is cut down to 78" and used as a scenic divider. A scenic divider such as this makes a small oval layout appear to be a stretched-out scene, since you're unable to look across the width and see the entire railroad.

All mainline and yard tracks are at one level, but the 1/2"-thick plywood base should be cut to depress spurs and sidings 3/16" lower. The switchback spur to the mine is designed with a 5 percent grade. Cut away the plywood at various spots to position some scenery contours below the track grade. While the yard is small, it can easily be extended to provide additional storage space.

BENCHWORK

L-girder benchwork is specified because of the versatility in adjusting the outer shape of the layout. It also provides the most flexible track-supporting structure. Cutting and reassembling the plywood pieces and extending the 1 x 4 stringers provides added scenery base outside the track and, again, eliminates the sterile rectangle form. Also, the layout shape can be easily changed at any time by cutting back, or further extending, the stringers.

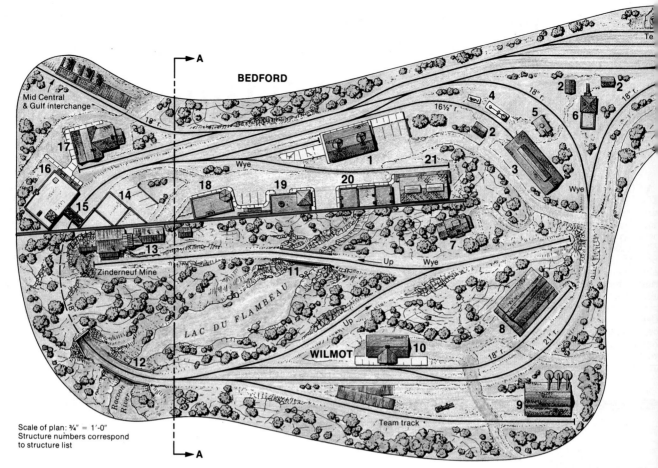

BEDFORD

Mid Central
& Gulf interchange

17

16

15

14

18

19

20

1

21

3

5

6

2

2

4

2

16½" r.

18" r.

18" r.

18" r.

7

Wye

Wye

Up

Wye

Te

13

Zinderneuf Mine

11

8

10

WILMOT

21" r.

18" r.

LAC DU FLAMBEAU

12

Racoon River

9

Team track

Scale of plan: ¾" = 1'-0"
Structure numbers correspond
to structure list

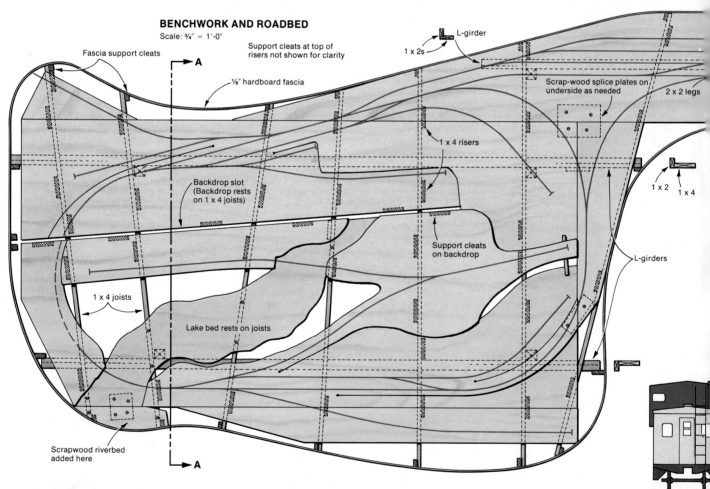

BENCHWORK AND ROADBED
Scale: ¾" = 1'-0"

Fascia support cleats

⅛" hardboard fascia

Support cleats at top of
risers not shown for clarity

L-girder

1 x 2s

Scrap-wood splice plates on
underside as needed

2 x 2 legs

1 x 4 risers

Backdrop slot
(Backdrop rests
on 1 x 4 joists)

Support cleats
on backdrop

1 x 2

1 x 4

L-girders

1 x 4 joists

Lake bed rests on joists

Scrapwood riverbed
added here

LOCOMOTIVE COLOR SCHEME
N scale

OPERATION

The BVRR uses hood units both as switchers and road engines. An older hood unit could be added to serve the mine and the town of Wilmot. The rolling stock is a mixture consisting mostly of boxcars, with flats, gondolas, hoppers, and a tank car or two.

There are two team tracks: one at the Bedford yard and the other on the spur across from the Wilmot station. These sites, along with the interchange track, provide spots where almost any type of freight car can be spotted. Small town team tracks often have unloading docks, a small crane, a portable elevator for covered hopper cars, and a small pump unit for tank cars.

Two interchanges are provided. These railroads can be renamed to suit your preferred locale. The MC&G does not enter Bedford, but leaves and picks up (in theory) cars at the interchange track. The T&NE (again theoretically) runs a train in and out of Bedford Yard. In an operating scheme BV crews set out cars at the interchange point at the first operating session and pick up the same ones at the next session, assuming them to be new arrivals. Another alternative is to replace the cars at the interchange points by the 0-5-0 (hand) method.

One regular train could be assigned to a short run to the MC&G interchange and servicing the industries. Another train would be a way freight picking up and delivering cars to the industries all along the main line. A third train could work the yard to the mine, hauling ore, gravel, or timber.

To complete the image of a specific railroad entity, about half the rolling stock is to be painted and lettered for the BVRR. (The Sweepstakes winner will get his equipment painted and lettered by members of the MR staff.) Floquil Signal Red is the standard freight car body color with white lettering. Locomotives and cabooses are SP Armour Yellow and Signal Red with black undergear and black and red heralds.

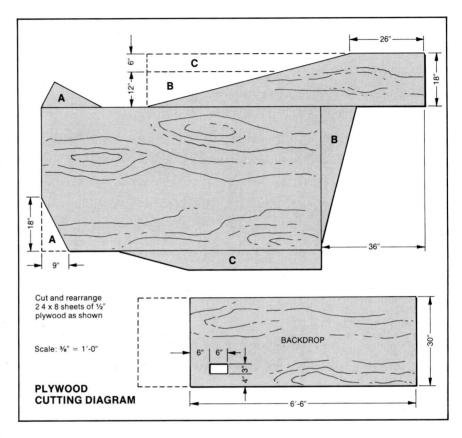

Cut and rearrange 2 4 x 8 sheets of ½" plywood as shown

Scale: ⅜" = 1'-0"

PLYWOOD CUTTING DIAGRAM

BACKDROP

STRUCTURES AND TRACK

1 AHM (Regal Way), no. J15811 Station
2 Pikestuff, no. 5 Yard Office (3)
3 Heljan, no. 404 Enginehouse
4 Stewart, no. 183 Sand and Fuel
5 Vollmer, no. 5518 Storage Tank
6 Atlas, no. 704 Signal Tower
7 Model Power, no. 433 Farmhouse
8 Campbell, no. 377 Seebold & Sons
9 Heljan, no. 360 Chemical Plant
10 Kibri, no. 9494 Station
11 AHM (Regal Way), no. 18052 Truss Bridge
12 Atlas, no. 855 Girder Bridge
13 Campbell, no. 429 Red Mountain Mine
14 Heljan, no. 922 Ford Motor Co.
15 Bachmann, no. J2634 Signal Bridge

16 Model Power, no. 455 Burlington Mills
17 Heljan, no. 914 Wright Bros. Cycle Shop
18 Heljan, no. 901 Two Brothers Restaurant
19 Heljan, no. 905 Firehouse
20 Walthers, no. 545 Merchant's Row III
21 Heljan, no. 1780 Appliance Warehouse

Midwest cork roadbed, 2 boxes
Shinohara Code 70 track
  1-meter flex-track, 35
  No. 4 right-hand turnout, 8
  No. 4 left-hand turnout, 10
  Wye turnout, 3
  Rail joiners and spikes, 5 boxes each
  Insulated rail joiners

CABOOSE COLOR SCHEME
N scale

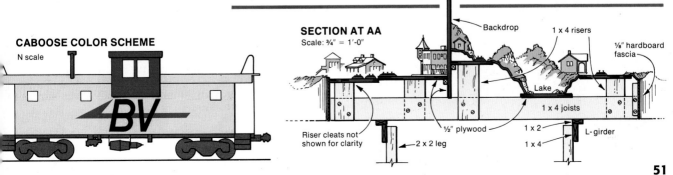

SECTION AT AA
Scale: ¾" = 1'-0"

Backdrop
1 x 4 risers
⅛" hardboard fascia
Lake
1 x 4 joists
½" plywood
1 x 2
1 x 4
L-girder
Riser cleats not shown for clarity
2 x 2 leg

Peace River RR

A small northern bridge route in HO featuring mainline trains

BY BILL BAUMANN

SOME PEOPLE INSIST that a point-to-point layout is the only kind to design and build. Everyone knows that real railroads move goods from point A to point B to earn their keep. Well, for a while I had myself convinced that anything less than a pure point to point design was less than the state of the art layout design and to be avoided.

Then, my rediscovery of some of the simpler pleasures of

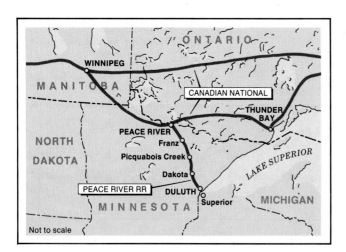

model railroading took root when I took my son, who was four at the time, to the local annual model railroad show. I watched his delight as trains repeatedly made their way over the display layouts, all of which were designed with continuous run. I hated to admit it, but I found I too was quite content to see trains just go round and round without the obligatory switching and reshuffling at each end of a short mainline run. Was it possible that my carefully designed two-deck point-to-point layout, complete with handlaid Code 70 rail and scratchbuilt iron ore dock, was not the layout of my dreams after all?

Now don't get me wrong. I'm not trying to talk anyone out of a point-to-point layout. What I *am* saying is that a desire for extended mainline running in conjunction with realistic operation, and a relatively small space, are not mutually exclusive. I think the HO scale, 9'-3" x 11'-1", Peace River RR I've designed to fit into a downstairs room in my house demonstrates that point.

The inspiration for the Peace River RR came from an article on the Algoma Central RR in the September 1984 issue of TRAINS Magazine. I found the concept of a moderately busy bridge route running through sparsely populated northwoods country to be very appealing. The PR is a free-lance line connecting its fictional namesake on the Canadian National route, through northern Minnesota with various unnamed railroads at Duluth, Minn.

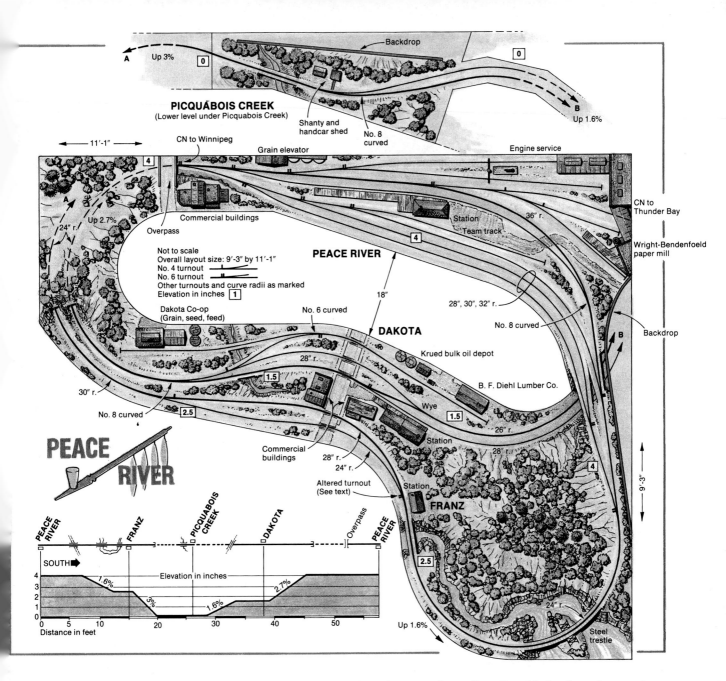

Not to scale
Overall layout size: 9'-3" by 11'-1"
No. 4 turnout
No. 6 turnout
Other turnouts and curve radii as marked
Elevation in inches [1]

On the track plan, one end of the Canadian National (to Thunder Bay, Ont.) is hidden by a paper mill structure, while the other end (to Winnipeg, Man.) disappears under a highway overpass after the junction with the Peace River RR. The Yard at Peace River is the exchange point with the Canadian National. There are basic engine facilities here in addition to a couple industries and a team track.

The commercial buildings at the back-to-back towns of Franz and Dakota do double duty portraying both communities. Opposite sides of the structures can be painted and lettered differently. The two depots are separated by a scenic barrier of tall trees.

Piquabois Creek (pronounced Peek-a-boo) is just a small opening in the layout fascia to provide access to the turnout located at this lower level. By adding a backdrop and scenery a short distance to each side of the station, the area becomes a mini diorama (albeit one with a low ceiling). On each side of this diorama the track disappears behind bushes and shrubs.

I've specified nos. 6 and 8 Shinohara curved turnouts in the plan. The curved no. 6 at Franz needs to be altered to fit into 24" and 28" radius curves. Cut through the plastic spacer bars under the outside rails and bend the rails to fit smoothly into the specified curves.

This model railroad can be set in any time period you choose by adjusting the motive power and rolling stock.

Through trains have Canadian National engines and cabooses. Peace River motive power can be CN leased four-axle hood units or units painted and lettered for the Peace River. In the steam era any small steam locomotive up to a 2-8-2 would be suitable.

OPERATION

The layout can be operated in a more-or-less point-to-point method with Peace River used as a staging/receiving yard. Trains with Canadian National motive power are assumed to be traveling from Winnipeg to Duluth and back. With this in mind, after leaving cars at Peace River yard, a train departs southbound to the lower right, traverses the layout, and after passing through Dakota heads upgrade into a tunnel. From there it theoretically continues on to Duluth. Actually, it reappears at the junction with the CN at Peace River, now representing a new train just arriving from Winnipeg.

Similarly, a northbound train leaving Peace River for Winnipeg becomes a northbound train from Duluth. A Peace River RR local freight is used to serve industries as far south as Dakota, passing through Franz and Picquabois Creek on the way.

Of course, operation is a lot of fun, but when the mood strikes, you can just sit back, put your feet up, and watch 'em roll, just like I intend to do. ❧

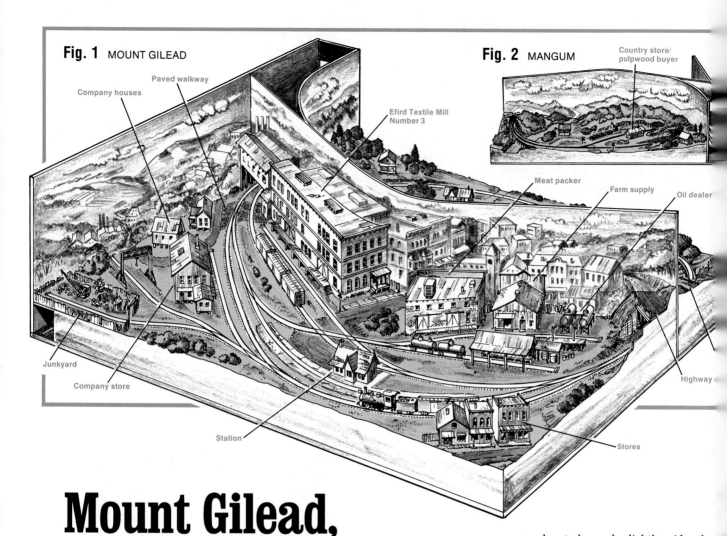

Fig. 1 MOUNT GILEAD

Company houses

Paved walkway

Efird Textile Mill Number 3

Fig. 2 MANGUM

Country store/ pulpwood buyer

Meat packer

Farm supply

Oil dealer

Junkyard

Company store

Station

Stores

Highway

Mount Gilead, a town on the move

An interesting portable layout section
that uses the middle of the room

BY MICHAEL ROGERS

LAYOUT PLANNING has always been an exercise in selective compression and compromises. All of the elements must be balanced against each other to create an impression of space and time in a relatively confined area. As a career Air Force officer, I have always had to consider the additional problems of coping with a mobile lifestyle.

Over the years, I have designed a number of sectional shelf-type layouts designed to fit against the wall. In each case I planned things so the sections could be easily rearranged to take advantage of whatever space I had available. All of these around the wall arrangements were somewhat frustrating to me since they failed to make efficient use of the middle of the layout room.

During a recent planning session, I turned my efforts toward designing a semiportable layout section that would make use of the middle of a room. To begin with, I examined exactly what I wanted the railroad section to accomplish, and then I listed the physical constraints that were necessary to maintain the layout's portability.

Any layout section that extends peninsula fashion, into a room from a shelf-type railroad must either be a dead end (terminal), or it must be wide enough to contain a turnback curve to get the main track out of the section. Since my personal hobby interest is in shortline-style railroading (using a series of portable sections that may be combined to simulate several towns connected by the railroad), a dead-end shelf is only useful as a terminal or as an industrial switching area leading off the main line. For this reason I designed my new layout section as a larger unit that would serve as an intermediate portion of the layout.

Any layout section with a turnback curve has to be made slightly wider than the diameter of the curve to allow for proper clearances. This would be 4 feet or more for an HO scale minimum radius of 20" (which is about as tight as I desire even for my small shortline equipment). This width can create serious problems when it comes to moving the railroad. In fact, I have experienced some difficulty at times when it came to getting my 2 x 8-foot layout sections into or out of houses which have winding stairways or rooms leading off narrow hallways.

Some years ago I remember reading an item about possible sizes for portable layout modules in relation to the problem of door sizes (which are about 6'-6" tall in most homes). If a wide layout section is limited to an overall length of about 6 feet, it can be moved through residential doorways on end. With this in mind, I settled on a 4½ x 6-foot layout section that gives me a little extra room for a wider radius and better track positioning.

I am primarily interested in layout sections that may be rearranged and combined in various ways to make an interesting short line. To accomplish this, each layout section has a center of operations such as a yard or a switching area. Whenever I finally retire and settle down, I will be able to connect these activity centers with simple scenicked sections of railroad.

On this larger section I wanted one

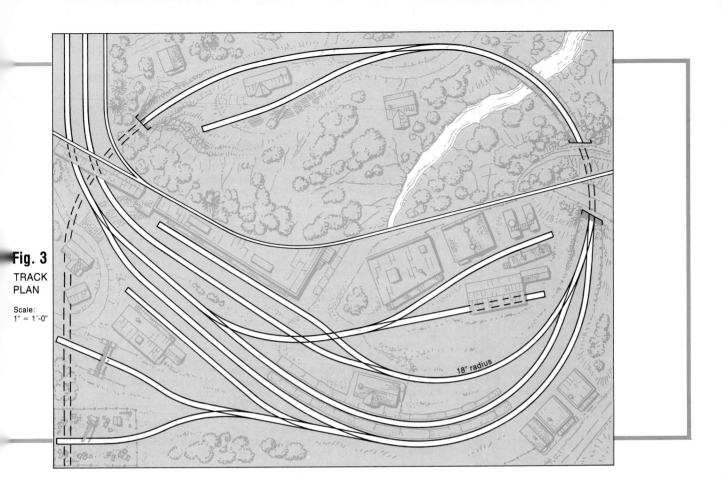

Fig. 3
TRACK
PLAN

Scale:
1″ = 1′-0″

18″ radius

side to have a small town with lots of switching while the other side would have a countryside setting to give a sense of distance. To accomplish this I used a scenic divider through the main portion of the layout section. An appropriate background painting would give the rural side a feeling of distance, while building flats set near the backdrop would help increase the apparent size of the town on the other side of the section.

MOUNT GILEAD

Figures 1, 2, and 3 show the track plan I developed to meet these requirements. I named this layout section Mount Gilead after a small town near my home town in North Carolina. Like its prototype, the model Mount Gilead is a textile and farming town typical of many found in the rural south. The track enters the section at the right rear corner and comes through the scenic divider into town. As it leaves town, the track again passes through the scenery divider, descends through the rural area and disappears into a tunnel under the town scene.

The minimum radius through Mount Gilead is 20″. I curved the scenic divider to provide more room for the town scene and to make it easier to blend the rural scenery into the backdrop. This divider is also split at the right rear corner to conceal the tracks from the town scene while allowing access from above. This makes it possible to exchange cars on this track if it is used to simulate an interchange point.

Any movable layout section must be designed to protect the interior during

moves without adding excessive weight. Mount Gilead has a bottom made from a solid piece of plywood that is reinforced by side pieces and ribs under the town area. A lot of primary strength comes from the scenic divider and the plywood back which are the same height. These parts make it easy to add removable plywood covers (mounted with screws) for moving protection. Removable panels under the town provide wiring access and the turnouts are controlled with ground throws to minimize complication.

Working out the grade necessary to bring the main line under the town proved to be a major design challenge. I wanted to keep the town switching area level so cars would not roll away. This meant the grade could not begin until the track entered the rural scene. Since there was no room to add more track, I searched for a way to reduce the thickness of the overhead supporting structure at the point where the lower track passed underneath it. I wound up removing the town level's plywood trackboard where it passed over the bottom track and then used thin metal or plastic to support the town tracks and scenery over the gap. This reduced the effective grade in the area to 3.75 percent.

Mount Gilead is now a major operating center for the railroad. The town is dominated by Efird Mill No. 3, a three-story textile plant which is the area's biggest employer and source of revenue for the short line. This mill is actually only a few inches thick, with most of the structure built as a flat along the center divider. The tracks curve back under an extension of the mill to make a visual transition.

Since my railroad is set in the 1950s, a series of mill houses is appropriate. These company-owned homes are across the track from the mill with a paved walkway connecting the properties. This walkway also serves as an easy way to conceal the different construction I used over the hidden lower track. A nearby company store receives durable goods and food products by rail as well as fuel and other supplies.

Both the company houses and the store are simple wooden structures, unadorned but sturdy. They were generally built on brick pilings to keep their wooden floors away from termites and to allow air to circulate underneath during the hot weather.

One of the spur tracks passes under the mill beside the main line. It may be treated as a mill siding or as an interchange with another railroad. There are five other spurs in the area serving a variety of industries. One track serves the rear docks of a group of stores and wholesalers which face the town (toward the divider). These include a farm supply house and a meat packer. Diagonally across town is a junkyard and a retail oil dealership. All of these industries were chosen to use a variety of car types and be fairly typical of what one might find in a small town.

My own preference is for local freight operation, but Mount Gilead is certainly large enough to have its own switcher. An EMD SW1 or Baldwin S-12 diesel switcher, or an 0-4-0 or 0-6-0 steam switcher would fit right in. In such cases, the local freight would simply drop off a group of inbound cars and pick up the outbound cars on its way through town. Then the local yard engine would handle the industrial switching. A small gas electric car or a mixed freight and passenger train could add some interesting variety. During the harvest season, a couple of old coaches might be used to run an extra local to transport townspeople out to the farms.

If the track under the hill is treated as an interchange, a train from the "other"

railroad could come into town, exchange cars, and disappear again. So there would be room for enough city structures to give the feeling of a complete town, I deliberately did not crowd every nook and cranny with switching tracks. The single track curving out of Mount Gilead is hidden by a highway overpass.

The rural crossroads scene is named Mangum after a "wide spot in the road" near the real Mount Gilead. I use this area primarily as a scenery technique test area, but it does have a single spur track to give some operating interest. This spur serves a small country store which receives shipments of feed and fertilizer by rail. The store also doubles as an office for a pulpwood buyer. Back in the 1950s, pulpwood was often loaded on bulkhead flats by hand with the cars spotted on team tracks or small country sidings. All this "industry" requires is a rutted muddy roadway next to the track where the trucks can pull up alongside the flatcars.

Scenery in the Magnum area is constrained by the need to hide or at least reduce the visual impact of trains passing through the divider at two different locations. At one end the track appears from a deep foliage-filled cut with the view of the track restricted by the heavy foliage, a foot bridge, and angle of the cut. A nearby scene includes a curved trestle spanning the river to further divert the viewer's attention from the cut. The opposite end of the scene has a normal tunnel approach and portal so everything remains fairly visible. A lot of foliage is built around the track in this entire scene to help conceal the steepness of the grade.

ROCKINGHAM

Rockingham is a 2 x 8-foot yard section complete with engine facilities, a car repair shed, and a work-equipment storage track (fig. 4). It can take care of the required switching for a short line or a small division point on a regular railroad. Although the turntable and enginehouse are restricted to engines shorter than 12" long, larger engines can work through the yard since it is built with Atlas no. 4 Customline turnouts, except for a single three-way switch and the sharper turnouts

leading to the coal supply track and a industry track.

ELLERBE JUNCTION

Ellerbe Junction is built in two section which are always used together as show in fig. 5. This area includes two tow and hidden trackage which represents th Norfolk Southern branch line that onc served the real town of Ellerbe. The na row end of the area is built on a 2 x foot section and contains a pair of hi den storage tracks, part of the junctio and the upper level town of Jackso Springs which has industries and an en gine facility.

The other end of Ellerbe Junction i built on a 3½ x 4-foot section that ha industrial spurs, a hidden interchang track, and a steep branch line up t Jackson Springs. The track connection between these two sections are prett complex, but they are all straight, and link them with short removable track pieces concealed by scenery and th branchline bridge. I don't mind this com plication as the two sections are only separated when I move. As it is, Ellerb Junction has an 18" radius curve, bu this could be tempered by slightly in creasing the width of the layout section

FITTING IT ALL TOGETHER

These three layout sections can be fit ted together in a variety of ways depend ing upon the room configuration. Figure 6 (A, B, and C) shows three possibilities with the major towns connected by short sections of simple benchwork I custom fit as needed.

In version A the town sections are connected so the trains travel from Rocking ham, through Mount Gilead, to reach the hidden storage tracks of Ellerbe Junction. This scheme will just barely fit into a 10 x 12-foot room. It has no turning facilities at Ellerbe Junction, so operations would be difficult unless diesel road switchers are used.

I like the arrangement in version B better, but it would require a 10 x 12½-foot room if 24"-wide operator spaces are used. In this setup Mount Gilead is set out about 3" from the wall so a hidden track may connect the upper-level branch (Jackson Springs) to the track from Rock-

Fig. 4 ROCKINGHAM

Scale: 1" = 1'-0"

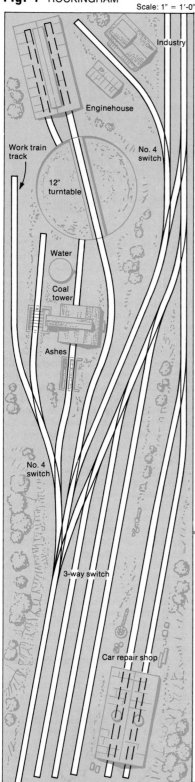

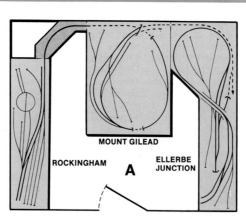

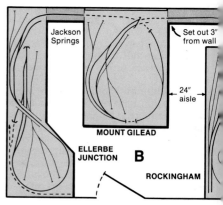

Fig. 6 MODULE COMBINATIONS

Not to scale

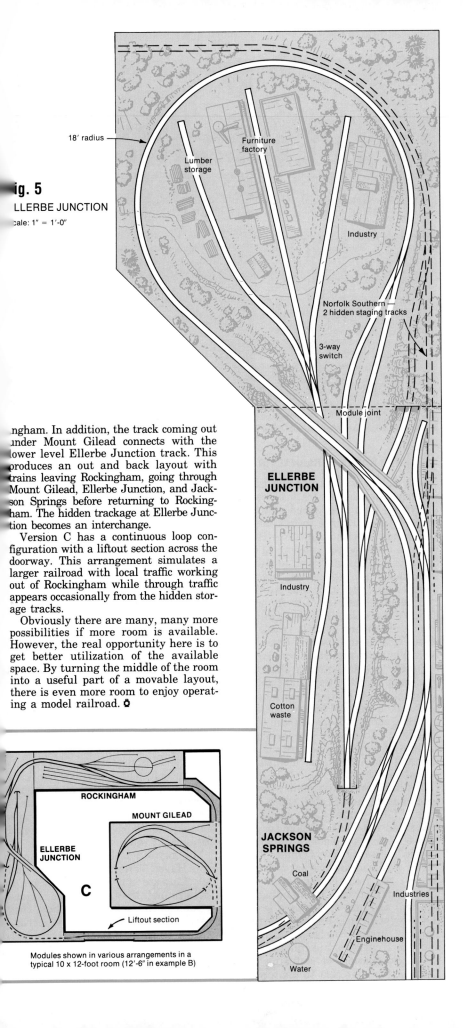

18′ radius

Lumber
storage

Furniture
factory

Industry

Norfolk Southern —
2 hidden staging tracks

3-way
switch

Module joint

ELLERBE
JUNCTION

Industry

Cotton
waste

JACKSON
SPRINGS

Coal

Industries

Enginehouse

Water

ngham. In addition, the track coming out
under Mount Gilead connects with the
lower level Ellerbe Junction track. This
produces an out and back layout with
trains leaving Rockingham, going through
Mount Gilead, Ellerbe Junction, and Jackson Springs before returning to Rockingham. The hidden trackage at Ellerbe Junction becomes an interchange.

Version C has a continuous loop configuration with a liftout section across the
doorway. This arrangement simulates a
larger railroad with local traffic working
out of Rockingham while through traffic
appears occasionally from the hidden storage tracks.

Obviously there are many, many more
possibilities if more room is available.
However, the real opportunity here is to
get better utilization of the available
space. By turning the middle of the room
into a useful part of a movable layout,
there is even more room to enjoy operating a model railroad. ✿

ROCKINGHAM

MOUNT GILEAD

ELLERBE
JUNCTION

C

Liftout section

Modules shown in various arrangements in a
typical 10 x 12-foot room (12′-6″ in example B)

By the beautiful sea

Track plan for an HO railroad serving a busy port

BY RUSSELL SCHOOF

RAILS AND WATER go together. In part that has to do with economics: Water transport is by far the cheapest mode of travel. For some commodities and for most intercontinental trade it is the *only* economically feasible mode. A very large proportion of land transportation — and this is especially so of railroads — is devoted to carrying goods between inland areas and ports. It's no accident that many early railroads in this country were built by port cities to carry trade to and from interior areas. The significance of all this for model railroaders is that the junction of the two great transportation modes, the rail/water terminal, is a wonderful subject for a layout. It offers a heavy flow of traffic over densely packed, complicated tracks winding through a variety of interesting facilities and structures.

FREE HAVEN TERMINAL RR

MODEL RAILROADER has published a number of waterfront track plans over the years, both free-lanced and based on prototypes. I chose to free-lance in designing the terminal at Free Haven, because I wanted the freedom to select facilities and lay out track to suit certain model railroad goals. My aims were to pick facilities that would require a large amount of traffic and to design a track plan that would allow efficient movement of that traffic. The object was to keep two or three operators busy with realistic operation.

Take a look at the track plan, fig. 1. You'll see that the terminal has three distinct areas: a wharf, an industrial park, and a railroad area consisting of a yard, freight house, and team tracks. The wharf absorbs by far the greater amount of traffic in the terminal. The different piers and their facilities are described in fig. 2.

The industrial park behind the railroad yard is laid out with three industries of fairly large size by model railroad standards. The total siding capacity here is seven cars, enough to handle a modest but steady flow of traffic.

The yard has seven tracks. Track 1, nearest the front of the layout, is a thoroughfare track (no standing cars allowed) and also serves as a lead for the freight house and team tracks. Tracks 2 through 6 serve for the arrival and classification of incoming cars and the accumulation of outgoing cars. Track 7, the spur next to the terminal

office, is for storage of service cars, bad orders, and the like.

Two team tracks with capacities of six cars each provide rail access to off-line customers. A door-level dock, a small pillar crane, and an end-loading ramp are in place for customer convenience.

The freight house for less-than-carload freight is really two houses, one for incoming and one for outgoing. Each has its own covered loading dock and track long enough for six cars. This substantial facility is a busy spot.

EFFICIENT OPERATION

I mentioned earlier that my main objective in designing this terminal was to create a facility that could efficiently accommodate a large volume of traffic. No "switching problem," this — quite the opposite, in fact. The tracks are designed to process the traffic efficiently and directly. The interest for the operators comes from planning and executing the movements necessary to keep heavy traffic flowing, not from solving puzzles or performing unnecessarily complicated maneuvers. Each move should have a purpose, and each should advance the work of the terminal.

The key words in the operation of Free Haven Terminal are *process* and *flow*. Cars are in *process*: they arrive at the terminal; they are spotted, loaded or unloaded, and pulled; then they leave. They should spend little time just sitting idle, but should *flow* through the process, in action most of the time. Several design features work to maintain that flow.

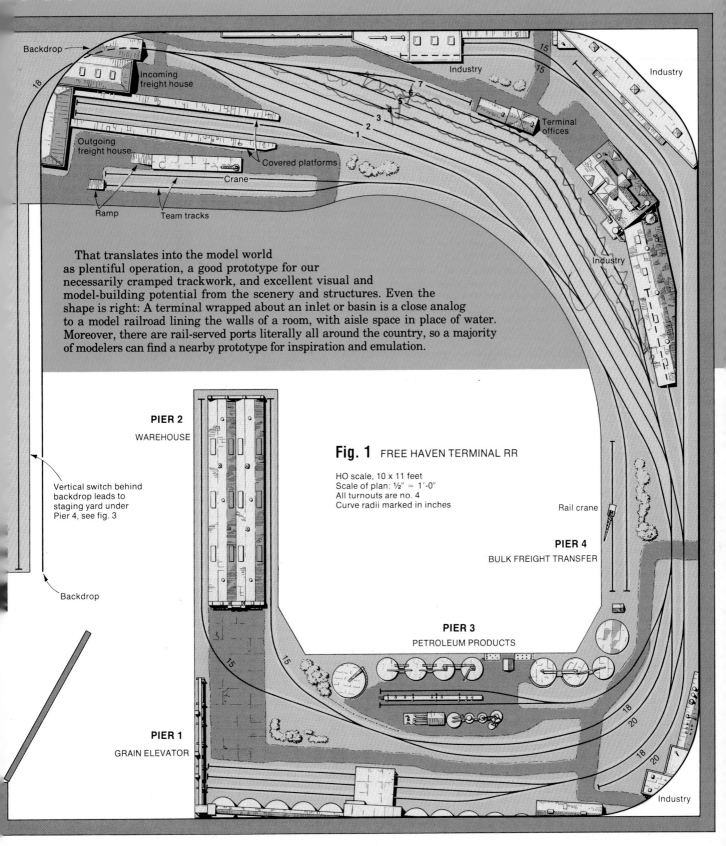

Backdrop

Incoming freight house

18

Industry

15

15

Industry

6 7
5
4
3
2
1

Terminal offices

Outgoing freight house

Crane

Covered platforms

Industry

Ramp

Team tracks

Industry

That translates into the model world as plentiful operation, a good prototype for our necessarily cramped trackwork, and excellent visual and model-building potential from the scenery and structures. Even the shape is right: A terminal wrapped about an inlet or basin is a close analog to a model railroad lining the walls of a room, with aisle space in place of water. Moreover, there are rail-served ports literally all around the country, so a majority of modelers can find a nearby prototype for inspiration and emulation.

PIER 2

WAREHOUSE

Fig. 1 FREE HAVEN TERMINAL RR

HO scale, 10 x 11 feet
Scale of plan: ½″ = 1′-0″
All turnouts are no. 4
Curve radii marked in inches

Rail crane

Vertical switch behind backdrop leads to staging yard under Pier 4, see fig. 3

PIER 4

BULK FREIGHT TRANSFER

Backdrop

PIER 3

PETROLEUM PRODUCTS

15

15

18
20

PIER 1

GRAIN ELEVATOR

18
20

Industry

Fig. 2 THE WHARF

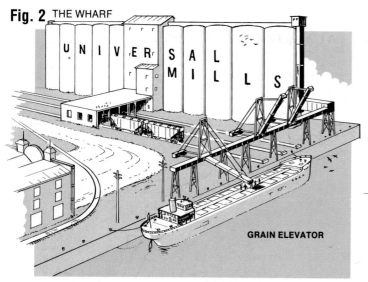

GRAIN ELEVATOR

WAREHOUSE

A large grain elevator is an asset to any railroad, whether prototype or model. The great volumes of grain it handles can fill many trains fast — that means money for the real-life roads, operating fun for the model. The heavy season comes during the harvest (June-August), but traffic moves at other times, even all year round at an ice-free port. The Universal Mills elevator at Free Haven can handle a dozen cars on three sidings. The cars are pulled through by a car puller unloading three at a time under the shelter.

Pier 2 at Free Haven has two slips with a multistory warehouse between for handling packaged (as opposed to bulk) freight. One track along each slip allows transfer directly between car and vessel, or car and warehouse. Rail traffic need not coincide precisely with vessel movements, though it should be expected to peak when vessels are at the docks so as to reduce double-handling of the freight. Capacity is six cars on each track.

• Wherever possible within the space limitations, track is arranged to keep cars moving in one direction, with few or no reverse moves. Cars bound for the docks meet that ideal, moving directly through the double-ended yard to the piers. Industrial park, team and freight house cars fall short of it, each requiring one reverse move.

• Two engines can work with minimal conflict. There are separate switching leads for each working area, numerous alternate routes and tracks throughout the terminal, and a thoroughfare track that is kept free of standing cars to allow unobstructed movement from end to end.

• All spurs within each area are trailing-point — there are no switchbacks, and no running around is required.

The FHT can employ three operators: two switch-engine "crews" and a terminal superintendent. The switch crews move the cars into, through, and out of the yard under the supervision of the superintendent, who oversees the entire operation.

The superintendent takes care of traffic management. He schedules cars into the terminal, assigns their places within it, and schedules them out. He sees that his plans are carried out through assignments to the switch crews for work, both within the terminal and between it and an adjacent classification yard.

OPERATING CONVENTIONS

This is a *model* railroad, of course, so the operators do some things that aren't done in the real world. The superintendent makes his plans in response to imagined rather than real demands, which may involve some unprototypical method of traffic generation like file cards or tabs on the cars. As in all such cases, the key to what we regard as realistic operation is to treat those "unreal" devices like stage props or conventions in the theater. That is, we ignore the fact that they are not what they purport to be and respond to them as if they were genuine.

Another such case arises when the switchers supposedly take cuts of cars to

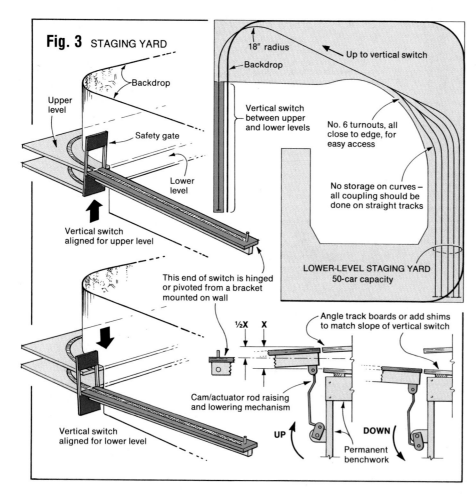

Fig. 3 STAGING YARD

Backdrop

Upper level

Safety gate

Lower level

Vertical switch aligned for upper level

18" radius

Backdrop

Up to vertical switch

Vertical switch between upper and lower levels

No. 6 turnouts, all close to edge, for easy access

No storage on curves – all coupling should be done on straight tracks

LOWER-LEVEL STAGING YARD
50-car capacity

This end of switch is hinged or pivoted from a bracket mounted on wall

Vertical switch aligned for lower level

Cam/actuator rod raising and lowering mechanism

½X   X

Angle track boards or add shims to match slope of vertical switch

UP   DOWN

Permanent benchwork

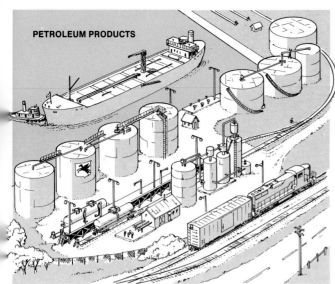

PETROLEUM PRODUCTS

Petroleum products also keep the trains moving. There's a constant, though somewhat seasonal, demand for gasoline, fuel oil, heating oil, and kerosene products. Shipped in bulk by water, they are stored and blended in the tank farm at Free Haven, then distributed inland by tank car. The loading tracks can accommodate six cars at a time.

BULK FREIGHT

The facility for handling bulk freight (coal, sand and gravel, clay, and the like) is a simple affair. A self-powered crane with a clamshell bucket unloads cargoes from vessels directly into railroad cars. In addition, bulky items such as farm or industrial machinery, construction materials, and lengths of pipe occasionally are handled by use of a hook in place of the bucket. The crane runs on its own isolated railroad track. This is a fairly low-volume operation, with siding capacity of three cars.

and from the classification yard, but are actually traveling in and out of a staging yard hidden below the benchwork. The staging yard, shown in fig. 3, is reached by means of a vertical switch, an idea from John Armstrong's *Creative Layout Design*. [Kalmbach has now reissued this book under the title, *Creative Model Railroad Design. — Ed.*]

The staging yard represents a substantial classification yard not far from the waterfront. The switch engines shuttling between the two remain within yard limits and so do not formally operate as trains. No cabooses are required, and since only short distances are involved the switchers can back their cuts of cars without restriction. This particular bit of fiction allows the simplest arrangement for the hidden tracks by avoiding the need for runaround moves. The engines always lead their cuts of cars into the tail of the vertical switch, and so reach the "subterranean" staging yard in one simple backing move.

THE FHT AT WORK

For a good idea of how the FHT works, look at fig. 4. It's summer, and the grain harvest rush is on, so the elevator is running at full capacity. One crew is working the team tracks, while the other is busy at the merchandise pier. This is the general operating pattern:

● Incoming cars are spotted on track 2, then classified by destination on tracks 4, 5, and 6.

● Cars are spotted at their destinations as space and crew time become available.

● Outgoing cars are accumulated on track 3. They are moved from there to the classification yard on frequent runs by the switch crews.

This isn't the only way to run this railroad; indeed, I wouldn't think it a successful design if it were so limited. You could start with different assumptions as to geographical location, period, property owner, time of year, operating procedures, and many other factors, and from them develop very different patterns. There's lots of room for imagination and variety. ⚓

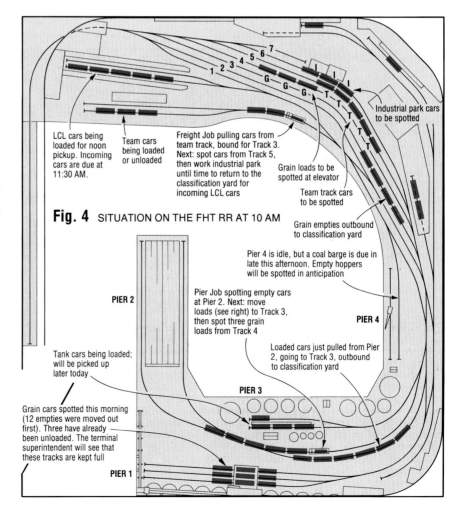

Fig. 4 SITUATION ON THE FHT RR AT 10 AM

LCL cars being loaded for noon pickup. Incoming cars are due at 11:30 AM.

Team cars being loaded or unloaded

Freight Job pulling cars from team track, bound for Track 3. Next: spot cars from Track 5, then work industrial park until time to return to the classification yard for incoming LCL cars

Industrial park cars to be spotted

Grain loads to be spotted at elevator

Team track cars to be spotted

Grain empties outbound to classification yard

Pier 4 is idle, but a coal barge is due in late this afternoon. Empty hoppers will be spotted in anticipation

Pier Job spotting empty cars at Pier 2. Next: move loads (see right) to Track 3, then spot three grain loads from Track 4

PIER 4

Loaded cars just pulled from Pier 2, going to Track 3, outbound to classification yard

Tank cars being loaded; will be picked up later today

PIER 2

Grain cars spotted this morning (12 empties were moved out first). Three have already been unloaded. The terminal superintendent will see that these tracks are kept full

PIER 3

PIER 1

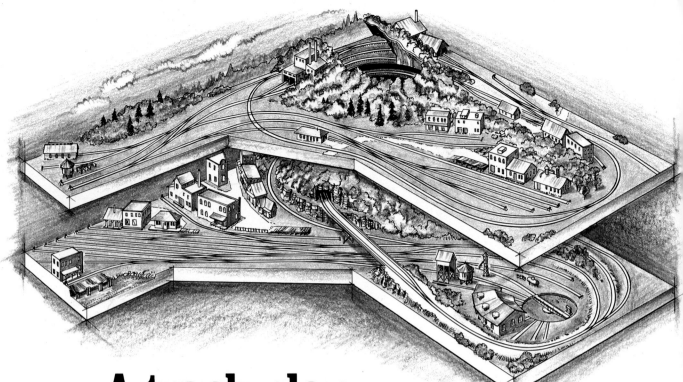

A track plan
for the Muss, Cuss & Fuss RR

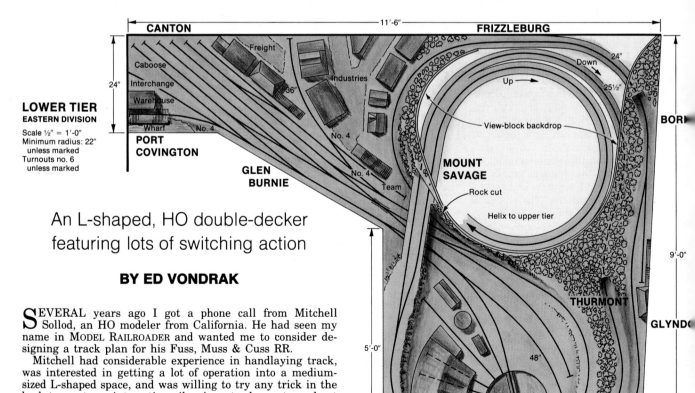

CANTON ·························· 11'-6" ·························· FRIZZLEBURG

Freight

Caboose
Interchange
Warehouse
36"

24"

Industries

LOWER TIER
EASTERN DIVISION

Scale ½" = 1'-0"
Minimum radius: 22"
unless marked
Turnouts no. 6
unless marked

Wharf   No. 4
PORT
COVINGTON

GLEN
BURNIE

No. 4

No. 4

Team

Down   24"

Up

25½"

View-block backdrop

MOUNT
SAVAGE

Rock cut

Helix to upper tier

BOR

9'-0"

THURMONT

GLYND

5'-0"

48"

Up

Down

5'-6"   6"

An L-shaped, HO double-decker featuring lots of switching action

BY ED VONDRAK

S EVERAL years ago I got a phone call from Mitchell
Sollod, an HO modeler from California. He had seen my
name in MODEL RAILROADER and wanted me to consider designing a track plan for his Fuss, Muss & Cuss RR.

Mitchell had considerable experience in handlaying track,
was interested in getting a lot of operation into a medium-
sized L-shaped space, and was willing to try any trick in the
book to create an interesting pike. An extra bonus turned out
to be that he enjoys a good pun as much as I do — several of
the names used on the track plan reflect that type of humor.

Many modelers shy away from trying to build a multitiered
layout, but Mitchell was willing. He wanted a plan that
would encompass both his boyhood in the Baltimore area and
his present romance with the gold country of California. The
FM&C would be a transcontinental railroad, with the East

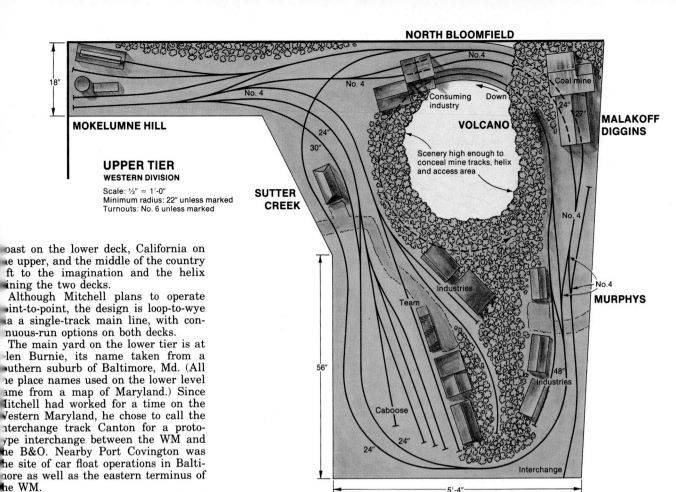

18″

MOKELUMNE HILL

UPPER TIER
WESTERN DIVISION

Scale: ½″ = 1′-0″
Minimum radius: 22″ unless marked
Turnouts: No. 6 unless marked

No. 4

No. 4

No. 4

Consuming industry

Down

24″

27″

Coal mine

MALAKOFF DIGGINS

VOLCANO

Scenery high enough to conceal mine tracks, helix and access area

SUTTER CREEK

24″

30″

No. 4

No. 4

MURPHYS

Industries

Team

56″

48″

Industries

Caboose

24″

24″

24″

Interchange

5′-4″

FIDDLETOWN   HALLELUJAH JUNCTION

coast on the lower deck, California on the upper, and the middle of the country left to the imagination and the helix joining the two decks.

Although Mitchell plans to operate point-to-point, the design is loop-to-wye via a single-track main line, with continuous-run options on both decks.

The main yard on the lower tier is at Glen Burnie, its name taken from a southern suburb of Baltimore, Md. (All the place names used on the lower level came from a map of Maryland.) Since Mitchell had worked for a time on the Western Maryland, he chose to call the interchange track Canton for a prototype interchange between the WM and the B&O. Nearby Port Covington was the site of car float operations in Baltimore as well as the eastern terminus of the WM.

For the Glen Burnie yard I developed two drill tracks and several runarounds, making it possible for two operators to simultaneously work the yard and the Canton and Port Covington interchanges.

The several runarounds in the Glen Burnie yard are partly a result of trying to fit the Timesaver switching puzzle into the plan. Mitchell had said he would like to have a Timesaver somewhere on the layout, and there is indeed one hidden in the Glen Burnie yard trackage. [The Timesaver was a switching game developed by John Allen. Author Vondrak enjoys working the Timesaver track configuration into his layout designs. For a fuller explanation see Vondrak's article "The Timesaver in a loop" in the February 1979 MR. — Ed.]

A train departing the Glen Burnie yard can go directly around to Mount Savage and enter the helix, or it can first make several circuits around the Mount Savage/Thurmont loop.

The track through Frizzelburg is part of a large reversing loop. It's a long reach back to that part of the layout, so I located no turnouts there. The backdrop between Mount Savage and Frizzelburg should extend toward the wall just far enough to block any view of the ascension helix. It should then be possible to reach around the edge of the backdrop from the access area to build and repair scenery, work on track, reach derailed cars, etc.

THE UPPER LEVEL

As a train climbs the helix the engineer can envision a long trip through the Alleghery Mountains, across the Midwest's

amber waves of grain, through the Rocky Mountains, and finally arriving in California's gold country.

On the upper deck the locomotive bursts out of Volcano tunnel, appropriately named for the open-top access area located within the helix. Strange as they may sound, all of the names on the upper tier of the FM&C can be found on a map of northern California.

Mitchell wanted another Timesaver on the upper tier of the layout, and I was able to fit one in at Murphys. The real Murphys was a stage stop between Sheep Flat Ranch and Sonora, but Mitchell dubbed the Timesaver Murphys because of Murphy's Law: "If anything can go wrong, it will." To help keep things from going wrong at Murphys, though, I added extra track and introduced an interchange track (Hallelujah Junction), positioning it so it also could be used to drill the mine tracks without fouling the main line.

Proceeding westward, we enter Sutter Creek, named after John Sutter, on whose land gold was discovered in 1848. For the terminus of the line Mitchell chose the name Mokelumne Hill. He says local folks never use the whole name, but simply call it Moke Hill. I made the benchwork narrow at Moke Hill to provide good visibility of the lower deck.

The switchback at Moke Hill serves

several purposes. It is one of the tail tracks of the scissors wye, and it is also part of the yard lead and drill tracks. It is also a lead to both the Sutter Creek industrial area and the loads in/empties out operation that Mitchell wanted and that I provided with the coal mine at Malakoff Diggins.

Mitchell called the hidden leg of the scissors wye North Bloomfield because the prototype North Bloomfield is a ghost town hidden in the hills of northern California.

I certainly would not design the track configuration near Sutter Creek for the novice. Those four curved crossings would spell trouble for most modelers, but Mitchell told me he wants it that way. He looks forward to the challenge of handlaying those curved crossings. To each his own.

I included an interchange track in the industrial area at Sutter Creek, running it into the greenery where a few cars could be concealed. The end of this track would be shielded from view on all sides, but it would be accessible from above. It could serve as a one-track fiddle yard using the old 0-5-0 switcher, hence the name Fiddletown.

Well, there you have it, Mitchell Sollod's two-tiered FM&C. Modelers who don't like our corny humor may want to change some of the names to protect the innocent. ⚙

The Northern Pacific's Cascade Line

The inspiration for a double-deck N scale track plan

BY KENNETH L. GENTILI

TO ME, the primary strength of scale is that it allows you to operat long trains in mainline movements in reasonable-size layout room. The North ern Pacific Line across Stampede Pas from Pasco to Auburn, Wash., is an exce lent area to model if you want to incluc these characteristics on your layout.

This double-deck track plan is de signed to fit an 11 x 11-foot spare bec room plus its closet. Even with thi fairly large space for an N scale layou some compromises had to be made. Fc example, parts of the hump yard ar folded over itself.

Spokane, the eastern-most end of th system, is found at the bottom of the he lix, while Auburn is located at the top Access is from the inside of the helix The longest mainline length within th helix is only one-and-one-half turns. Th time that a train will remain hidde from the operator will be tolerable, I be lieve, for most model railroaders.

Hidden sections of the main line ar appropriately placed so that visitors wil sense a time lapse between towns or re gions with climatic changes, but will no lose interest in railroading. There ar also three hidden reversing tracks a each end of the main line.

To enhance the image of a Class railroad, a large minimum radius of 20 was used. Allowing for a rise of 4" per loop on the helix, the maximum grade for this railroad becomes a reasonable 2.7 percent. Under these conditions two diesels can easily pull the normal train length of 15 to 20 50-foot cars.

On mountain layouts such as this one, train length will appear to be much longer than it is. A train of much longer length would tend to connect the scenes together, and the railroad would actu- ally appear to shrink.

THE STAMPEDE PASS LINE IN 1968

In 1968, the time period selected for this layout, the single-track main line across Stampede Pass was the Northern Pacific's major east-west route serving Puget Sound. The hump yard at Pasco had been opened for only a short time. It was here that all cars were sorted. Set in the desert with rolling sagebrush hills, the hump yard was a bustle of activity.

Westbound trains departing this area crossed over the Columbia River and pro- ceeded up through the Yakima Valley.

J. M. Fredrickson

NP train no. 26, the eastbound *North Coast Limited*, photographed in 1963 at New Stampede, Wash.

Northern Pacific photo, Kalmbach collection

An eastbound Northern Pacific freight, with a classic A-B-B-A consist of F7s at the point, winds along the Yakima River east of Cle Elum, Wash.

eveloped with irrigation water from he Yakima River, this rich valley was aded with fruit trees, hops, grapes, and her produce. Surrounding this lush alley were brown hills where herds of attle roamed.

This area was a great source of reve-ue for the NP. Long trains of reefers rowled this valley with produce des-ned for the eastern markets. All that eems left is the beautiful cut stone sta-ion at Yakima, truly a monument to he past.

The line continued along the Yakima River through a long deep canyon, so nar-ow and twisting that a more recent deci-ion was to construct the new interstate ighway over the surrounding hills. A imilar decision was made for I-90 to by-ass the canyon between Ellensburg and Cle Elum.

The small towns along the way pro-luced very little revenue for the NP. Ellensburg was a college town and cattle enter. The afternoon winds that rolled ff the Cascade Mountains made it diffi-ult to grow anything but the hay that was needed to support the cattle indus-try. Up the line at Cle Elum was a ser-vice facility for the steam engines that once pounded the rails. However, during this time period the facility still served as a storage location for maintenance-of-way cars and snow removal equipment.

Trains entered the east portal of Stampede Pass Tunnel in a pine tree for-est. At the time that this portal was con-structed, a creative crew diverted a wa-terfall to flow over the portal. NP created a station called "Martin" to con-trol activity through this portal. After CTC systems were installed, Martin be-came redundant.

Trains emerged from the western por-tal in a different climatic region. The mountains were heavily forested with the familiar spruce, douglas fir, hem-lock, cedar, alder, and maple that grow on the west side of the Cascades. The main line followed a huge "S" as it wig-gled its way down the mountain to the Green River Valley below. A magnifi-cent steel trestle marked the entry to the railroad town of Lester, which was accessible in winter only by railroad. On the way to Auburn the line disappeared into the Green River watershed, the main source of water for Tacoma. The railroad personnel and passengers were the privileged few who ever saw this area. A fence and gate were patrolled by Tacoma City employees.

Today, under Burlington Northern, this route has been closed, and all east-west traffic is sent over the more direct Great Northern line across Stevens Pass. There is still limited railroad activity in the Yakima Valley, which is accessible only from Pasco. There is some talk that per-haps coal trains will travel along the line as far as Cle Elum and then over Snoqualamie Pass along the former Mil-waukee Road right-of-way. But the town of Lester will see "no trains no more."

OPERATING THE LAYOUT

The characteristics of the NP line I just described were chosen because they can be modeled so well in an N scale layout. The long main line will create many train movements with many meets. Only a lim-ited amount of wayside switching will be needed. The ability to store several trains in the hidden yards will supply the many cars needed to keep the Pasco hump yard busy. The hump yard sorts the cars much more rapidly than could be done by a con-ventional yard and will support heavy traffic movements over the layout.

The passage of an occasional transcon-tinental passenger train will break up the abundance of freight activity.

The limited number of structures on the layouts, like the steel trestle at Les-ter, the portal with its waterfall, and the cut stone station at Yakima will become focal points on the railroad. The track density, except at Pasco, is low. The sin-gle main line will be impressive against the mountainous background as the trains gain elevation and move to the highest level.

It was the practice of the Northern Pa-cific to sort all east-west trains at Pasco. Westbound trains to Puget Sound were blocked according to their city of des-tination. At Auburn Yard cars were sorted and formed into transfer cuts destined for Tacoma or Seattle. Trains were dispatched from Tacoma to other points to the south as well as to the Pa-cific coastal towns. Northbound trains were dispatched for Seattle, Everett, and Sumas, B. C.

Eastbound cars arriving at Pasco were only partially sorted. They would then be blocked for various points east, such as Spokane, Butte, Silver Bow, and Minneapolis.

The inbound tracks on our N scale layout will receive all arriving trains,

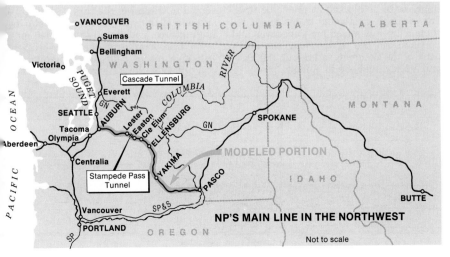

NP'S MAIN LINE IN THE NORTHWEST

Not to scale

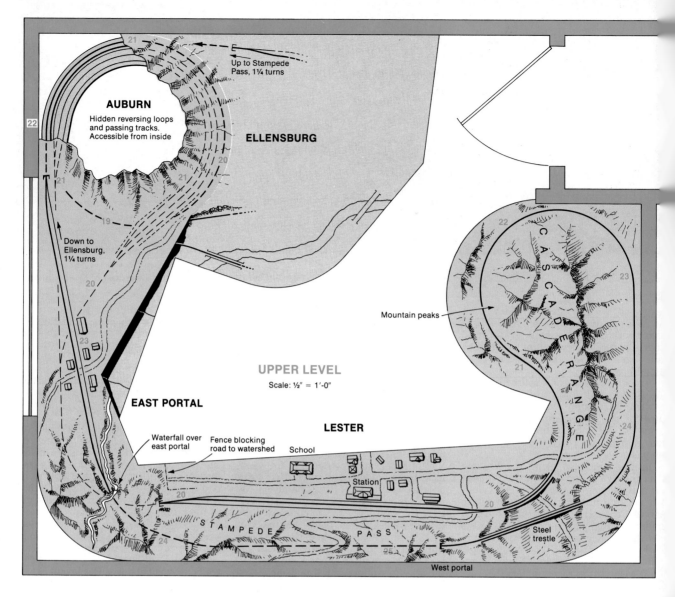

AUBURN
Hidden reversing loops and passing tracks. Accessible from inside

ELLENSBURG

Up to Stampede Pass, 1¼ turns

Down to Ellensburg, 1¼ turns

EAST PORTAL

Mountain peaks

CASCADE RANGE

UPPER LEVEL
Scale: ½″ = 1′-0″

LESTER

Waterfall over east portal

Fence blocking road to watershed

School

Station

Steel trestle

S T A M P E D E   P A S S

West portal

typically about 20 standard 50-foot cars. The road diesels will be uncoupled and sent to the engine service facility for refueling and inspection. The cabooses will be cut by the yard switchers and stored.

The remaining cars will be moved as soon as possible to the lead tracks of the hump yard, thus freeing up the inbound yard so that it can also serve as the outbound makeup yard.

As the cars are pushed over the hump, they are uncoupled individually or in blocks. A missorted car can be picked up later by the yard diesel and pulled back up over the hump and released again. The hump is strong enough to support the weight of the diesel. The vertical arc of the hump is too small for three-axle units, so Geeps should work the hump. Actual activity on the prototype hump would use the retarders to hold a missorted car, while the diesel would move out of the way.

The sorting yard has ample tracks to sort and hold more than one complete train at a time. This allows several destinations to be blocked at the same time. For instance, westbound trains might include a train destined for Vancouver and Portland via the SP&S along the north bank of the Columbia, a local up the Yakima Valley, and one to Auburn.

Bad-order cars need to be sent to the rip track to await repair. The bad-order and maintenance-of-way storage tracks will be able to hold these cars until space is available.

To efficiently run the hump yard without backing up the main line, two sets of yard diesels need to be employed. One set should work the hump and the sorting of cars. The other will be assigned to trimming the cars on the opposite end of the yard, cutting and storing the cabooses, and moving bad-order cars.

The transportation system described here will give model railroaders many busy and enjoyable hours of entertainment. ☉

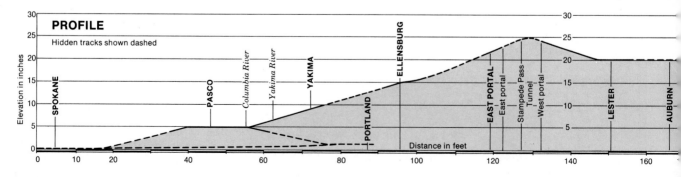

PROFILE
Hidden tracks shown dashed

Elevation in inches

Distance in feet

SPOKANE   PASCO   Columbia River   Yakima River   YAKIMA   PORTLAND   ELLENSBURG   EAST PORTAL   East portal   Stampede Pass   Tunnel   West portal   LESTER   AUBURN

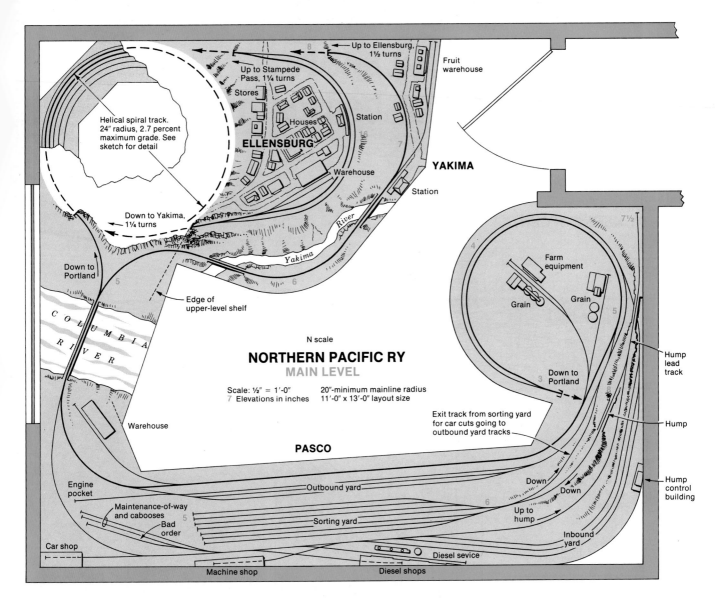

Helical spiral track. 24" radius, 2.7 percent maximum grade. See sketch for detail

Up to Ellensburg, 1½ turns

Fruit warehouse

Up to Stampede Pass, 1¼ turns

Stores

ELLENSBURG

Houses

Warehouse

Station

YAKIMA

Station

Down to Yakima, 1¼ turns

Down to Portland

Edge of upper-level shelf

Yakima River

COLUMBIA RIVER

N scale

NORTHERN PACIFIC RY
MAIN LEVEL

Scale: ½" = 1'-0"
7 Elevations in inches

20"-minimum mainline radius
11'-0" x 13'-0" layout size

Warehouse

Farm equipment

Grain

Grain

Down to Portland

Hump lead track

Hump

PASCO

Exit track from sorting yard for car cuts going to outbound yard tracks

Hump control building

Engine pocket

Outbound yard

Down

Down

Maintenance-of-way and cabooses
Bad order

Sorting yard

Up to hump

Inbound yard

Car shop

Diesel sevice

Machine shop

Diesel shops

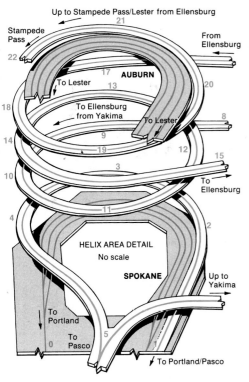

Up to Stampede Pass/Lester from Ellensburg

21

Stampede Pass

22

From Ellensburg

To Lester

AUBURN

17

13

20

18

To Ellensburg from Yakima

To Lester

8

14

9

19

12

15

10

3

To Ellensburg

4

11

2

HELIX AREA DETAIL
No scale

SPOKANE

5

Up to Yakima

To Portland

To Pasco

To Portland/Pasco

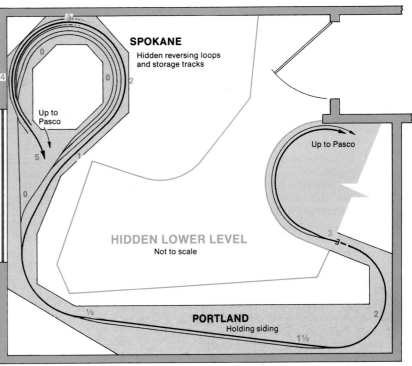

SPOKANE

Hidden reversing loops and storage tracks

Up to Pasco

Up to Pasco

HIDDEN LOWER LEVEL
Not to scale

PORTLAND
Holding siding

A track plan to share a family room or bedroom

The HO scale
Spokane, Pasco & Wallace

BY KENNETH GENTILI

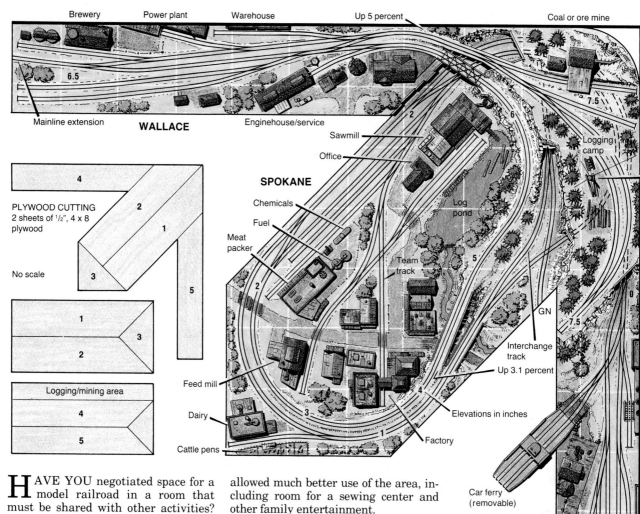

Brewery   Power plant   Warehouse   Up 5 percent   Coal or ore mine

6.5

Mainline extension   **WALLACE**   Enginehouse/service

PLYWOOD CUTTING
2 sheets of 1/2", 4 x 8
plywood

No scale

Logging/mining area

Sawmill
Office

SPOKANE

Chemicals
Fuel
Meat
packer

Log
pond

Team
track

Logging
camp

7.5

GN

Interchange
track
Up 3.1 percent

Feed mill

Dairy

Cattle pens

Elevations in inches

Factory

Car ferry
(removable)

Norm's Landing

PASCO

Layout size:
11'-0" x 11'-0"
One square = 12"
19 1/2" minimum radius
No. 4 turnouts

Railed crane

Mainline extension

HAVE YOU negotiated space for a model railroad in a room that must be shared with other activities? Then the HO scale Spokane, Pasco & Wallace RR is for you. It features lots of operating possibilities, yet is relatively easy to build.

The inspiration for the SP&W is a layout I designed for three brothers, ages 8, 11, and 15. Their original layout was built as a fold-up design in the middle of a family room. It turned out that the railroad was down all the time, so the space wasn't available for other family use. Shifting the layout into the corner allowed much better use of the area, including room for a sewing center and other family entertainment.

As designed, this model railroad can also fit into an 11-foot-square bedroom, but either of its wings can be easily changed to fit other spaces. All it really needs is two plain walls in the corner of a room. As long as the layout is positioned in a corner, there will be good access to its operating areas.

The SP&W is a fictitious subsidiary of the Northern Pacific Ry. It's a small point-to-point railroad that runs between Pasco, Wash., on the Columbia

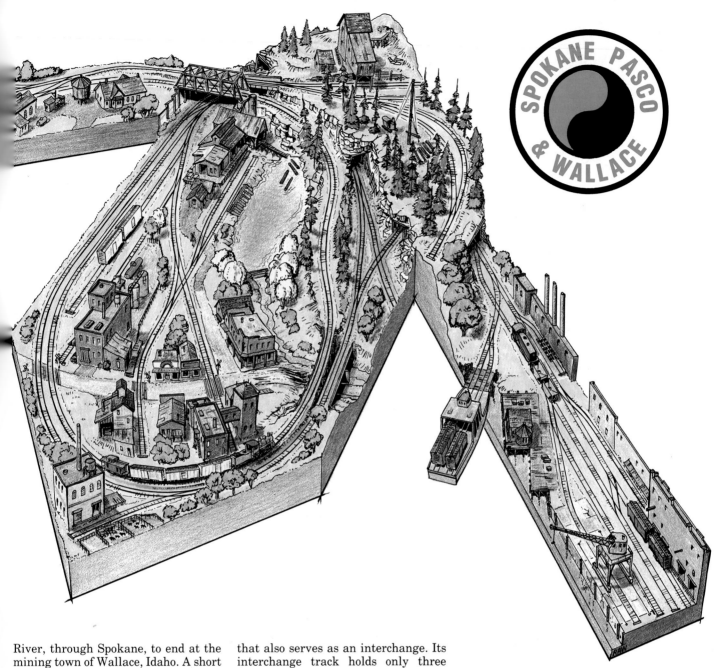

River, through Spokane, to end at the mining town of Wallace, Idaho. A short branch line serves the mines and logging camps nestled in the pine forests above Wallace.

INTERCHANGE TRAFFIC

A car ferry operation, simulated by a number of movable barges, brings cars into the harbor at Pasco for interchange. These barges serve as a staging area to link the SP&W to other railroads and distant destinations. Such an interchange allows traffic to move off-line instead of simply having the same cars shuffling back and forth. It also makes the model railroad seem more plausible as "foreign" cars appear and disappear.

Near Spokane, the Great Northern Ry. crosses the SP&W at a small junction that also serves as an interchange. Its interchange track holds only three cars, but additional ones could be hidden in the tunnel until needed. This short bit of GN track enhances operating realism and provides a route for cars headed to Seattle or Canada.

An interesting operation takes place where the branch line joins the main line at Wallace. The branchline crew brings their log flats or ore cars into the yard while the conductor checks on their next move. If the job terminates at Wallace, they shove the cars into a yard track and leave the engine on the service track. If they are to continue southward, a runaround must be performed to get the engine on the south end of the train. Then the caboose has to be switched to the other end before the train is ready

for departure. This may sound like a lot of effort, but these extra maneuvers add running time to a small railroad and make a good thing last longer.

ON-LINE INDUSTRIES

There isn't enough space to model both a sawmill and a smelter. The sawmill was chosen because it offered more traffic for the railroad. Log cars may be cycled through loading, moving to the mill, and returning for another load, while boxcars and flatcars would need to be switched in and out of the mill for finished lumber products.

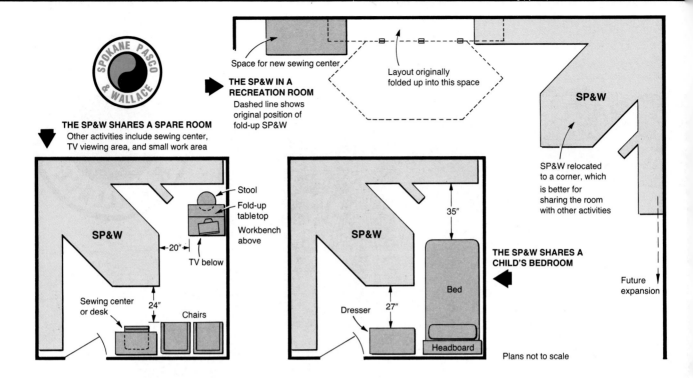

THE SP&W IN A
RECREATION ROOM
Dashed line shows
original position of
fold-up SP&W

Space for new sewing center

Layout originally
folded up into this space

SP&W

SP&W relocated
to a corner, which
is better for
sharing the room
with other activities

THE SP&W SHARES A SPARE ROOM
Other activities include sewing center,
TV viewing area, and small work area

SP&W

Stool
Fold-up
tabletop
Workbench
above

—20″—

TV below

Sewing center
or desk

24″

Chairs

SP&W

35″

THE SP&W SHARES A
CHILD'S BEDROOM

Future
expansion

Bed

Dresser

27″

Headboard

Plans not to scale

To provide a destination for the ore cars, the smelter is located "off-stage," somewhere along the GN main line. This means loaded ore cars must be moved down the branch line to Wallace where they're turned over to the main-line crew. Then the ore travels on the SP&W to the junction where it's delivered to the GN interchange for further movement to the smelter.

In a different setting, the mining operation might be coal instead of ore. In that case, the loaded coal cars could be sent to either of the two power plants on the railroad.

ADDING MILEAGE

An oval of track on the peninsula is used as a special feature in this track plan. During an operating session, trains are required to go around the loop at least once so the train travels over every section of the main line without repeating its path.

The loop is disguised by hiding one end beneath the mine and log camp. In addition, the track climbing toward Wallace forms a scenic divider making it difficult to see both sides of the layout at the same time. The GN crossing gives a feeling of track going someplace, and the S curve near the tunnel helps the illusion that the main line is heading away from the peninsula. Placing the two tracks parallel to each other in Spokane makes them look like a double-track line.

At Spokane, the "double track" emerges from a tunnel, runs through a pair of crossovers, and splits into two branches. One heads uphill toward Wallace, and the other continues toward the Great Northern interchange. In reality, when the crossovers are ignored, each of these parallel tracks represents a different location on the run between Pasco and Wallace. However, the crossover near the tunnel may be used to route trains around the continuous loop to build mileage as desired.

Because the loop is flat, trains can be run without tending to the throttle. This makes it a great place to break in locomotives or just train-watch if you get tired of switching. A second crossover at the opposite end of town allows trains to meet at Spokane and provides a runaround for local switching.

CONSTRUCTION

The SP&W is designed for construction from two sheets of 1/2″ plywood. By following the cutting diagrams, you'll see that one sheet takes care of the peninsula and the other covers the wings and provides material for the Wallace Branch and its mine and lumber camp area.

The overall width of the benchwork determines the minimum radius of any track plan. In this case, there must be sufficient room for passing trains to clear each other on the two peninsula tracks. Allowing 2 1/2″ for car overhang on the tight curves, this works out to 19 1/2″ and 22″ radii.

I recommend using the cookie-cutter technique to build this layout. With this method, you first draw the track plan on the plywood and then cut alongside the tracks for the various changes in elevation with a saber saw. Next, the grades and upper-level sections are raised and supported on risers added beneath the plywood. Careful transitions need to be made where the grades begin and end to avoid kinking the track and causing derailments.

OPERATIONS

As designed, the SP&W uses conventional wiring for three control cabs. One local cab operates the Wallace spur, and the other two handle trains on the rest of the layout.

The SP&W is a small railroad so its train size needs to be kept in proportion. A typical HO engine can haul about seven cars and a caboose up the 3.1 percent mainline grade. That's about right for this layout as a longer train would look out of place and shorten the apparent run. After all, an engine chasing its own caboose doesn't look right on any layout. Even if the sidings could handle longer trains, there isn't enough business to justify them.

Like any small model railroad, the SP&W can serve as the nucleus for an expanded system. More small towns can easily be added by lengthening the shelf along the wall. The trick would be to keep the new town(s) in proportion to the existing ones. By doing this, the run can be lengthened without making the train size unmanageable when it reaches the original layout.

Building a small railroad like the SP&W can serve as a great learning experience for any builder. Its size makes it relatively easy to transport if a move comes along. Later, it could become a branch line or a short line tied into a future "ultimate" super railroad. ✿

Just for fun!

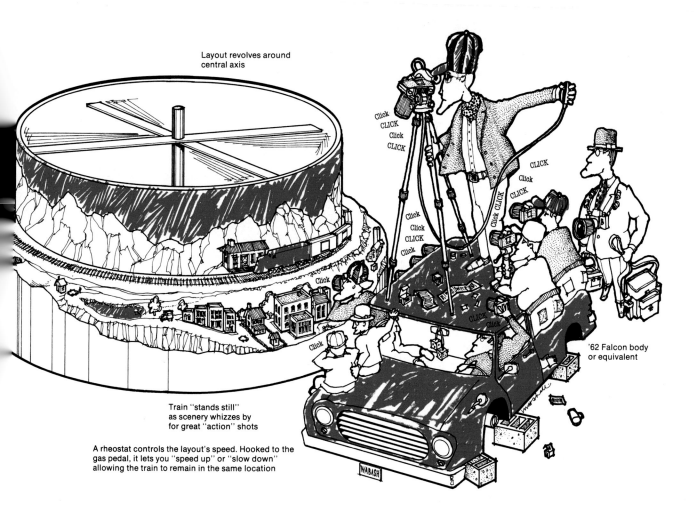

Layout revolves around central axis

Click CLICK Click CLICK

CLICK Click

Click Click CLICK Click

Click CLICK Click

CLICK Click

Click

'62 Falcon body or equivalent

Train "stands still" as scenery whizzes by for great "action" shots

A rheostat controls the layout's speed. Hooked to the gas pedal, it lets you "speed up" or "slow down" allowing the train to remain in the same location

WABASH

A railfan's dream layout

Designed with the model photographer in mind

BY RAYMOND F. SPENCER

ONE of the most dramatic photographs a railfan can take is that of a locomotive running at speed. The idea is to drive alongside the engine, match its speed exactly, and take the photograph. The image of the locomotive on the processed film will be sharp and crisp while the background is blurred, giving the impression of great speed. Achieving this effect in model photography is a problem I have long struggled with. My proposed solution is illustrated in the accompanying sketch.

This layout works on the "lazy susan" principle, with the layout revolving in the opposite direction of travel of the train, thereby creating a net locomotive speed of 0 mph. You can see in the sketch that, with appropriate props, one could create the strong illusion of pacing a train. By altering the speed of the layout and/or the train, various dramatic effects could be created. ⚙

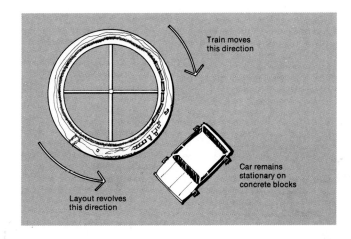

Train moves this direction

Car remains stationary on concrete blocks

Layout revolves this direction

A. L. Schmidt

The Merrimac SouthEastern RR.

From module to model railroad and back again

BY GORDON ODEGARD

MODULAR model railroad systems, beginning with Ntrak and Interail, have sprung up all around us. One of the main concerns of those who build modules is how to incorporate a section into their home model railroads, making the best use of a piece of modelwork that has taken considerable time to build. The Merrimac SouthEastern RR. track plan was designed to accommodate the 30" x 72" HO module that the MR staff built after studying various modular systems. [Since no national set of standards seems to have emerged as the favorite for HO scale, we built our module to the standards established by the local WISE (Wisconsin Southeast) Division of the NMRA.] The MSE is only one of an infinite number of layouts that could be built incorporating this module. Or for that matter, it could be built without making the section modular.

Depending on the track design, a module may be easy or difficult to fit into a complete track plan. I found the interlocking arrangement to be somewhat of a problem in designing a layout. I kept coming up with too many reversing sections and an unreasonable traffic arrangement. The plan I chose seems to solve these problems.

A second removable portion was incorporated to facilitate the removal of the 30" x 72" piece. There shouldn't be more

than a few times each year when the section will be removed, so the fit is close and tight. A couple of men can easily take out the small removable section and then slide the module toward the center and up.

Figure 1 is the track plan I designed for the MSE, while fig. 2 shows the general arrangement of the tracks on the module itself.

The Merrimac SouthEastern represents a common-carrier prototype (dealing in no particular commodity) located Anywhere, U.S.A. The plan includes 7 stations, an interlocking, 15 industries, 2 interchange tracks, and 11 highway crossings. The maximum grade (shown in fig. 3) is 2.5 percent westbound between Chatfield Jct. and Merrimac. Outside of the lumberyard near Johnson Creek and the fuel depot at Merrimac, the types of industries are unspecified. I leave these to your own discretion.

There are a number of interesting scenic possibilities available. At Stearn's Slough you might try Art Curren's swamp-modeling techniques as described in the June 1979 MR. At Hollins a line of tall industrial buildings conceals a tunnel portal, and near Tyler a high, forested hill partially shields the rear double-track curve. There are a number of stream and river

crossings where trestles, culverts, and bridges of various styles can be featured.

The single yard at Merrimac is adequate for most home operations. A few more tracks could be added to increase the storage capacity, and a small yard could be built at Cedar Bluff by increasing the benchwork width. About 30 to 35 freight cars and a half dozen locomotives would be adequate for the MSE as shown.

Modelers working in other scales will have to do a little reworking of the track plan. The conversion factors are: .55 for N scale; 1.36 for S; and 1.8 for ¼" scale. Figure 4 offers some possibilities to get you started. For the most part, N scale presents no problems; the HO plan can be reduced almost intact. The left half would have to be lengthened slightly to provide adequate operator space. Also — and this applies to all scales — aisle width should not be less than 36".

In S and ¼" scales the mainline arrangement has to be changed considerably and the curve radii reduced proportionately. The main line at Chatfield was cut to two tracks in both cases.

Another factor that cannot be ignored, particularly in the larger scales, is the space available. The average house is 23 to 25 feet wide (or long), so the ¼" plan has been held to 25 feet. In the length of main

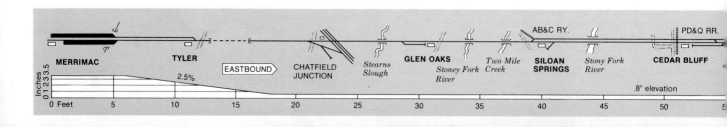

Inches											
MERRIMAC		TYLER	EASTBOUND	CHATFIELD JUNCTION	Stearns Slough	GLEN OAKS Stoney Fork River	Two Mile Creek	SILOAN SPRINGS	Stony Fork River	CEDAR BLUFF	

AB&C RY.   PD&Q RR.

2.5%

.8" elevation

0 Feet   5   10   15   20   25   30   35   40   45   50

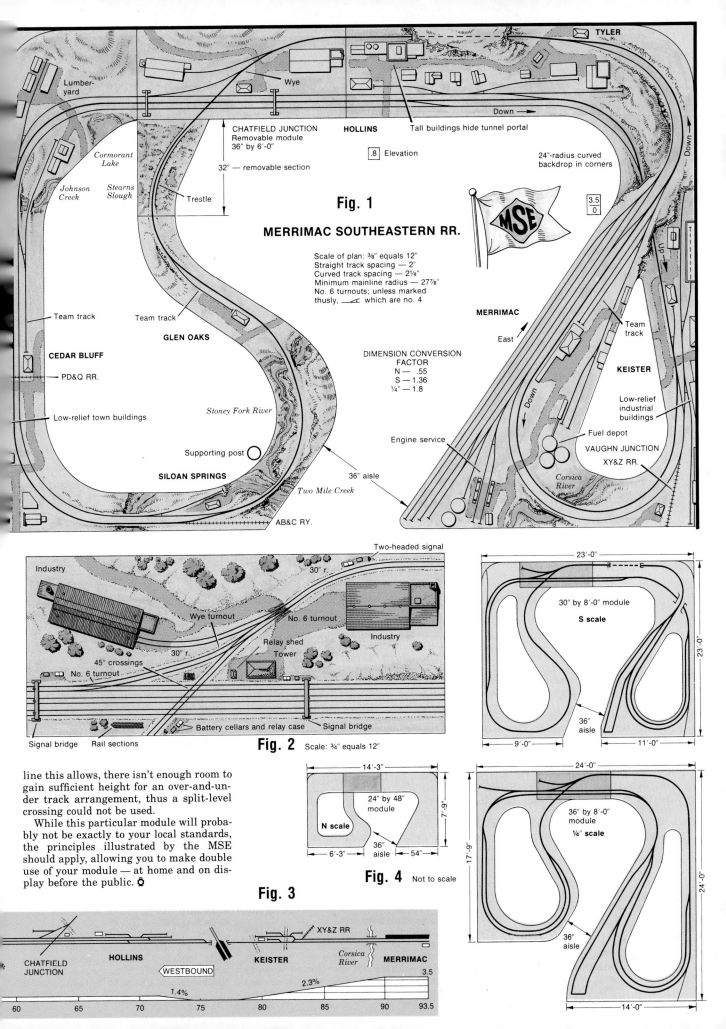

Fig. 1

MERRIMAC SOUTHEASTERN RR.

Scale of plan: 3/8" equals 12"
Straight track spacing — 2"
Curved track spacing — 2 1/8"
Minimum mainline radius — 27 7/8"
No. 6 turnouts; unless marked
thusly, ⊸ which are no. 4

DIMENSION CONVERSION
FACTOR
N — .55
S — 1.36
1/4" — 1.8

TYLER

Down →

Down

Up

24"-radius curved
backdrop in corners

3.5 / 0

MERRIMAC

East

KEISTER

Team track

Low-relief
industrial
buildings

Fuel depot

VAUGHN JUNCTION
XY&Z RR.

Corsica
River

Engine service

36" aisle

Lumberyard

Wye

CHATFIELD JUNCTION
Removable module
36" by 6'-0"

32" — removable section

Trestle

HOLLINS

.8   Elevation

Tall buildings hide tunnel portal

Down →

Cormorant
Lake

Stearns
Slough

Johnson
Creek

Team track

Team track

GLEN OAKS

Stoney Fork River

Supporting post

SILOAN SPRINGS

Two Mile Creek

AB&C RY.

Cedar Bluff

PD&Q RR.

Low-relief town buildings

CEDAR BLUFF

Industry

Two-headed signal

30" r.

Wye turnout

No. 6 turnout

Industry

Relay shed

Tower

30" r.

45° crossings

No. 6 turnout

Battery cellars and relay case

Signal bridge

Signal bridge   Rail sections

Fig. 2   Scale: 3/4" equals 12"

line this allows, there isn't enough room to
gain sufficient height for an over-and-un-
der track arrangement, thus a split-level
crossing could not be used.

While this particular module will probably not be exactly to your local standards,
the principles illustrated by the MSE
should apply, allowing you to make double
use of your module — at home and on display before the public. ⚲

Fig. 3

CHATFIELD
JUNCTION

HOLLINS

WESTBOUND

KEISTER

Corsica
River

MERRIMAC

XY&Z RR.

1.4%

2.3%

3.5

60   65   70   75   80   85   90   93.5

23'-0"

30" by 8'-0" module
S scale

36"
aisle

9'-0"   11'-0"

23'-0"

14'-3"

24" by 48"
module

N scale

36"
aisle

7'-9"

6'-3"   54"

Fig. 4   Not to scale

24'-0"

36" by 8'-0"
module
1/4" scale

36"
aisle

17'-9"

24'-0"

14'-0"

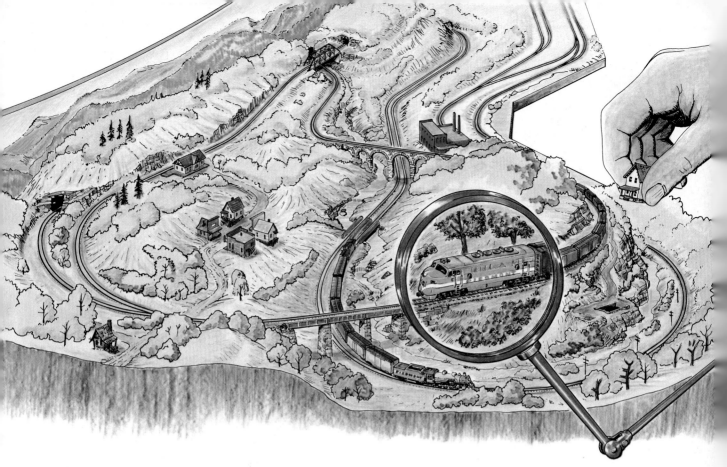

Starting a second 50 years – with Z scale

The dean of track planners comes up with a knockout fold-up layout for the smallest scale

BY JOHN ARMSTRONG

Z SCALE (1:220) has one big thing going for it and one big thing going against it.

Going for it is the fact it's so *small* — a typical American boxcar is 2½" long. A 4 x 8-foot sheet of plywood swells to an impressive 35 acres.

Going against it is the fact that it's so !@#$% small! Looking at that boxcar from a distance close enough to see its exquisite detail means your eyeballs are as far apart as the car is long — and that can do funny things to the perspective. When you gasp in amazement at the detail you can blow the car clear down the track!

Of course, each scale and gauge has its advantages and disadvantages, and effective layout planning is largely a matter of emphasizing the strong points and minimizing the shortcomings. As American scale model railroading enters its sixth decade, let's look at the current tiniest of the tiny: Z scale.

THE STATE OF Z

Z scale was introduced by Märklin, the German company, some 10 years ago, and Märklin's Mini-Club remains the sole source of Z scale locomotives.

They have produced a generous selection of steam, diesel, and electric motive power, almost all of them German prototype. Many of these could be kitbashed into American-looking engines.

Full-length European passenger cars of all eras abound. The freight cars are primarily four-wheelers, but there are also some eight-wheelers.. The Märklin catalog even shows a Schnabel car that, spliced with its transformer load, scales 111 feet long. In deference to Märklin Z's minimum 5¾"-radius curves, all but two of the Schnabel's axles on each end are dummies. No aquarium cars or other *really* offensive items are offered.

The Walthers N scale catalog includes a section on Z. Most structures available are distinctively European and not readily adaptable to an American layout. Kibri offers some oil tanks, a grain elevator, a freight house, a traveling crane, and some other buildings that have good possibilities. Still, the Z scale modeler will be scratchbuilding a lot of structures for the foreseeable future, one reason why the plan I'll be discussing has few structures on it!

There are lots of bridge kits in all shapes and sizes. Rather suprisingly, dozens of Z scale figures are available. Preiser and Merten offer Z-sized versions of most of the same folks seen on HO

layouts. A good selection of automobiles and trucks (mostly modern though) is on the market.

Z COULD TAKE OFF

The principal interest in Z among modelers of North American practice has been in adapting it to N scale narrow gauge. Just recently, though, Kadee announced their intention to enter the Z scale market, a development that could lead 1:220 scale modeling into the big time in this country.

Having bought Nelson Gray's line of American prototype equipment, Kadee is now tooling up to make an F unit and several freight cars. They have also developed a Z scale coupler, although immediate plans call for introducing equipment with Märklin-style couplers.

You could handlay Z scale track. Code 40 rail (equivalent in Z to the oversize but widely used Code 100 in HO) is available, and the techniques of spikeless tracklaying with adhesives are established. However, if this sort of activity doesn't exactly thrill you in HO or N, it's not likely to in Z either.

Peco has introduced Z scale flexible track, but for the time being most Z scale modelers will use Märklin track because only Märklin makes turnouts. Rolling stock likely to be available in

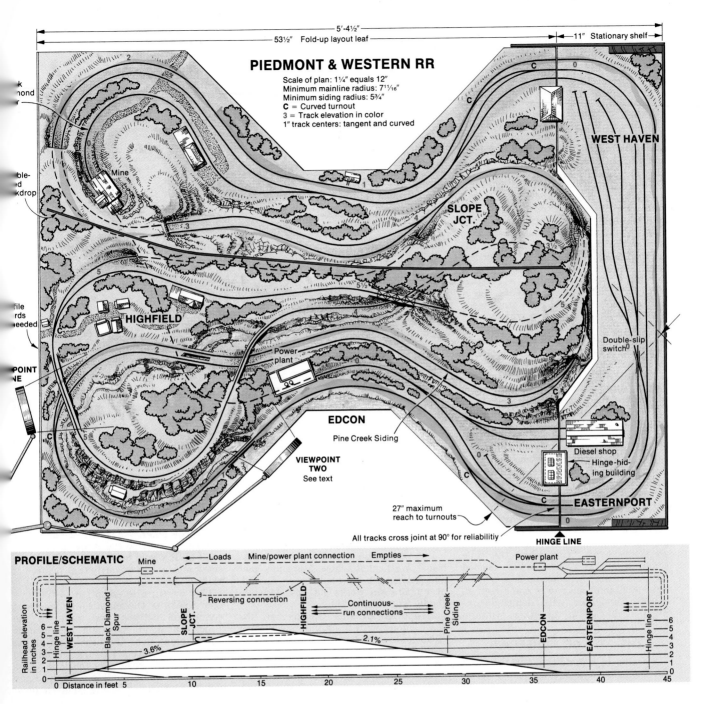

PIEDMONT & WESTERN RR

Scale of plan: 1¼" equals 12"
Minimum mainline radius: 7¹¹/₁₆"
Minimum siding radius: 5¾"
C = Curved turnout
3 = Track elevation in color
1" track centers: tangent and curved

5'-4½"
53½" Fold-up layout leaf
11" Stationary shelf

WEST HAVEN

Mine

SLOPE JCT.

HIGHFIELD

Power plant

Double-slip switch

EDCON

Pine Creek Siding

VIEWPOINT TWO
See text

Diesel shop

Hinge-hiding building

EASTERNPORT

27" maximum reach to turnouts

All tracks cross joint at 90° for reliabilitiy

HINGE LINE

PROFILE/SCHEMATIC

Mine
Loads Mine/power plant connection Empties
Power plant

Railroad elevation in inches

Hinge line
WEST HAVEN
Black Diamond Spur
Reversing connection
SLOPE JCT.
HIGHFIELD
Continuous-run connections
Pine Creek Siding
EDCON
EASTERNPORT
Hinge line

3.6%
2.1%

0 Distance in feet 5   10   15   20   25   30   35   40   45

the near future will be designed to run on Märklin. Is this a serious restriction?

The key element is the turnout, and here Z is in enviable shape. Märklin's standard turnout is about a no. 4½, a very usable size. Its effective radius is a liberal 490 mm or 19¼", more than broad enough to accept any class of rolling stock and look super in the process.

Märklin's rail visible above the ties resembles Code 60 — about 50 pecent more oversize for mainline trackage than Code 100 is for HO. The 39" center-to-center tie spacing is also outsized, so all in all, the off-the-shelf track is on the coarse side. Once ballasted and painted, however, its overall appearance should not be far out of line. Humongous switch machine housings and psychedelic-colored connecting plugs are part of the tinplate heritage which must be subdued, but we have become accustomed to overcoming

similar irritations in the larger scales.

Märklin's curved track sections come in radii of 145 mm, 195 mm, and 220 mm; that's about 5.7", 7.7", and 8.7" in the measure still preferred by us Colonials and approximately equivalent to 14", 19", and 22" in HO. The F units and 40-foot freight cars coming should operate fine over the 195 mm curves and not look too horrible doing it, so adopting that radius as our minimum seems a reasonable first step in exploring the opportunities Z offers for getting out of the armchair.

OVER THE MOUNTAINS ON A SHELF

If we could fold the railroad up out of the way when not using it, that old reliable "no space" excuse would pretty well disappear. If, in addition, the layout were no more of an excrescence in the decor than a paneled-in chimney, any remaining resistance should crumble. What are

some Z scale planning considerations?

Though we can comfortably reach into a layout about 30" or so to paint scenery or retrieve rolling stock in distress, these trains are so small that looking at them from that distance insults their detail. Providing close-up access to the trains and structures is even more essential in Z than it is in the other scales!

Also, one of the gimmicks that is so effective in the larger scales — the hidden helix to gain an impressive altitude in a minimum of space — won't work with such a small minimum radius. A circle of 8"-radius track at 3 percent rises only 1½". Now in theory this is enough to clear a train (a Z scale F unit is less than ⅞" tall), but the practical difficulties of building roadbed and track in the remaining space, to say nothing of re-railing equipment within such a finger-height gap, are forbidding.

To depict moderately extensive diesel-era American railroading successfully on a simple fold-down shelf, we will do well to pick a prototype that has itself squeezed lots of track into a small area. Rather than admit we're doing another Clinchfield, let's claim it's the more indefinitely located Piedmont & Western. The area we're modeling still represents the most convoluted (and therefore most modelable) section of a reasonably busy mountain-crossing main line.

DON'T FORGET THE EARTHQUAKE!

Putting wheels back on track that's only ¼" wide can be tricky, even with a rerailing ramp. So for starters our track plan should allow the rolling stock to stay on the rails, ready to go, when the railroad is folded up. The P&W's modest yard, located on the stationary part of the layout, will double as a roosting place for trains between sessions.

The base elevation of P&W trackage is a low 40" above the floor, with reason. This railroad is to be operated *sitting down* — a "roll-around" rather than a "walk-in" if you please. The leaf itself is somewhat wasp-waisted, simply because it would be a shame not to be able to look at these little trains from as close up as your reading glasses will permit.

The P&W picks up most of its 1.8-scale-mile mainline run by emulating the Clinchfield's descent of the east side of the Blue Ridge mountains. Schematically, the P&W is a continuous-run plan. A point-to-point would be questionable since Z is probably going to remain a train-running rather than a car-switching scale, and at best our main line is a bit short for a loop-to-loop scheme. The continuous-run plan also makes it easy for the trains to reach the security of nontilting terra firma when the time comes to put the railroad away. Loaded open-top trains (assuming hoppers become available) can run in one direction, empties (weighted with depleted uranium, perhaps?) in the other, with no turning, no fuss.

THE JOYS OF PIONEERING

Working in a scale that's in the early development stages takes some faith, since it's hard to predict the direction it will take. Experience-based data you'd like to have on such matters as car weights, grades, and tonnage ratings is lacking — *you're* the one who will be developing these numbers.

Distances are short (a Z scale mile is only 24 of our big feet!) and steep grades are therefore highly desirable if we're going to accumulate any worthwhile elevation before running off the end of the table. But how steep is practical? What's reasonable to expect, considering the sharp curves and their effects on both stability and flange friction?

As the profile shows, the P&W features asymmetrical ruling grades on its continuous main line. Westbound the slope to the bridge at the summit is a mere 2.1 percent. Eastbound the tracks reach the summit by means of a 3.6 percent route. Do pushers work in Z scale? I don't know . . . try 'em, and if the consist buckles conduct your own "track-train

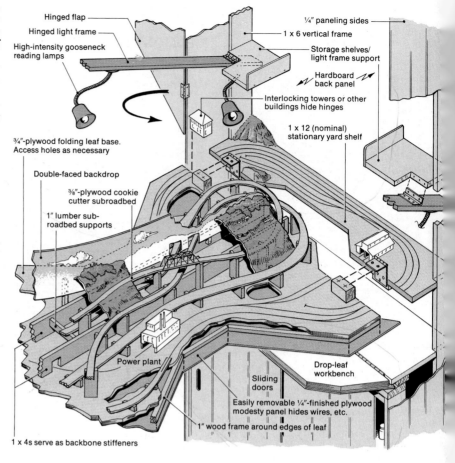

dynamics" studies to find out how to get the tonnage over the hill efficiently! That's the way it's done in full scale; it can be equally challenging in Z, even if a lot less destructive.

But where did that 3.6 percent come from? Well, that's how Märklin's pier and bridge set for ready-made up-and-over operation works out, and Märklin should know *something*!

Wrapping all this trackage in the space, along with the minimum number of turnouts to get trains past each other, could be almost impossible were it not for Märklin's turnouts. These let you put crossovers wherever needed without introducing curvature any sharper than that 195-mm-radius standard. These fellows are no beauties — the short, wide-swinging points have an undeniably tinplatish look — but they do the job with minimal damage to the geometry.

HOLD THE TURNOUTS

The P&W is relatively stingy with turnouts. One reason is they're expensive. As you may recall from your tinplate days (if you got started that way), you could quickly determine the wealth of the new kid on the block by asking "How many switches *you* got?" One pair of remote-control jobs will knock as much out of the budget as four or five freight cars. Incidentally, in Z they're still sold only in pairs, but both may be lefts or rights.

A better reason for few turnouts is that relatively little local freight traffic is called for on this pike. Lots of spurs on the fold-up portion would be both a nuisance and a hazard. They'd create more

places for cars to hide and be missed when everything runs for cover before a fold-up. The weight-to-size ratio of Z scale equipment makes it remarkably survivable, but before flipping the railroad up it would be best to audit all the track on the leaf to verify that it's free of rolling stock.

One worthwhile exception to the few-spurs rule is the empties-in / loads-out connection between the mine on the Black Diamond spur and the electric power plant near the other end of the main line at Edcon. This track should be handling strings of cars too long to be overlooked and profitable enough to pay for its turnouts and electromechanical uncoupling ramps.

That double-slip switch at Easternport certainly isn't typical of American practice, but it does maximize use of space in a critical area, letting us store several more cars. It also illustrates one of the peculiarities of Z scale in its present state: compared to its schematic equivalent of two turnouts point-to-point, one remote-control Märklin double-slip is about 40 percent *cheaper*! (Double-slips are only available powered; one of them is still only slightly more costly than a pair of manual turnouts.) What we won't do to save a little money.

IT DOESN'T HAVE TO FOLD UP

A nonfold-up, conventional version of the Piedmont & Western is also a compact railroad, of course — at 4 x 5½ feet it would slide under a double bed. If full-time space-saving isn't an overriding consideration, most of the complexities

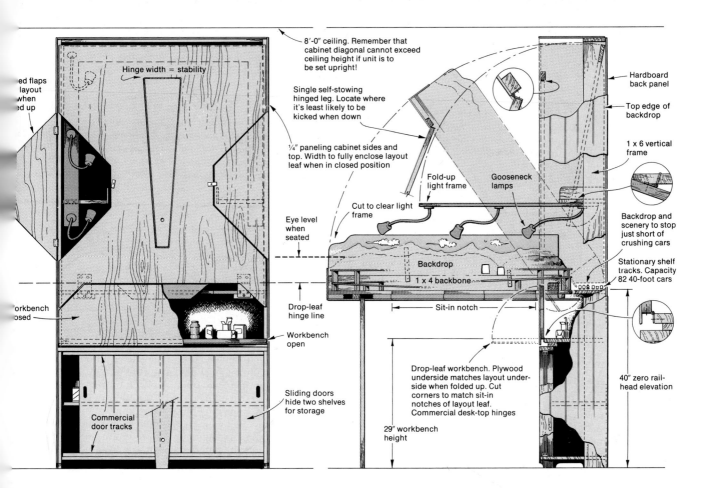

...ed flaps
layout
when
...d up

Hinge width = stability

8'-0" ceiling. Remember that cabinet diagonal cannot exceed ceiling height if unit is to be set upright!

Hardboard back panel

Single self-stowing hinged leg. Locate where it's least likely to be kicked when down

Top edge of backdrop

¼" paneling cabinet sides and top. Width to fully enclose layout leaf when in closed position

1 x 6 vertical frame

Fold-up light frame

Gooseneck lamps

Cut to clear light frame

Backdrop and scenery to stop just short of crushing cars

Eye level when seated

Backdrop

Stationary shelf tracks. Capacity 82 40-foot cars

1 x 4 backbone

Drop-leaf hinge line

Sit-in notch

Workbench closed

Workbench open

Drop-leaf workbench. Plywood underside matches layout underside when folded up. Cut corners to match sit-in notches of layout leaf. Commercial desk-top hinges

40" zero rail-head elevation

Sliding doors hide two shelves for storage

Commercial door tracks

29" workbench height

of the swing-up version can be eliminated. If it does do the disappearing act, though, double use of its dedicated floor area for a model-building workbench as shown is only logical.

The degree of cabinetmaking elegance employed is obviously a personal matter. Going far beyond the configuration indicated can become a hobby in itself; limiting fold-up complexity to that sufficient to get the railroad out of the way can salvage considerable time for modeling. On the other hand, compromising the quality, sturdiness and rigidity of construction would be a serious error — minor unintended hills and valleys in the roadbed foundation will look awful in comparison to the size of the trains themselves.

LIGHTING

What can we do to enhance the enjoyment of operating those little wonders? For one thing, we could provide sunbright lighting to show up their detail.

Lighting up the entire room to get enough foot candles on those tiny mountains and trains would not only be inefficient in the extreme but distracting as well, with all those nonrailroad things in the room clamoring equally for attention. Local lighting is to be preferred; the construction notes and Section A-A suggest a way of providing it which also has the advantage of creating directional effects and shadows more representative of sunlight. Expensive? Compared to a couple of big fluorescents overhead or a few incandescents, yes. Compared to a square foot covered with Z scale rolling stock, not at all!

Planning the location of each light source to achieve the best effect is at best laborious and, for those of us who are not trained stage technicians, of uncertain effectiveness as well; with the goosenecks it becomes a matter of enjoyable experimentation.

As Z scale matures, the trains are going to run better and get closer to scale. More of the prototypes we want will become available. By definition, they are not going to get any bigger, though they will undoubtedly *seem* bigger to their aficionados as memories of such huge beasts as HO SD45s fade with time. Are there ways to get something of the feel of the bigger scales while retaining the compactness of Z?

OPTICAL AMPLIFICATION, ANYONE?

Well, how about watching them run *under a magnifying glass?* You can't expect to enlarge the whole railroad, of course, but a little experimentation with a medium-power, "action-arm" mounted drafting magnifier indicates that under certain limited conditions it definitely *is* possible to turn the Z scale train into something a size or two bigger. (You can get some idea of the effect by looking at one of the little ones through your Optivisor if it's equipped with one of the stronger lenses.)

There are two principal restrictions:

Depth of field is limited. For best effect, the magnified scene should either be shallow — a single track against a vertical cliff, for example — or the background should be far enough behind the

train to be completely out of focus and therefore nonintrusive.

Three-quarter views don't work. Magnification messes up perspective; a boxcar viewed from an angle acquires a distinctly unrealistic "Manx cat" (higher in the rump) appearance.

On the P&W I have tricked up two places as candidates for effective magnification — a bridge scene to the right of Highfield where there's no nearby background, and an adjacent location (to the left of Edcon) where the close-cliff gimmick is attempted. A well-placed socket for an arm-mounted magnifier should be able to cover them both.

So much for *optical* amplification in making bigger ones out of the littlest. What about sound? Even if it becomes possible to put sound units aboard Z scale equipment without displacing so much weight that tractive force is destroyed, the fact that a train actually moves only a few feet in going from one end of the railroad to the other will prevent much of that "here it comes —there it goes" effect we are after.

With microprocessors busting out all over in this business, though, maybe it is not unreasonable to foresee binaural sounds fed into your ears and synchronized with the progress of a train to duplicate convincingly the roar and rumble of a big-scale counterpart.

If Z is to make itself felt big over here, the process has to start about now. So, if you want the chance to be in the thick of it, consider the possibilities offered by something like the Piedmont & Western — a railroad for pioneers! ✿

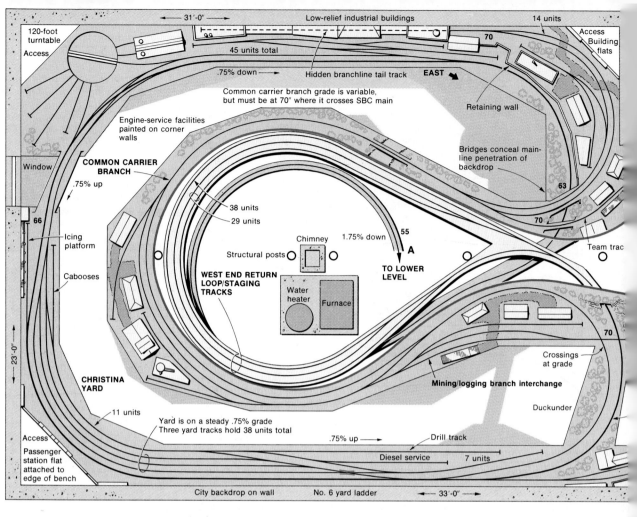

Upper Level (Top Diagram):

120-foot turntable

Access

← 31'-0" →

Low-relief industrial buildings

14 units

Access Building flats

70

45 units total

.75% down →

Hidden branchline tail track

EAST

Common carrier branch grade is variable, but must be at 70" where it crosses SBC main

Retaining wall

Engine-service facilities painted on corner walls

COMMON CARRIER BRANCH

Window

.75% up

66

Icing platform

Cabooses

38 units

29 units

Bridges conceal main-line penetration of backdrop

63

70

Team trac

Chimney

Structural posts

WEST END RETURN LOOP/STAGING TRACKS

1.75% down

55

A

TO LOWER LEVEL

Water heater

Furnace

23'-0"

CHRISTINA YARD

11 units

Yard is on a steady .75% grade
Three yard tracks hold 38 units total

.75% up →

Mining/logging branch interchange

Crossings at grade

Duckunder

70

Access

Passenger station flat attached to edge of bench

Drill track

Diesel service

7 units

City backdrop on wall

No. 6 yard ladder

← 33'-0" →

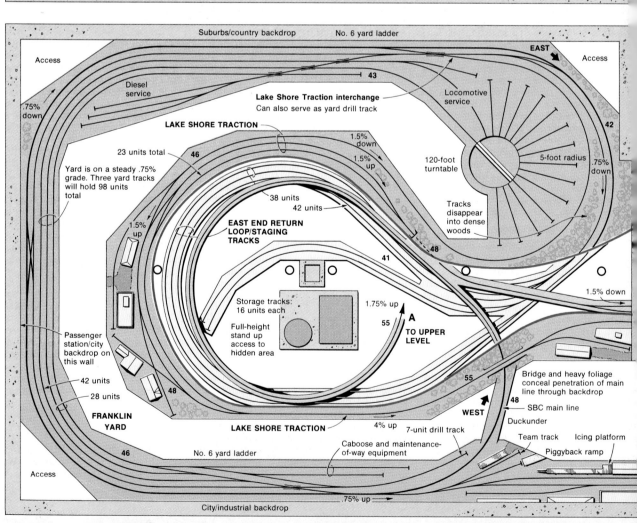

Lower Level (Bottom Diagram):

Suburbs/country backdrop

No. 6 yard ladder

EAST

Access

Access

Diesel service

43

Lake Shore Traction interchange
Can also serve as yard drill track

Locomotive service

42

.75% down

LAKE SHORE TRACTION

1.5% down

1.5% up

23 units total

46

120-foot turntable

5-foot radius

.75% down

38 units

42 units

EAST END RETURN LOOP/STAGING TRACKS

Tracks disappear into dense woods

48

Yard is on a steady .75% grade. Three yard tracks will hold 98 units total

1.5% up

41

1.5% down

Storage tracks: 16 units each

Full-height stand up access to hidden area

1.75% up

55

A

TO UPPER LEVEL

Passenger station/city backdrop on this wall

42 units

28 units

48

55

Bridge and heavy foliage conceal penetration of main line through backdrop

48

SBC main line

Duckunder

WEST

FRANKLIN YARD

LAKE SHORE TRACTION

4% up

7-unit drill track

Team track

Icing platform

Piggyback ramp

46

No. 6 yard ladder

Caboose and maintenance-of-way equipment

Access

.75% up →

City/industrial backdrop

The South Bay Central RR.

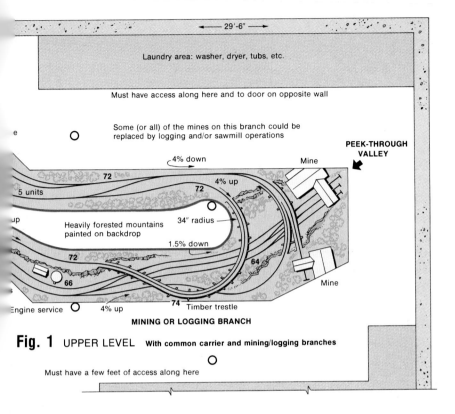

Laundry area: washer, dryer, tubs, etc.

Must have access along here and to door on opposite wall

Some (or all) of the mines on this branch could be replaced by logging and/or sawmill operations

PEEK-THROUGH VALLEY

4% down   Mine

4% up

72   72

Heavily forested mountains painted on backdrop

34" radius

1.5% down

72   64

66   74   Timber trestle

Engine service   4% up

Mine

5 units

MINING OR LOGGING BRANCH

Fig. 1 UPPER LEVEL **With common carrier and mining/logging branches**

Must have a few feet of access along here

Scale in feet
0 1 2 3 4 5 6

Minimum mainline radius: 5'-6"
Mainline turnouts no. 8 or larger
Backdrops shown by red lines
Bold numbers are elevations in inches from the floor

A large ¼″ scale layout, with ideas for smaller track plans

BY ED VONDRAK

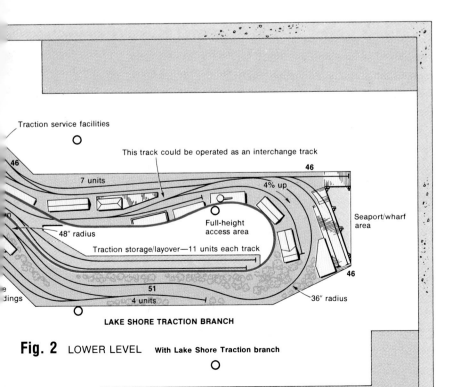

Traction service facilities

This track could be operated as an interchange track

46   46

7 units   4% up

48" radius

Full-height access area

Traction storage/layover—11 units each track

Seaport/wharf area

51   4 units   36" radius

46

dings

LAKE SHORE TRACTION BRANCH

Fig. 2 LOWER LEVEL **With Lake Shore Traction branch**

---

*O*NE thing sometimes leads to another in an interesting way. "Railroads in the Mountains," an article by Dr. Robert Rothe in the October 1974 MODEL RAILROADER, triggered my imagination. Over a period of several months following the appearance of that article I designed a track plan that was published as the "Dover Hill Western RR." in the August 1975 MR.

In the spring of 1977 I received a telephone call from a Michigan modeler named Dale Stanford. Dale wanted to build about two-thirds of the DHW track plan, but his space was slightly smaller than the dimensions of the published plan. I redesigned the plan for him, and a few months and hundreds of man-hours later the modified Dover Hill Western became a reality.

Other modelers soon learned of Dale's railroad, and in the spring of 1978 I heard from Dale again. He asked if I would consider designing a large ¼″ scale layout for his friend Frank Sniecinski. I had not designed anything for that scale before, but I thought I'd like to try. Frank and I subsequently carried on a considerable correspondence, and the result is this track plan for Frank's South Bay Central RR. It has been an enjoyable chain of events, and all because Dr. Rothe wrote an article for MR about mountain railroading.

PLANNING THE SBC

When Frank Sniecinski and I first corresponded about a track plan for the SBC, I wondered if I could adapt my thinking to ¼″ scale. It proved to be relatively easy to do, requiring only a rescaling of my rule-of-thumb sense of what would fit in what space. Frank's basement seemed very large at first, but he had grand ideas about what he wanted to fit into it.

Frank initially told me that he wanted a point-to-point main line with provision for continuous running, a minimum radius of 6 feet, and passing sidings and yard tracks long enough to accommodate 50-car trains. He also wanted three branch lines using smaller minimum radii: a common-carrier branch line, a switchback logging or mining branch that would use Shays for motive power, and a traction line — to be called the Lake Shore — serving both a mining area and a seaport. There were to be at least three towns, other than the large mainline yards, and plenty of industrial spurs wherever possible.

As Frank and I discussed possible configurations for his main line, we discovered that he really didn't want a point-to-point track plan. What he was after was a railroad that appeared to go somewhere instead of just around in circles. He wanted doubled-ended yards, and he said I could bridge the walk-in aisles once or twice. The

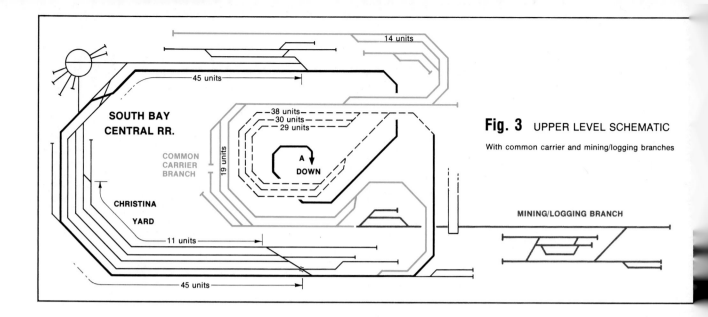

SOUTH BAY CENTRAL RR.

14 units

45 units

COMMON CARRIER BRANCH

38 units
30 units
29 units

19 units

A DOWN

CHRISTINA YARD

11 units

45 units

MINING/LOGGING BRANCH

Fig. 3 UPPER LEVEL SCHEMATIC

With common carrier and mining/logging branches

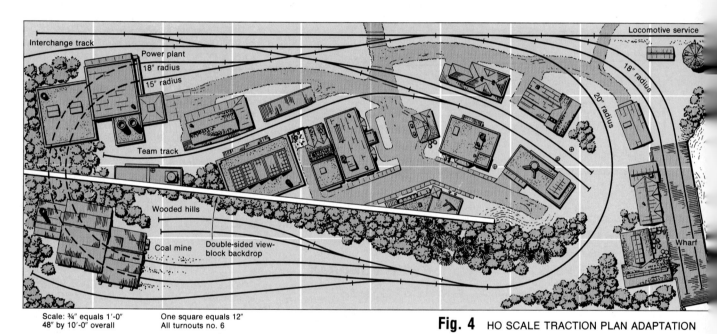

Interchange track

Locomotive service

Power plant
18" radius
15" radius

Team track

18" radius

20" radius

Wooded hills

Coal mine

Double-sided view-block backdrop

Wharf

Scale: ¾" equals 1'-0"
48" by 10'-0" overall

One square equals 12"
All turnouts no. 6

Fig. 4 HO SCALE TRACTION PLAN ADAPTATION

---

43 units

29 units

LAKE SHORE TRACTION

7 units

FRANKLIN YARD

SOUTH BAY CENTRAL RR.

23 units total

38 units
42 units

A UP

16 units

11 units

LAKE SHORE TRACTION

43 units

Fig. 5 LOWER LEVEL SCHEMATIC

With Lake Shore Traction branch

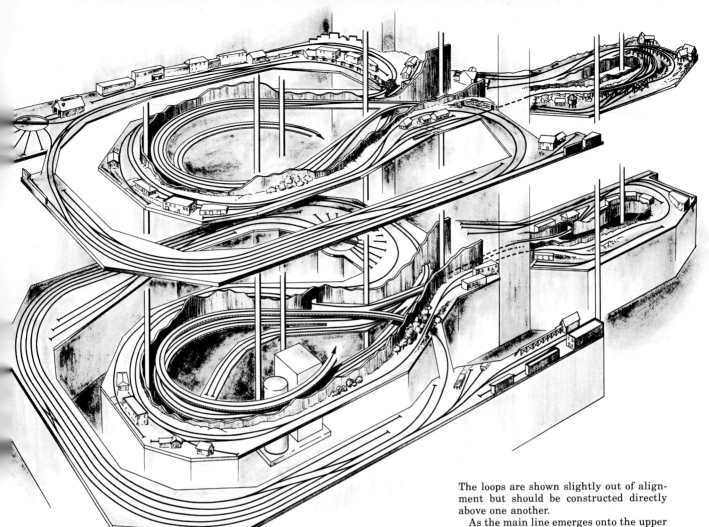

schematic that I ultimately used for the main line was loop-to-loop, with a division point plus another smaller yard.

The two-tiered track plan I developed for the SBC is shown in figs. 1 and 2, with the schematic shown in figs. 3 and 5. The plan satisfies modified criteria that Frank adjusted as the planning progressed. Notice that even a large space becomes crowded when a layout must include such a variety of features.

The loop-to-loop main line has a minimum radius of 5½ feet, but there is no continuous running connection. If a smaller minimum radius were used, it would be possible to double-track the whole main line. It would then be a version of the dogbone, a continuous-run schematic.

The hidden loops on the lowest level are the eastern end of the South Bay Central RR. See fig. 2. I used to put double loops at the ends of the main line in track plans like this until I realized that triple loops allow storing more trains and require only a little more space. Now I try to include triple loops whenever possible. Fig. 2 also shows two stub-end storage tracks within the lowest loops. If you wanted to increase the storage capacity, I think three or four tracks would fit in the space available.

Turnouts on the main line are no. 8 or larger, with no. 6s in the yards. I didn't worry too much about turnout sizes except to allow plenty of space as I drew the plan,

because Frank said that all the turnouts would be custom built. He also said I could freely use curved turnouts, and I did. The track plan could be modified to use only standard turnouts, but there would be reductions in track capacities and a smaller minimum radius would be necessary.

Track capacities are shown on the plan in terms of 40-foot units, so that each equals approximately one car. These capacities would have to be adjusted for the larger cars of contemporary railroading; current employee timetables often list track capacities in terms of 50-foot cars.

As the main line comes into view on the lower tier near the basement stairs (fig. 2), it immediately enters the large division-point yard at Franklin that stretches around three sides of the room. The shortest body track in this yard holds 29 units. The main line leaves the western end of Franklin Yard near an industrial area, proceeds across the aisle, and disappears into the backdrop that surrounds the furnace area in the center of the room.

Inside the backdrop the main line makes two complete loops around the furnace on a 1.75 percent grade to reach the level of the upper tier, where the track elevations are generally between 20 and 22 inches above those of the lower tier. Point A in fig. 1 is the same place as point A in fig. 2, but some liberties were taken in drawing the ascending helix to make the plan easier to read.

The loops are shown slightly out of alignment but should be constructed directly above one another.

As the main line emerges onto the upper tier, fig. 1, it goes through an industrial area and then past the smaller Christina Yard before crossing the aisle once more. Disappearing again into the central backdrop, the main reaches the hidden loop with triple staging tracks at the western end of the main line — see figs. 1 and 3. A smaller space dictated smaller track capacities on the upper-tier loop than on the lower one. Also, no stub-end storage tracks are shown within the upper loop, but some could be added directly above those on the lower tier.

There are yards alongside most of the visible main line of the SBC, but that's what Frank wanted. Some won't like the SBC's lack of open-country scenery, but that's a point of personal preference.

My personal preference is not to bridge aisleways at all, but in this plan bridging one aisle enabled me to efficiently stack the end loops and the tier-transition helix one above the other. The design also provides west-toward-the-left orientation at all visible parts of the main line.

BRANCH LINES

The complete track plan tries to make more of the branch lines than of the main, and the branches should be more scenic. On the upper tier, the common-carrier branch connects to the main at the west end of Christina Yard, where the interchange track parallels the main as both bridge the aisle. This branch heads west around the central backdrop and ends up in a town along the north wall near the basement stairs. Operationally there are

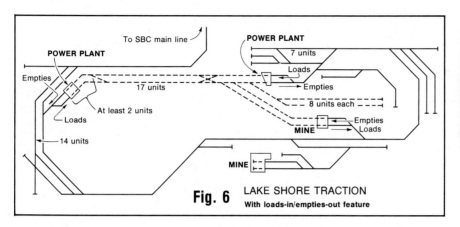

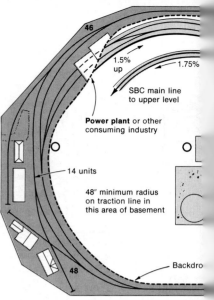

Fig. 6 LAKE SHORE TRACTION
With loads-in/empties-out feature

two towns along this wall, between the turntable and the stairs, but visually it would be one large town.

The switchback mining and logging branch leaves the common-carrier line across the aisle from Christina, fig. 1, and heads eastward through the closet to the right half of Frank's basement. It would likely be the scenic highlight of the whole layout, with timber trestles and a peek-through valley. I haven't seen such valleys on many track plans, but can remember first seeing this idea in John Armstrong's Pueblo & Salt Lake plan in the January 1962 MR.

The Lake Shore Traction line interchanges with the SBC at the east end of Franklin Yard, near the large turntable and locomotive service facilities on the lower tier. The Lake Shore, shown in figs. 2 and 5, has both a continuous running connection and its own staging tracks. The wharf tracks and both the real and simulated interchanges provide plenty of operating action for the LS.

IDEAS FOR SMALLER SPACES

Very few people have space for a railroad as large as the one described here, but even large track plans may include ideas that can be used on smaller layouts. Let's consider a couple of steps in going to smaller plans. One would be to build only the parts of Frank's plan shown in the left half of the

basement, but even that measures a large 23 x 33 feet.

The areas shown in figs. 2 and 5 present more likely possibilities for a small layout. As a specific example of what I'm talking about, consider the 4 x 10-foot HO scale track plan shown in fig. 4. This layout is adapted from the portion of the traction line shown in fig. 2. In a similar fashion the logging and mining branch line shown in fig. 1 could be built as a complete small railroad, either keeping the point-to-point arrangement of fig. 1 or altering it for continuous running as I did in fig. 4.

The HO layout incorporates several track planning features usually reserved for larger designs. A center backdrop is used to visually separate the town from the rolling hills. Not many people seem to use center backdrops on small layouts, but the idea has been discussed in MR in articles by John Armstrong, the late Don Myatt, and Jack Work — whose delightfully complex 4 x 8-foot layout appeared in the December 1974 issue. Center backdrops make layouts appear larger by keeping you from seeing everything at once and allow seemingly distant and distinct scenes to be built close together.

In a 1963 MR article Dr. Roy Dohn said that the best spurs to include in a track plan for operational flexibility are a team track, an interchange track, and a wharf. Team tracks are used to load and unload

freight cars from and into trucks (originally teamsters' wagons, hence the name) and so serve industries not located directly on the railroad. Almost any kind of car can thus be spotted on a team track, whether or not you actually model an industry needing that type of car.

Interchange tracks are connections to other railroads, and again almost any type of car can appear on an interchange. "Overhead" traffic, cars moving across your railroad from one interchange to another, doesn't have to have any relation to the kind of industries you serve on your layout.

A wharf track for transloading between freight cars and ships or barges has many of the advantages of team and interchange tracks. There is also the point that even a small shipload of freight equals a lot of railroad carloads. All three of these are incorporated in the HO plan, with a good bit of switchback and runaround shunting required to get from one to another.

The loads in/empties out arrangement for handling open-top cars has been grow-

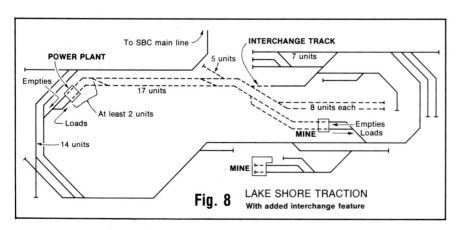

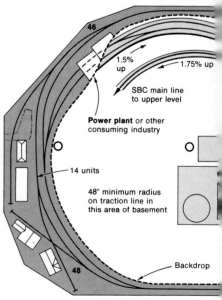

Fig. 8 LAKE SHORE TRACTION
With added interchange feature

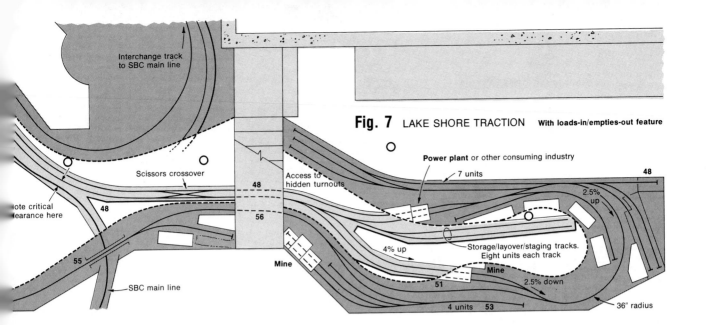

Fig. 7 LAKE SHORE TRACTION **With loads-in/empties-out feature**

Interchange track to SBC main line

Scissors crossover

48

48

56

Note critical clearance here

55

SBC main line

Access to hidden turnouts

Mine

Power plant or other consuming industry

7 units

48

2.5% up

4% up

Storage/layover/staging tracks. Eight units each track

Mine

51

2.5% down

4 units   53

36" radius

---

ng in popularity, and the railroad in fig. 4 has that too, similar in arrangement to the mine/power plant combination on MR's Clinchfield RR. If you didn't want that kind of operation, the tracks through the back-drop could be modified to serve as func-tional interchange tracks instead. I would maintain the continuous-run connection for occasions like breaking in a new loco-motive or showing a lot of action to visitors who aren't model railroaders.

IDEAS FLOW BOTH WAYS

Working these features into the HO track plan led me to go back and speculate on possible modifications of my ¼" scale plan for Frank, particularly in regard to including more interchanges and team tracks. Some are already included on the SBC as shown, but many other locations are possible. Several of the industrial tracks could be used either as team or in-terchange tracks, and there is even space for additional spurs to serve these func-tions.

One interesting possibility would be to

use the hidden tail track at the end of the common carrier branch line as an inter-change track. One could then run the branch as a bridge route between the South Bay Central and some other railroad lo-cated offstage at the west end of the branch. The possibilities are limited only by your space and imagination.

Another idea from the HO layout is to incorporate the loads in/empties out in-dustry arrangement into the Lake Shore Traction system. An alternate layout for the traction line which does this is shown in figs. 6 and 7. In fact, I was able to ar-range a multiple scheme where loaded cars from one mine can go to two power plants, with empties returning from both in the proper fashion. I also added a reverse loop to the traction line but had to give up the simulated interchange trackage.

The best of both worlds would be a design for the traction system that would have both the interchange to hidden tracks *and* the loads in/empties out operation. I couldn't figure out how to do this in the SBC plan because of the limitations of

clearances, gradients, and minimum radii.

I did find a way to work in one of each of these operating features. The simulated in-terchange track will fit near the seaport at the eastern end of the Lake Shore line, with the loads in/empties out industry pair near the western end. This design for the traction line is shown in figs. 8 and 9. The LS could thus be built in any number of ways, depending on what kind of operation it is to emphasize.

IDEAS ARE EVERYWHERE

Some readers complain every time a large and complex track plan is published in MODEL RAILROADER, claiming that such plans are useless to most people. Quite the contrary is the case, as I found when de-signing the 4 x 10-foot HO track plan. It was inspired by the large and complex South Bay Central, and it in turn gener-ated some useful improvements for the traction line that forms only a small part of the large layout. I like to study both large and small track plans with an open mind, as useful ideas can be found everywhere. ◊

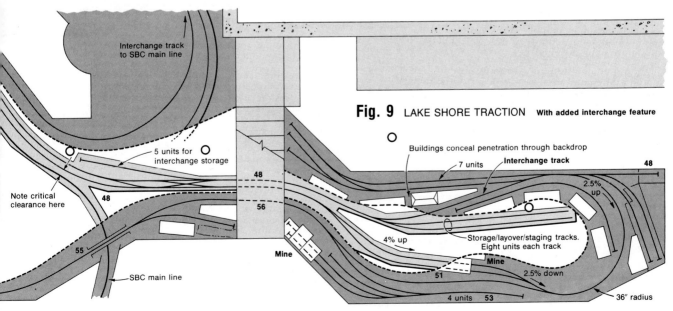

Fig. 9 LAKE SHORE TRACTION **With added interchange feature**

Interchange track to SBC main line

5 units for interchange storage

48

56

Note critical clearance here

48

55

SBC main line

Mine

Buildings conceal penetration through backdrop

7 units

Interchange track

48

2.5% up

4% up

Storage/layover/staging tracks. Eight units each track

Mine

51

2.5% down

4 units   53

36" radius

The Iowa Centra

Class 1 operation on a simple S scale layout

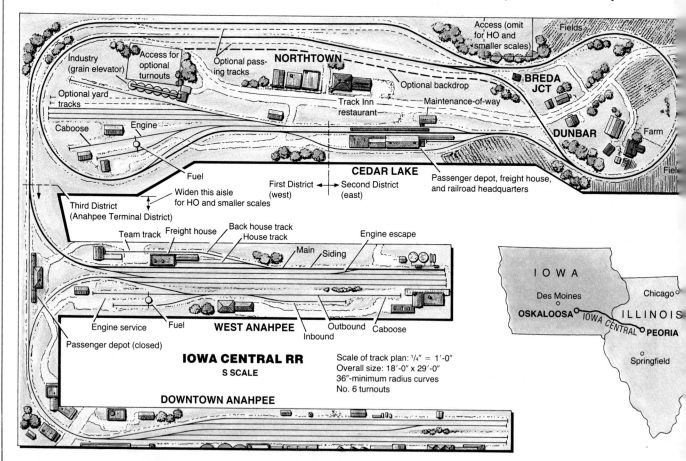

Access (omit for HO and smaller scales)

Fields

Industry (grain elevator)

Access for optional turnouts

Optional passing tracks

NORTHTOWN

Optional yard tracks

Caboose   Engine

Track Inn restaurant

Optional backdrop

Maintenance-of-way

BREDA JCT

DUNBAR

Farm

Fuel

Widen this aisle for HO and smaller scales

CEDAR LAKE

First District (west) ←→ Second District (east)

Passenger depot, freight house, and railroad headquarters

Third District (Anahpee Terminal District)

Team track   Freight house

Back house track

House track

Engine escape

Main   Siding

Engine service   Fuel

Passenger depot (closed)

WEST ANAHPEE

Outbound   Caboose

Inbound

IOWA CENTRAL RR

S SCALE

DOWNTOWN ANAHPEE

Scale of track plan: 1/4" = 1'-0"
Overall size: 18'-0" x 29'-0"
36"-minimum radius curves
No. 6 turnouts

I O W A

Des Moines

OSKALOOSA

Chicago

I L L I N O I S

IOWA CENTRAL

PEORIA

Springfield

A railroader's track plan

BY ROBERT NICHOLSON

MANY MODEL RAILROADS seem to be tight-knit little empires apparently run without regard to human intervention, limitations, or imperfections — other than what comes through the control cable. Now, before everybody starts throwing things, let me explain.

What I look for in a model railroad track plan is the potential for realistic operation as I know it, influenced by my profession as a locomotive engineer. This goes for design, traffic justification, and possibility of continuous running.

IOWA CENTRAL RR

The Iowa Central RR is a good example. It offers no breakthroughs in model railroad technology or design. Nor is it in the advanced category, although it has a wye and a reverse loop.

I conceived the Iowa Central a few years ago as a place to operate my small but hard-won roster of S scale locomotives and rolling stock. A high-density main line was out of the question, and a short line wasn't what I wanted either. However, a secondary Class 1 main line, like Baby Bear's porridge, was just right.

Discussions with a former Minneapolis & St. Louis employee nailed down the prototype example. My Iowa Central track plan is based on the M&StL line between Oskaloosa, Iowa, and Peoria, Ill., that was once really called the Iowa Central RR.

A LITTLE HISTORY

The model Iowa Central RR is a fictitious midwestern Class 1 railroad. The Anahpee Division is a vine-like secondary extension that reaches out to industries and a river terminal and interchanges with other railroads in the small city of Anahpee. The year is 1962, and motive power is strictly first-generation diesels.

The Anahpee Division consists of three districts. The First District is about 125 miles long and runs from Dunbar to Cedar Lake. The Second District, only 50 miles long, runs from Cedar Lake to West Anahpee. West Anahpee Yard and the trackage to the metropolitan area (downtown Anahpee) make up the Third District, known as the Anahpee Terminal District.

Anahpee once figured prominently in company fortunes. However, in recent years the business from a once-extensive coal industry has dwindled or been diverted to trucks, and its status has declined. Consequently, traffic on the Iowa Central has been reduced to one daily freight train in each direction, with extra trains handling occasional surges in business.

Cedar Lake is the boundary between the First and the Second Districts as well as the division headquarters. The daily trains change crews here, a practice held over from the days when the entire length of the division was more than a crew could cover in a working day. There's no longer an assigned yard engine, and many of the yard tracks have been taken up. A small service facility takes care of engines left here. It also services the cabooses used by the train crews.

Activity on the Anahpee Terminal District has dwindled as well. One yard shift a day, with occasional extra jobs called out, is a far cry from the 24-hour hum that existed as recently as the mid-1950s.

THE LAYOUT

The Iowa Central RR is designed for point-to-loop operation, with continuous running possible via the connecting track at Breda Junction. A single operator could manage the whole layout by letting a train run off laps on the main line while switching on the Anahpee Terminal District.

When the operating crew comes over, there's room for at least three operators, one serving as the First District crew, another as the Second District crew, and the third as the West Anahpee yard crew.

A fourth person, if the optional passing

Minneapolis & St. Louis Ry.

The small "IC" that you see at the corners of the depot in Oskaloosa, Iowa, hints at the Iowa Central heritage of this part of the former Minneapolis & St. Louis Ry. The small town of Cedar Lake included in author Robert Nicholson's S scale Iowa Central plan is based on Oskaloosa.

tracks are added, could serve as operator for BJ Tower, being responsible for proper routing of trains per instructions from the dispatcher at Cedar Lake. Okay, make it five people.

Passenger train operation can be discontinued or in its final days, with no loss of credibility either way. If passenger service does exist, a single diesel pulling a short ragtag mixture of old and new passenger equipment would be appropriate.

Representing a last-ditch effort to appease the rigid terms of an expiring mail contract, the passenger train would need more head-end cars than coaches.

On the Anahpee Terminal District, West Anahpee is a flat classification yard where road trains originate and terminate. Except for passenger crews, road crews don't run east of West Anahpee.

Downtown Anahpee is a fiddle and storage yard served by the yard engine. It's designed so cars can be pulled in and out as transfer blocks, switched with a yard engine, or lifted on and off the tracks by hand. New rolling stock makes its first appearance from here.

The Second District extends west (timetable direction) from the wye through Breda Junction and around the loop to the depot at Cedar Lake. The First District extends from there past Breda Junction, where it shares trackage with the Second District to Dunbar, the cutoff used to reverse trains and start the operating sequence again.

The First and Second District trackage along the back of the benchwork may be hidden so trains are out of sight until it's time for them to show up at Cedar Lake or West Anahpee. This creates the feeling that the trains are moving over two districts.

Hidden sidings in this area (shown as dashed lines on the track plan) for one or both districts would allow meets with reappearing trains at Cedar Lake and West Anahpee.

SETTING THE SCENE

Structures on the layout call back days not so long ago when activity on the railroad proceeded at a much faster pace. In line with this, the depot and freight house at Cedar Lake is an old two-story wood structure that also houses the division headquarters.

Northtown is a takeoff from North Chillicothe, Ill., a crew change point on the Santa Fe until 1991. Like "North Chilli," it's a small cluster of businesses north of the tracks, with a hardware store, grocery store, and Track Inn restaurant.

More switching opportunities could be added with the optional yard track at Cedar Lake. A grain elevator, fuel dealer, or lumberyard would fit right in alongside the yard.

A DAY ON THE IOWA CENTRAL

The daily trains are nos. 141 and 142 on the First District and 241 and 242 on the Second District. Three crews, each with an assigned caboose, work these trains.

Crews rotate jobs in turn — Cedar Lake to Dunbar on the first day, back on no. 142 the next. On the third day, they work no. 242-241, known as the Anahpee Turn, which uses one crew because the 50-mile district is short enough that they can make the round trip to West Anahpee and back in one day. The rotation begins all over again with no. 141 on the fourth day, with no days off.

The first train to run is no. 142, which leaves Dunbar in the wee hours of the morning. It lays over on the First District holding track. During the time it's moving over the First District towards Cedar Lake, the yard engine at West Anahpee begins rounding up cars for westbound no. 241.

This requires several trips to downtown as various connecting roads make deliveries and industries call for cars to be pulled, spotted, and reset. Cars for the outbound train are brought back to West Anahpee several times and lined up for departure in the two yard tracks.

MEANWHILE . . .

Back at Cedar Lake, no. 142 arrives and a new crew takes over. Cabooses are changed using an extra engine that's usually at Cedar Lake. Setouts and pickups are made, and maybe the engine consist gets rearranged (like setting out a unit for a work train). When that's finished, no. 142 leaves town as no. 242.

The caboose from no. 141 is spotted on the west end of the house track so it will be in position for a quick caboose change when it goes out on no. 242 the next day.

Train 242 arrives at West Anahpee and rolls down the yard main past the freight house. The engines are cut away from the train, slipped back through the siding, turned on the wye if needed, and sent to the service track.

The yard engine hangs the caboose on the rear of the outbound cars. As soon as the road engines are done at the pit, they couple onto the cars and no. 242 is made up for its return trip. Once no. 242 has departed, the yard crew switches out the cars from inbound no. 242 and begins making deliveries.

When no. 241 arrives at Cedar Lake, the third crew of the day takes over. Cabooses, train, and possibly engines are switched again. This time the inbound caboose is spotted on the east end of the house track in position for tomorrow's no. 141. After today's train leaves for Dunbar as no. 141, the inbound crew from no. 242 does its required switching around Cedar Lake.

At West Anahpee the yard engine goes off duty a short time later. Our day on the Anahpee Division closes a few hours later, when no. 141 arrives at Dunbar and the crew goes off duty before returning to Cedar Lake on no. 142 the next morning.

WHAT HAPPENED?

On that note the saga of the Iowa Central RR comes to a close. The layout was never built. It was rejected when I found a suitable basement for the "Big Dream." Since I'm still suffering the agony of its creation 8 years later, I wonder if I should've built the Iowa Central instead of the "Big Mistake." ◊

Layout Planning Contest Winners

The following 13 track plans were designed by the winners of two different MODEL RAILROADER track planning contests in the early 1980s. The first contest was for HO scale track plans. The nine winners were selected from 393 entries and represent the very best from an impressive field. The four winners of the N scale track plan contest were selected from 157 entries. The track plans represent a diversity of ideas but most include attractive prototype scenes, interesting research and planning, and practical layout design.

All of the HO plans had to be drawn to 3/4" = 1'-0" scale. The plans had to fit in an 8 x 9-foot room with a doorway and a ceiling height of 8 feet. The N scale plans could be no larger than 50 square feet and they had to fit in a 12 x 16-foot family room.

The Galena Division of the C&NW

A turn-of-the-century HO layout

BY ALAN CERNY

"ONLY eight by nine? You're kidding!" That was my first reaction when I quickly scanned the MODEL RAILROADER'S layout planning contest criteria. As small as that room is, however, with today's stratospheric lending rates many of us don't even have eight by nine feet of floor space to spare — I know I don't.

But I wasn't about to write off either the MR contest or model railroading. A two- or three-bedroom condominium, with a "down-sized" spare bedroom for the railroad, is realistically within reach of many of us whose

dream of owning anything so luxurious as a basement has long since vanished. So here's my idea for a historically interesting railroad designed to fit the quite reasonable space, all things considered, of eight by nine.

BLUFF CITY

The focal point of my layout plan is Elgin, Ill. Elgin's now rarely used nickname of Bluff City quickly sets the scene for this midwestern river town. Straddling the Fox River and located 38 miles slightly west and north of Chicago, this is the very same Elgin

known the world over for watches, clocks, and street sweepers.

It was also a major dairy center in the late 1800s and established national dairy prices with its own Board of Trade. Fortunately for Elgin's independent nature, Chicago's suburban sprawl was kept at bay by a buffer zone to the east, rolling farmland criss-crossed by railroads and dotted with gravel pits.

Elgin hosts two Chicago & North Western branch lines, one of which slices through the city's business district on the east side of the Fox River. On the river's west side, the Mil-

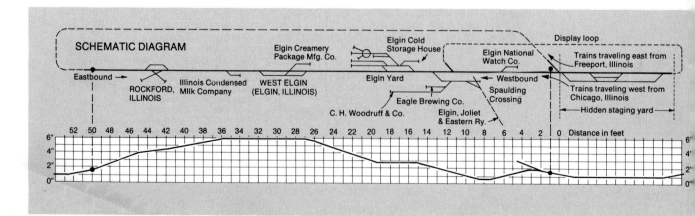

SCHEMATIC DIAGRAM

Display loop

Eastbound →

ROCKFORD, ILLINOIS

Illinois Condensed Milk Company

Elgin Creamery Package Mfg. Co.

WEST ELGIN (ELGIN, ILLINOIS)

C. H. Woodruff & Co.

Eagle Brewing Co.

Elgin Cold Storage House

Elgin Yard

Elgin, Joliet & Eastern Ry.

Elgin National Watch Co.

← Westbound

Spaulding Crossing

Trains traveling east from Freeport, Illinois

Trains traveling west from Chicago, Illinois

Hidden staging yard

52 50 48 46 44 42 40 38 36 34 32 30 28 26 24 22 20 18 16 14 12 10 8 6 4 2 0 Distance in feet

6" 4" 2" 0"

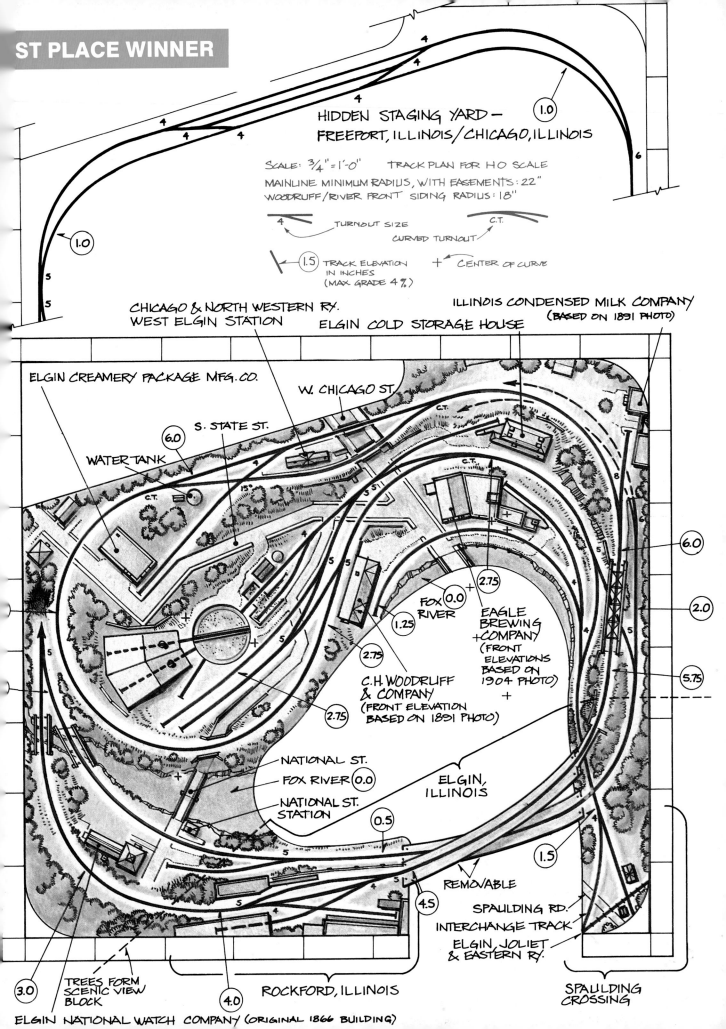

HIDDEN STAGING YARD —
FREEPORT, ILLINOIS/CHICAGO, ILLINOIS

SCALE: 3/4" = 1'-0"   TRACK PLAN FOR HO SCALE
MAINLINE MINIMUM RADIUS, WITH EASEMENTS: 22"
WOODRUFF/RIVER FRONT SIDING RADIUS: 18"

4 ──── TURNOUT SIZE
C.T. ──── CURVED TURNOUT

1.5 ──── TRACK ELEVATION
IN INCHES
(MAX GRADE 4%)   + ──── CENTER OF CURVE

CHICAGO & NORTH WESTERN RY.
WEST ELGIN STATION

ELGIN COLD STORAGE HOUSE

ILLINOIS CONDENSED MILK COMPANY
(BASED ON 1891 PHOTO)

ELGIN CREAMERY PACKAGE MFG. CO.

W. CHICAGO ST.

S. STATE ST.

WATER TANK

6.0

FOX RIVER 0.0

1.25

2.75

EAGLE
BREWING
+ COMPANY
(FRONT
ELEVATIONS
BASED ON
1904 PHOTO)
+

2.75

C.H. WOODRUFF
& COMPANY
(FRONT ELEVATION
BASED ON 1891 PHOTO)

2.75

6.0

2.0

5.75

NATIONAL ST.
FOX RIVER 0.0
NATIONAL ST.
STATION

ELGIN,
ILLINOIS

0.5

1.5

REMOVABLE

4.5

SPAULDING RD.
INTERCHANGE TRACK
ELGIN, JOLIET
& EASTERN RY.

3.0

TREES FORM
SCENIC VIEW
BLOCK

4.0

ROCKFORD, ILLINOIS

SPAULDING
CROSSING

ELGIN NATIONAL WATCH COMPANY (ORIGINAL 1866 BUILDING)

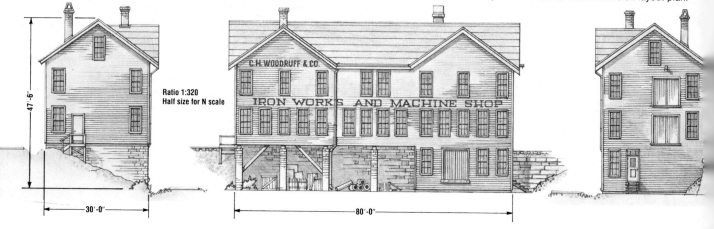

This is Alan Cerny's version of the C. H. Woodruff & Co. Iron Works and Machine Shop in Elgin, Ill. Alan worked from an 1891 photograph of the real building to come up with a selectively compressed but still recognizable front elevation to fit a spot on his C&NW Galena Division layout plan.

Ratio 1:320
Half size for N scale

waukee Road main line to the Mississippi threads its way along the industrialized riverfront. I borrowed industries and scenes from both of these routes, including the Elgin National Watch factory on the Fox River's east bank and the Milwaukee Road's interchange at Spaulding Crossing.

The layout's theme, though, comes from Elgin's other C&NW line, a route that clings to a bluff and hides behind large shade trees as it parallels the busy Milwaukee Road main just a few blocks east.

This single-track branch played an early role in Illinois railroad history as part of the main line of Chicago's first railroad, the Galena & Chicago Union. In 1836 the Illinois legislature chartered the G&CU to construct a railroad from Lake Michigan to the lead mine region of northwestern Illinois, and so to connect two promising cities — Galena and Chicago. Construction began only in 1848, but the Galena, as the new line was called, reached the city of Elgin by 1850.

The Galena got to Rockford in 1852 and Freeport in 1853, but never made it to its namesake city. Other Illinois railroads were winning the race for Galena's lead mines, and it was decided not to complete the route.

When the G&CU was consolidated with the Chicago & North Western Ry. in 1864, it was the C&NW's identity that defined the enlarged system. A further obscuring of the Galena's original plan occurred in 1873 when the Chicago & Pacific RR, later part of the Chicago, Milwaukee, St. Paul & Pacific, entered Elgin by a more direct route from the Windy City.

MODELING THE GALENA DIVISION: CIRCA 1900

I chose to set my version of the Galena Division in the turn-of-the-century era. My decision was prompted by talks with one of the keepers of Elgin history, retired architect and long-time Elgin resident Elmer Gylleck, and by two promotional books the city published in 1891 and 1904 to encourage industrial growth. After I'd been swimming for weeks through old photos, books, and maps, I settled on three key elements

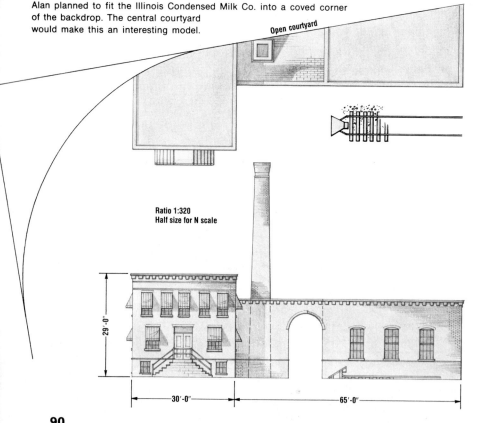

Alan planned to fit the Illinois Condensed Milk Co. into a coved corner of the backdrop. The central courtyard would make this an interesting model.

Open courtyard

Ratio 1:320
Half size for N scale

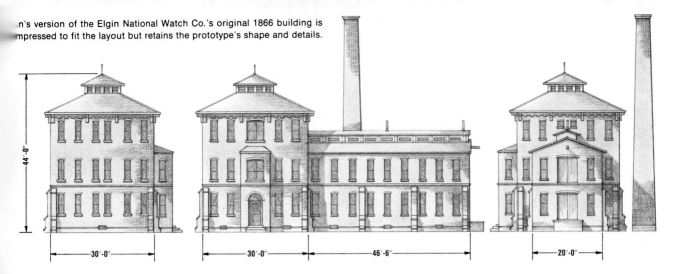

n's version of the Elgin National Watch Co.'s original 1866 building is
mpressed to fit the layout but retains the prototype's shape and details.

hat I wanted in the final layout plan:
• A track plan that traces the 121 mile
Galena Division route, at least in schematic diagram form that can be framed
and hung on the wall for visiting operators.
• Scenes based on Elgin's west side, spe-
cifically the Galena's almost theme-park-
like route along the bluffs contrasted with
the industrialized riverfront foreground.
• Models of Elgin industrial structures
as they were around 1900.

I was able to satisfy my first two requirements by designing a hidden staging yard,
and routing my main line first through the
industrialized river front and then back
along the paralleling bluffs. The Elgin promotional books helped meet the third requirement by providing information about
businesses and plenty of photos. I got carried away drawing buildings, but had fun
finding out what would and would not fit.

Almost all the structure drawings that
I've included are based on 1891 and 1904
Elgin photos, but they are selectively compressed and modified to fit the track plan.
The one exception is the Elgin National
Watch factory, which I've represented with
the original 1866 building instead of modeling the huge complex of 1907 that sprung
from all sides of the older structure.

Having all these structures accurately
planned will let me start filling shoeboxes
and closet shelves with Elgin industries
and C&NW equipment, such as the small

stable of 4-4-0s and 4-6-0s I plan to kitbash
using Charles Knudsen's book, *Chicago &
North Western Steam Power*, for reference.
I'm not alone in my plight, as many others
before me have overflowed apartment linen
closets with enough miniature real estate
and rolling stock for several rail empires
before obtaining suitable land rights.

An interesting twist to our problem can
be found in the history of the original Galena & Chicago Union RR. The builders
had such great faith in the future of railroading that the first 10 miles of track
were completed before acquiring a locomotive. Is it possible they too were waiting for
the prime lending rate to drop? ✿

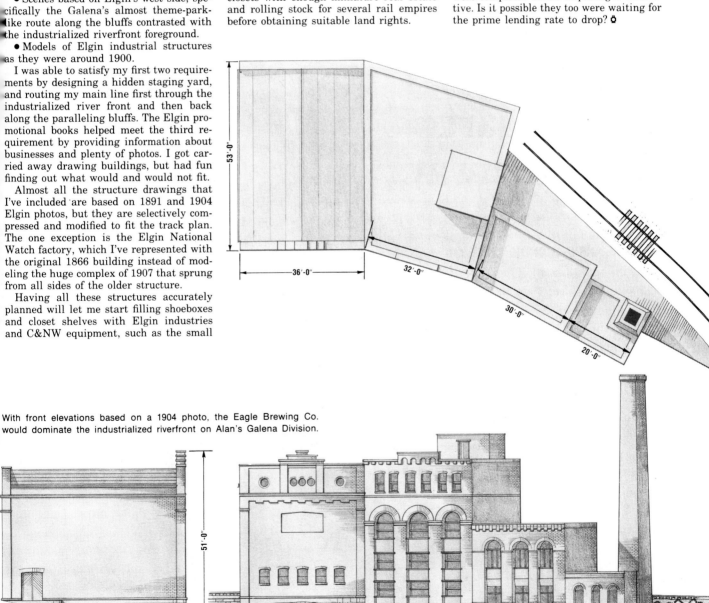

With front elevations based on a 1904 photo, the Eagle Brewing Co.
would dominate the industrialized riverfront on Alan's Galena Division.

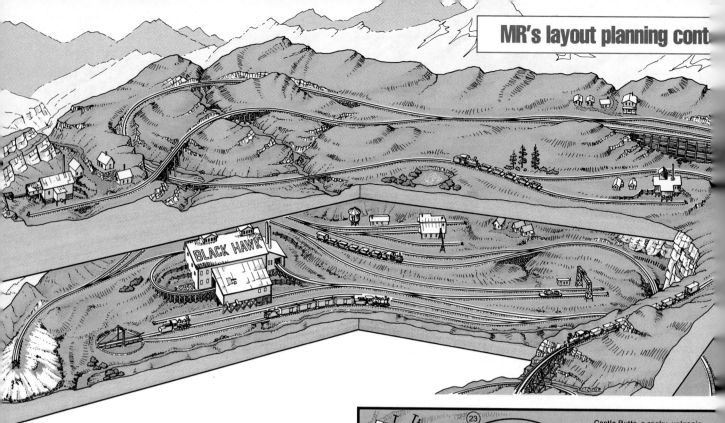

The Quartz Hill Tramway

HOn2½ in the Rockies

BY DON DE VERE

THE QUARTZ HILL Tramway is loosely based on the 2-foot-gauge Gilpin Tram in Colorado, circa 1910. This longest 2-footer in the West carried gold ore from several mines to a central stamp mill and smelter served by the 3-foot gauge Colorado & Southern. On the uphill trips the Tram hauled coal for mine hoists, mine timbers, machinery, and supplies.

For power the Tram used little two-truck Shays, which pulled long strings of unusual bottom-dump steel ore cars to and from mines perched high above the timberline on barren, rocky mountainsides. Its rolling stock also included a few flats, gondolas, homemade tanks, and small, boxlike cabooses. In addition it had some open-side passenger cars for excursion use.

The Tram's right-of-way was a convoluted series of steep switchbacks and loops cut out of barren rock and condensed into a relatively small area, so that its tracks were often farther apart vertically than horizontally. Grades were commonly as steep as 6 percent and curves were as sharp as 60-foot radius. See Ferrell's *The Gilpin Gold Tram* (Pruett) for photos, drawings, and more information on this Colorado 2-footer.

TRAMWAY MODELING

I chose extra-narrow gauge for the Quartz Hill Tramway for the same reason the prototype did: the slim track and small equipment permit sharp curves to get into tight places — such as MODEL RAILROADER'S 8 x 9-foot room! The mainline minimum radius is still a generous 15", although the equipment will turn much sharper. A few sharper wig-

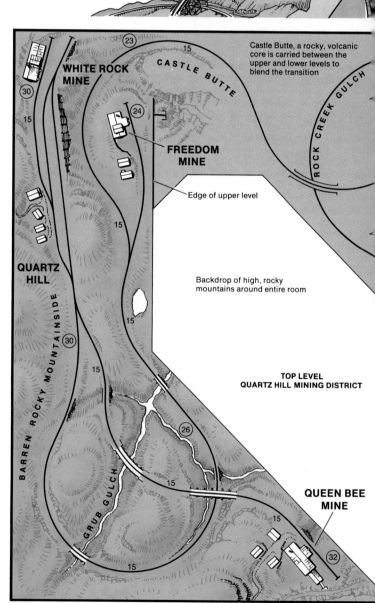

Castle Butte, a rocky, volcanic core is carried between the upper and lower levels to blend the transition

WHITE ROCK MINE

CASTLE BUTTE

ROCK CREEK GULCH

FREEDOM MINE

Edge of upper level

QUARTZ HILL

Backdrop of high, rocky mountains around entire room

BARREN ROCKY MOUNTAINSIDE

TOP LEVEL
QUARTZ HILL MINING DISTRICT

GRUB GULCH

QUEEN BEE MINE

gles and bends could be built into the route for character.

There is quite a bit of HOn2½ equipment available for such a model railroad. Joe Works offers little two-truck Shays and tiny rod engines that would also be appropriate, such as an 0-4-0T or 0-4-4T. Lambert imports Shinohara HOn2½ flextrack and turnouts with Code 60 rail. This is N gauge but with larger, wider spaced ties for use in HO scale. The 150 mm- and 200 mm-radius turnouts are very sharp and quite in keeping with the prototype.

The ore cars could easily be approximated by modifying N scale European-prototype open dump cars, removing their buffers, and adding brake staffs. In HO these would make ore cars of 4-yard capacity and would be quite impressive in strings of a dozen or more. You could use removable loads to differentiate between up and down trains.

RUNNING THE TRAMWAY

On the layout, Black Hawk is served by a branch of the C&S, which comes out of a hidden reverse loop and appears from a curving canyon. Daily, a 3-foot gauge mixed train arrives behind a Mogul or Consolidation. It swaps one or two empty boxcars for carloads of bagged concentrate at the mill, leaves gondolas of coal for the mines and occasional flats with machinery or timbers on the transfer track, and pushes coal gons into the mill's boiler house.

On the Tramway a typical up train out of Black Hawk consists of one or two small gons of coal and a flat loaded with timbers from the transfer track, together with a dozen or so empty ore cars from the mill. A diminutive caboose brings up the rear.

With a Shay on the head end the up train climbs through bleak, rocky high country typical of Colorado's Gilpin County, and past mining debris like tailing dumps, old head frames, and miners' cabins. Along the way it drops empty ore cars and loaded supply cars at the various mine spurs.

As the loading spurs at the California, Freedom, and Queen Bee mines are all trailing in the up direction, the up train spots the loaded ore cars so they'll be in position for the down train to pick up behind the engine. That is, it takes loads from the California to Upper Mongollon, and loads from the other two to Quartz Hill, which is on a second scenic level above Black Hawk.

These stations have runarounds where the loads can be switched behind the down-bound engine; the Tramway's rules call for the locomotive being on the low end of all down trains. With no air brakes and steep grades, this helps prevent runaways.

Easing back down to Black Hawk, the down train's Shay switches the strings of loaded and empty ore cars to and from the dump track at the rear of the mill. Access to the dump is by a switchback, which is also used to dispose of the mill tailings. Tailing cars are brought out of the mill in pairs on a curved trestle and pushed onto the dump by the small tank engine that does light switching around the mill.

With all the switching required by the hill rules added to that needed to get over the switchbacks, many pleasant hours of operation are assured on this small but dramatic extra-narrow-gauge system. ⊙

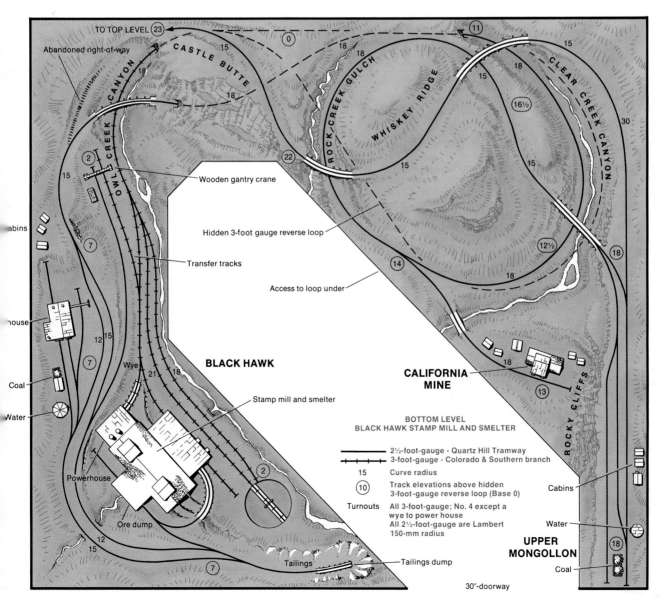

The Brooklyn East River Terminal Ry.

Turn-of-the-century waterfront railroading in HO

BY JOSEPH K. CREA

MY BROOKLYN EAST RIVER Terminal Ry. design is the result of my fascination with a particular building. I was in architectural design school in Brooklyn during the 1960s when I discovered a large block of old brick warehouses falling into ruin on the waterfront. Built in the 1850s beneath the Brooklyn Bridge, it had been vacant for many years before I found it.

Its most notable features were tiers of large arched doors, each with ponderous iron shutters, facing the East River. Above each column of doors a sturdy horizontal timber extended several feet beyond the cornice. These had once supported block-and-tackle rigs. Cargo unloaded from the sailing ships tied up here was evidently pushed across the cobblestones, and then the heavy crates and barrels were hoisted up and swung in through the doors!

As I surveyed the scene of rotted pilings, decayed brick, heaped trash, and derelicts sleeping off their morning bottles, in my mind's eye I saw the vitality of an age when steam and sail ruled the waterfront.

The trash and abandoned autos on those time-worn cobblestones were replaced by shouting stevedores, well-dressed businessmen, horse-drawn drays, and piles of crates, sacks, and barrels. The clusters of rotted pilings became wharves again, nudging the freshly painted hulls of the graceful wooden schooners and clippers that pushed their bowsprits over the street. A steam train moved slowly down the avenue, preceded by a walking flagman as required by law.

Hopeless romantic that I am, I've never forgotten that old warehouse block, and I hoped that sometime I might find a way to re-create its heyday. The result is this fictitious railroad, based on shortlines that still serve the Brooklyn waterfront.

WATERFRONT RAILROADING

The map shows where the BERT goes, and you can see how it serves waterfront businesses by distributing and collecting freight cars. Hauled by small dinky and tank engines, cars from the New York Central and its connections move to and from wharfside. Goods of all kinds are gathered for shipment to all parts of a developing America.

The BERT operates car floats too, ferrying cars to and from Manhattan Island for the Pennsylvania RR. Cars also go onto floats for the longer trip to New Jersey and interchange with the Erie RR.

Obviously, switching is the thing here: how to get two cars from point A to point C when point B is already occupied by a capacity string of empties; and

BROOKLYN EAST RIVER TERMINAL RY., CIRCA 1900

esides, point C won't allow both cars with the locomotive; and . . well, you get the picture!

I've included a complete loop to allow continuous running, and assing sidings to permit multitrain operation on the "main line." ong freights can drop strings of cars for the waterfront switchers to eliver. The car float makes a very handy interchange, since you an keep an extra barge or two loaded with additional cars. Grades re minimal, with just enough separation for scenic interest.

MODELING CITYSCAPE

You can tell from my layout plan that I like structures. Upon ntering the room by ducking under (or lifting out) the Old Ferry

Bridge the scene is dominated by the Brooklyn Bridge, with the Empire Warehouses — my memories — at the base of its far pier. The spidery rigging of sailing ships rises pleasantly in front. In my efforts to portray turn-of-the-century waterfront railroading, I scoured old photos and books to capture the look of rails twisting through narrow streets and strung along wooden wharves.

I've identified each of the structures to give you a better idea of the intended atmosphere. Most are kits, but some of the more interesting would be scratchbuilt.

Painted cityscape backdrops would enhance the overall effect. Notice that I've shown a backdrop applied directly to the rear side of the Brooklyn Bridge. This helps to destroy the visual effect of a continuous loop and provides a connection to the outside world for the harbor-bound sailing ships.

I hope you enjoy the BERT. I enjoyed planning it, especially since I was able to include one of my all-time favorite buildings! ✿

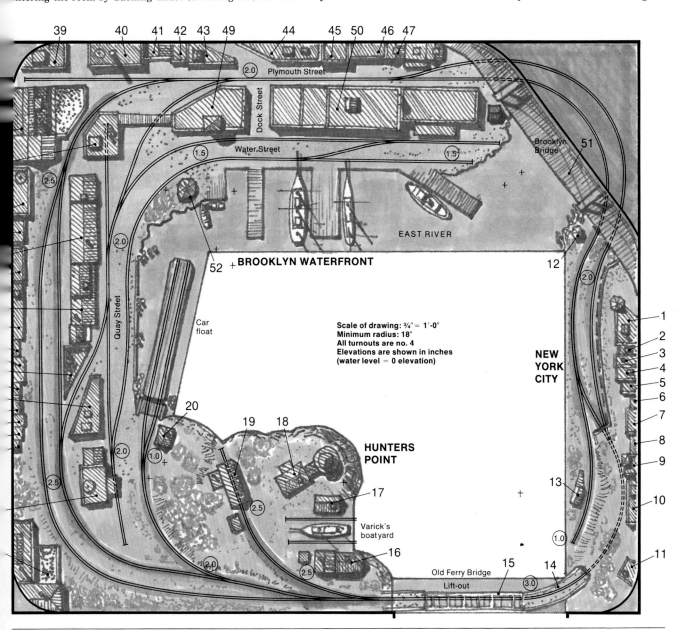

Key to structures

1. Heljan Two Brothers Restaurant, modified
2-5. Magnuson Victoria Street townhouses, front halves
6. Magnuson Don's Shoes, front half
7. Magnuson Gemini Bldg., front half
8. Magnuson Bill's Glass, front half
9. Heljan 1905 firehouse, front half
10. Heljan bank & stores, front half
11. Rear half of 9
12. Switchman's shanty, scratchbuilt
13. Atlas trackside shanty, modified
14. Masonry approaches, scratchbuilt
15. Old Ferry Bridge, Campbell single track truss
16. Campbell Hamilton's Dinghies

17. Campbell ice house
18. Hunters Point lighthouse and Coast Guard station, scratchbuilt
19. Engine shed, coal bin, and water column, all scratchbuilt
20. Float apron and operator's shed, scratchbuilt
21. Heljan brewery bottling plant, modified
22. Magnuson Burndout's Warehouse
23. Sinram Bros. Coal Co., scratchbuilt
24. Junkyard, scratchbuilt
25. Warehouse, modified Tyco freight station
26. Warehouse, Wabash Valley NKP freight house

27-30. Rear halves of 2-5
31. Rear half of 6
32. Rear half of 7
33. Rear half of 8
34. Rear half of 10
35. Magnuson Miners' Union Hall, rear half
36. Magnuson Grain Exchange, rear half
37. Magnuson Victoria Falls Hotel, rear half
38. Campbell talc factory, modified
39. Magnuson Wanglies Dept. Store, rear half
40. Front half of 37

41. Model Masterpieces Cimarron Supply, front half
42. Simms Hardware Co., scratchbuilt
43. Brooklyn Marine Supply Co., scratchbuilt
44. Front half of 39, modified
45. Front half of 36
46. Front half of 35
47. Magnuson Old Wisconsin Brewery
48. Brooklyn Dry Goods warehouse, scratchbuilt
49. Brooklyn Dry Goods, scratchbuilt
50. Empire Warehouses, scratchbuilt
51. Brooklyn Bridge, scratchbuilt!
52. Campbell cafe

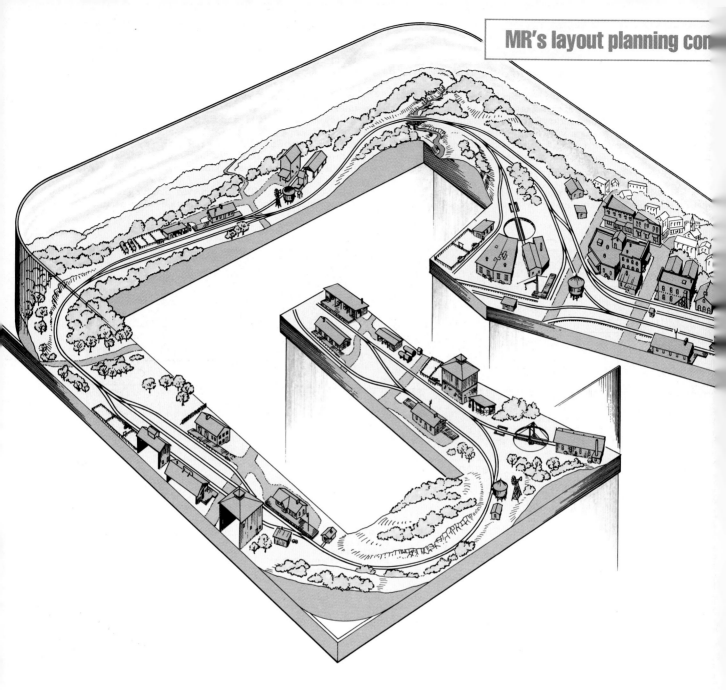

The Bellevue & Cascade RR

A Milwaukee Road branch in HOn3

BY ALBIN L. LEE

THE BELLEVUE & Cascade was a narrow gauge Milwaukee Road branch that ran from Bellevue, Iowa, on the Mississippi River 36 miles westward to Cascade, Iowa. It's a small, 3-foot gauge prototype that is ideal for a 1:87 scale railroad in an 8 x 9-foot room, and for many modelers could be a welcome break from Colorado-inspired HOn3.

I have a long-standing interest in this Iowa narrow-gauger, and my three-part article, "The Bellevue & Cascade Story," appeared in the July/August, September/October, and November/December 1979 issues of the *Narrow Gauge & Short Line Gazette*. I described the prototype and presented drawings and photos of its locomotives, cars, and right-of-way.

If modeling the B&C I would represent it as it was in 1926,

when the line rostered four small but distinctive steam engines:

No. 1, a secondhand 1889 Brooks 2-6-0.

No. 2, the original motive power of B&C predecessor Chicago, Clinton, Dubuque & Minnesota, an 1879 Pittsburgh 4-4-0.

No. 3, a secondhand 1908 Baldwin outside-frame 2-6-0.

No. 4, ex-Denver, South Park & Pacific no. 67, an 1882 Cooke 2-8-0 Consolidation.

Not only are these small engines perfect for a small layout, but the B&C's longest cars, two combines and a coach, were only 40-footers. Most of its freight cars were 24 feet long, the three exceptions being two 30-foot Union Tank Line tank cars and a caboose of the same length.

My B&C layout is a walk-in, point-to-point railroad that could be

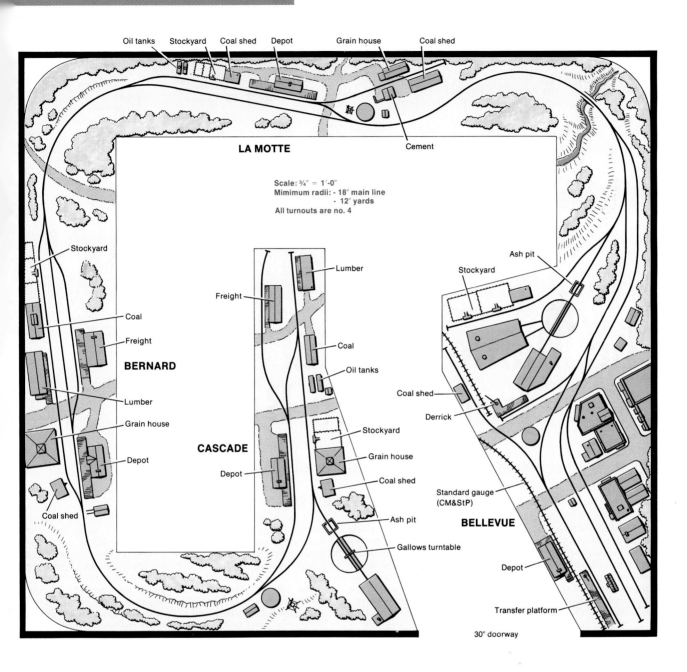

Oil tanks Stockyard Coal shed Depot Grain house Coal shed

LA MOTTE

Cement

Scale: ¾″ = 1′-0″
Mimimum radii: - 18″ main line
- 12″ yards
All turnouts are no. 4

Stockyard

Ash pit

Stockyard

Lumber

Freight

Coal

Freight

BERNARD

Coal

Oil tanks

Coal shed

Derrick

Lumber

Stockyard

Grain house

CASCADE

Depot

Grain house

Coal shed

Depot

Coal shed

Ash pit

Standard gauge
(CM&StP)

BELLEVUE

Gallows turntable

Depot

Transfer platform

30″ doorway

operated by one to four people, though it might be a little crowded with four rotund bodies! There are two narrow spots in the walkways, but I held both to an 18″ minimum. Except for the town of Bellevue, the scenery would be the rolling hills of Iowa with distant farms shown on the backdrop.

While the plan is necessarily a very condensed version of the prototype, I tried to include the essence of the B&C. The layout represents both terminals and, even though compressed, Bellevue and Cascade retain the characteristic track arrangements of the real towns. Naturally I couldn't include all the B&C's stations. I chose La Motte and Bernard because they could be shortened and still retain realistic switching patterns.

Operations might start with engine no. 1 at Cascade switching some freight cars and a combine into the early morning eastbound mixed. At the same time 4-4-0 no. 2 takes the westbound mail, a combine and coach, out of Bellevue. The mixed picks up empties at Bernard and waits for the mail to clear; then both trains proceed to their terminals.

Meanwhile, at Bellevue no. 4 is assembling a freight train with

a caboose to depart when the eastbound mixed arrives. This westbound freight delivers lumber and coal at La Motte, cement and coal at Bernard, and oil at Cascade. At the same time it spots empties on the sidings to be picked up on the return trip.

When the mail arrived at Cascade, no. 2 turned and recoupled to its consist, which then became the eastbound mail train. Heading back to Bellevue, the eastbound mail meets the westbound freight at Bernard. While all this is going on no. 3 puts together two l.c.l. (less-than-carload-lot) merchandise cars and a combine at Bellevue. This is the westbound mixed train, and it will be ready to get out of town as soon as the eastbound mail arrives.

Remember the westbound freight? When it arrived at Cascade, its 2-8-0 turned and delivered its cars. Then it assembled an eastbound freight and waited for the arrival of the westbound mixed.

On the way east the freight will pick up empties left at Bernard and La Motte. Back in Bellevue it will deliver its cars and bed down for the night, completing a day's running for a busy little railroad. To make this narrow gauger really hum, try throwing in some stock or grain extras! ✿

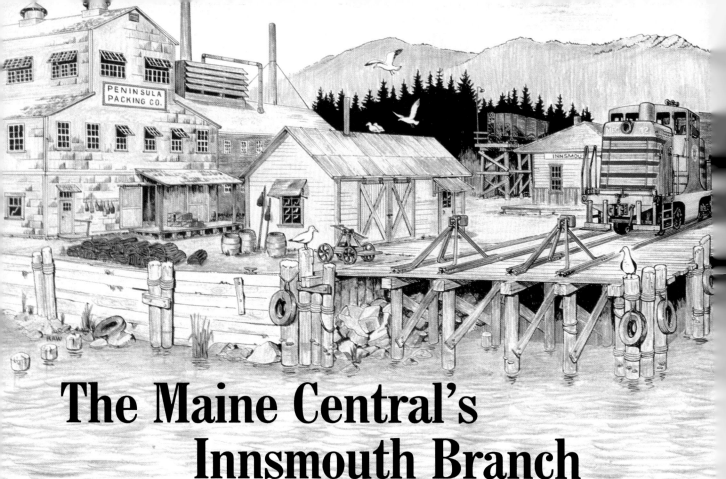

The Maine Central's Innsmouth Branch

Featuring a quarry, a cannery, and Maine's rocky shore

BY TED LEWTAS

WALDENBORO and Innsmouth, Maine, may not really exist, but the Maine Central RR certainly does. Let's imagine it's the late Forties and our fictional Innsmouth branch of the MEC leaves the Rockland line at Waldenboro and runs for a few miles among salt marshes and along granite cliffs to the fishing village of Innsmouth. Halfway along the route is a traprock quarry, the main economic justification for the continued existence of the branch. Most of the quarry's shipments go to the MEC itself for use as ballast. In the village of Innsmouth a small cannery, a lumberyard, and a coal yard provide the balance of the traffic.

The lightly constructed bridge over Innsmouth Narrows limits the branch to only the smallest of locomotives, so one of the Maine Central's newly acquired GE 44-tonners has quickly found a home on the Innsmouth job.

A typical day's operation consists of one or two turns to the quarry, with an additional run to Innsmouth to handle the business there.

DESIGN OBJECTIVES

The objective of my layout design was to provide a modicum of operation amid a realistic setting in a space that is really not very large for HO scale. A theme requiring short locomotives and cars was desirable. Another requirement which I considered extremely important was accessibility: there are no duckunders, and none of the track is more than 2 feet from the edge of the benchwork.

The basic configuration is point-to-point, with the action taking place at three principal locations: the interchange yard at Waldenboro, the quarry, and the industries at Innsmouth (the end of the line). These three locations are visually separated from each other by inlets or salt marshes.

The MEC main line is represented by a short segment of track across one corner of the layout. Hiding the two ends of this track where they run into the walls will be a bit of a scenic challenge.

Most of the structures at Innsmouth are typical New England wooden frame buildings. We'd have a church, town hall, post office, homes, enginehouse, depots (no longer used by passengers in the late Forties), freight houses, and section houses. Our cannery has grown and been added onto over the years, and is now a mixture of brick and wooden buildings cobbled together.

The crushing plant could be of either wood or steel. The quarry itself is represented only by the haul road to the primary crusher, although it would be possible to actually model some portion of the quarry itself in the corner behind the crushing plant.

OPERATION

Although I envision a 44-tonner, an SW7 switch engine could also be used. Rolling stock would consist of six or eight 34-foot hoppers, a few 40-foot boxcars, and a caboose.

An operating session could begin with the sorting of cars left at the interchange yard into cuts of empty hoppers for the quarry and a train for Innsmouth.

All trains would leave Waldenboro with the engine in front. A train going to Innsmouth would reverse direction at Quarry Point, so that the train is pushed into the stub yard in town. Returning from Innsmouth, the engine could use the quarry runaround so as to remain on the head end for the rest of the run back to Waldenboro.

A cut of cars for the quarry would be pushed past the quarry lead, then pulled into the track next to the loading track. The engine would then push the cars under the loading bin two or three at a time. When all of the cars were loaded, the engine would run around, pull the cut clear of the quarry sidings, push them past the "main" switch, then return to Waldenboro on the head end.

Because of the generous aisleways the operator can observe his trains close up and enjoy the nuances of operation, such things as coupler action and wheels riding up over rail joints. In fact, leaving so much room for the operator will make the railroad seem larger, simply because it can be looked at from so many different places. ✿

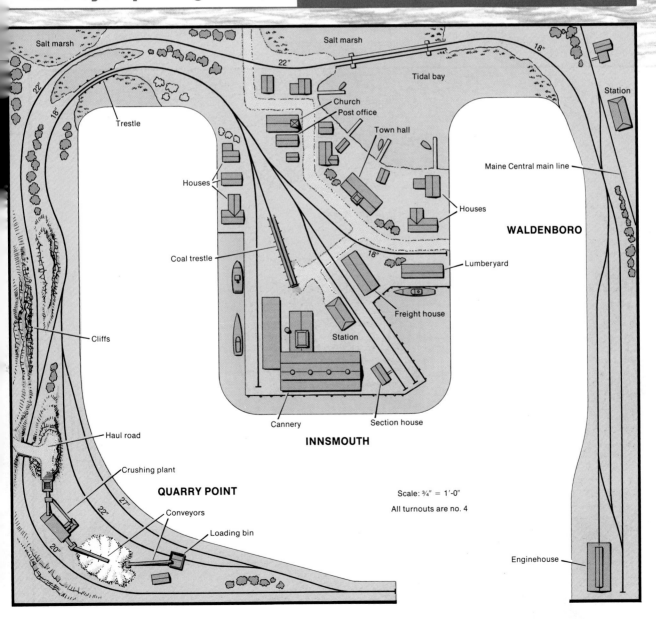

Salt marsh

Salt marsh

22"

18"

Tidal bay

Station

22"

18"

Trestle

Church

Post office

Town hall

Maine Central main line

Houses

Houses

WALDENBORO

Coal trestle

Lumberyard

Freight house

Cliffs

18"

Station

Cannery

Section house

INNSMOUTH

Haul road

Crushing plant

QUARRY POINT

Scale: ¾" = 1'-0"

All turnouts are no. 4

27"

22"

Conveyors

Loading bin

20"

Enginehouse

99

The Vos Mountain RR

BY SILAS KAYLE

WHY design a layout based on the long-vanished Vos Mountain RR? Well, you see, I inherited both my name and my love of railroads from my grandfather. The VM was always his favorite. I still have this report he wrote about her almost 70 years ago.

Date: Oct. 6, 1916
To: Directors, New England Ry. Corp.

In accordance with your instructions I interviewed Mr. Jasper Davidson, president and primary owner of the Vos Mountain RR. The VM is a feeder line with stable freight traffic, six commuter trains on weekdays, lucrative mail contracts, and milk traffic. Biggest shipper is world-famous Vos Mountain Natural Seltzer Water (also a Davidson family enterprise), with its famous slogan, "guaranteed to help you do what needs to be done."

According to Mr. Davidson, no paved automobile roads serve any of the communities on the VML, nor are any planned in the foreseeable future. I inspected the railroad with Paul Davidson, construction superintendent and Jasper's eldest son. I found the right-of-way to be well drained and cleared of brush. All bridges and other structures are in excellent condition.

Jasper's second son, Christopher, is master mechanic; he showed me the railroad's equipment. There are two locomotives: an 0-6-0 stationed at Mackenzie Junction, and a 2-6-0 stationed at Schel. Also rostered are a wooden combine, a coach, a side-door caboose, three Vos Mountain Natural Seltzer Water tank cars, and some maintenance-of-way equipment. I found all of these to be in impeccable condition.

Daniel Davidson, Jasper's youngest son, is vice-president for operations. Mackenzie is the last commuter stop on the NE Ry., but at least one coach a day continues to Schel on the VM, using NE power.

Recommendation: Purchase of the Vos Mountain RR would benefit the New England Ry. with a profitable branch, better utilizing commuter equipment as well as generating needed and steady freight traffic.

Respectfully submitted,
Silas Kayle, special agent

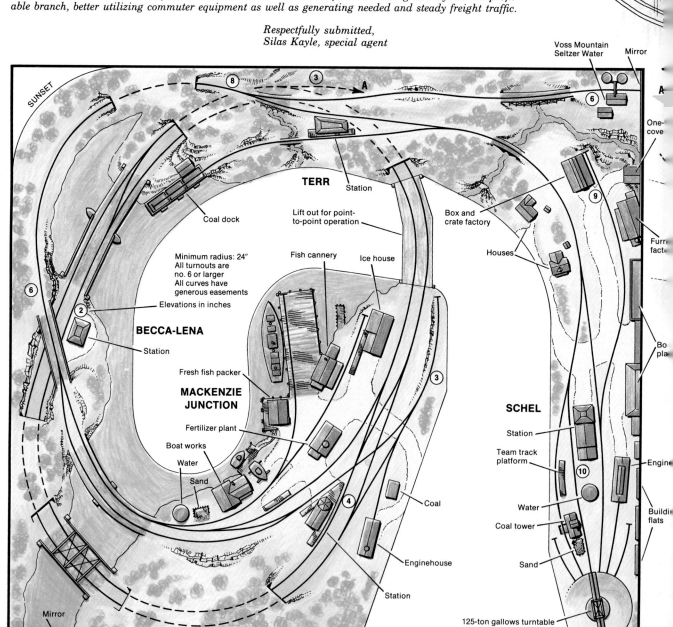

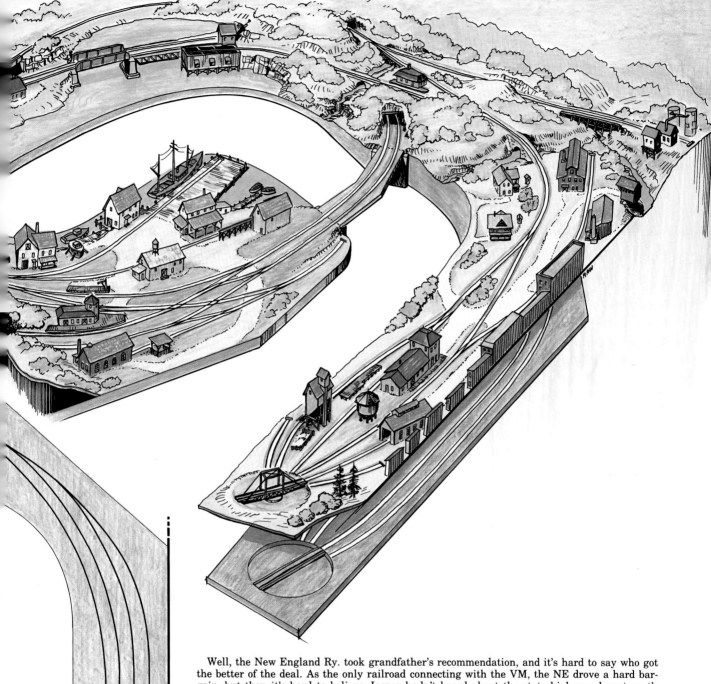

Well, the New England Ry. took grandfather's recommendation, and it's hard to say who got the better of the deal. As the only railroad connecting with the VM, the NE drove a hard bargain, but then it's hard to believe Jasper hadn't heard about the state highway department's plans. By 1920 Highway 13 was already finished and taking a big bite out of the VM's passenger revenue.

A TRACK PLAN FOR THE VM

I set the following criteria for my HO version of the Vos Mountain:
- Walk-in access (the liftout is required only for continuous running).
- Easy access to all turnouts.
- Interchange and hidden storage.
- Good scenic possibilities.
- Good switching possibilities.

Notice that there are really two railroads here, the New England Ry. and the Vos Mountain RR. They interchange at Mackenzie Junction. With the liftout removed, car transfer between lines will take careful coordination.

For those with a John Allen-like flair for the dramatic, I propose mirrors in the two locations shown and a simulated sunset above the high hill in one curved corner. The sunset could be achieved with red-orange lighting controlled by a dimmer switch.

Small though it is, the VM could keep three operators busy. Two tethered throttles anchored under MJ peninsula would allow operators to walk along with their trains and come close to enjoying the VM the way grandfather Silas did. ✿

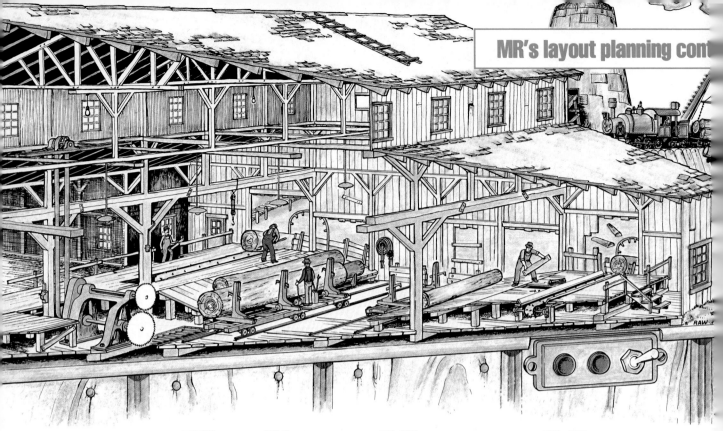

The Sierra Silverton RR

A switchback short line in HO scale

BY ROBERT W. PETHOUD

MY SIERRA Silverton RR plan depicts a mythical short line based on two dissimilar protoypes: the Sierra RR, movie star of California's Gold Rush country, and the Silverton RR of Colorado, a switchback-happy narrow gauger built by Otto Mears. The map shows what's modeled on the HO layout, the rugged country around Angels and Tuolumne that the Sierra Silverton can get through only by switchbacks. These are a bottleneck for a short line serving the booming sawmills and mines of the Sierras, and the reason for the layout's heavy traffic.

OPERATION

Above all, this is a model railroad to be operated. There are industries to switch, trains to meet or pass at Sonora, trains to turn at Angels and Tuolumne, locomotives to service at Angels, and more trains always emerging from the hidden storage tracks.

Those storage tracks represent the unmodeled portions of the SS main extending west from Tuolumne and east from Angels. A train sent to Oakdale from Tuolumne will wait on one of the tracks and appear later as another westbound arriving at Angels from Silverton. By the time this trickery occurs, several other trains will have been handled and we can assume that a viewer won't remember that he's seen the same consist before.

Stored trains line up one behind the other, up to three on each track. Each track contains three short, electrically isolated stopping sections controlled by on-off switches. The storage tracks are wired as single electrical blocks, but the stopping sections let you stop trains within the blocks.

Imagine a train about to enter the empty staging yard. You flip on all of the stopping-section switches except for the one at the forward end of the track. The train runs along the track until it stops at this dead section. Next you turn off the second stopping section, behind the train. This protects the first train and automatically stops the next one to enter the second of the three storage positions.

To pull the first train out of the staging yard, flip its switch on and apply power to the staging-track block. Any other locomotives on the track are sitting on dead sections, so only the first train pulls forward. After the first train has left, you can move the second train up to first position by flipping the first switch off and the second one on, and so on. Operating these hidden tracks can be nearly automatic, but a further refinement would be to place optical detectors between the rails to warn of trains longer than storage sections, stalled engines, or other problems.

TRACK, SCENERY, AND BUILDINGS

The Sierra Silverton can be built in either standard or narrow gauge. Of course, the 18″-radius curves would be easier on narrow gauge equipment. On the other hand in standard gauge all of the turnouts can be Atlas Custom Line no. 4s (actually 4½s), except for the four in the wye at Tuolumne. The wye needs some special trackwork to save space — see the detail drawing.

Small as it is, the Sierra Silverton can be made to look spacious with nearly vertical scenery. Tall pine trees, sheer rock faces, and terrain extending well below and above the track would all contribute to this effect.

Close clearances and things that appear to interfere with the tracks are points of scenic interest. Structures that extend over the track, loading docks, narrow rock cuts, through bridges, and grade crossings — both road and railroad — are good examples of this, and I've included all of them in the SS plan. Notice especially the covered walkway and sawdust conveyor over the tracks at Tuolumne, spurs entering open-sided buildings at Tuolumne and Sonora, and the oil loading trestle at Sonora.

The hidden staging tracks pass through the freight house and planing mill at Sonora. The places where the tracks enter these buildings will have to be concealed, perhaps behind clumps of trees.

Two structures will almost immediately arrest the visitor's attention: the turntable on trestlework at Angels and Tuolumne's imposing sawmill. Only part of the mill would be modeled, as if it were cut open diagonally. When you enter the room you'd see two exterior walls of what would look like a complete building. A walk around the room to Sonora would reveal the ruse: from the other side you'd be looking into the interior, complete with as much sawmill machinery and power transmission equipment as any modeler would care to create. ⚓

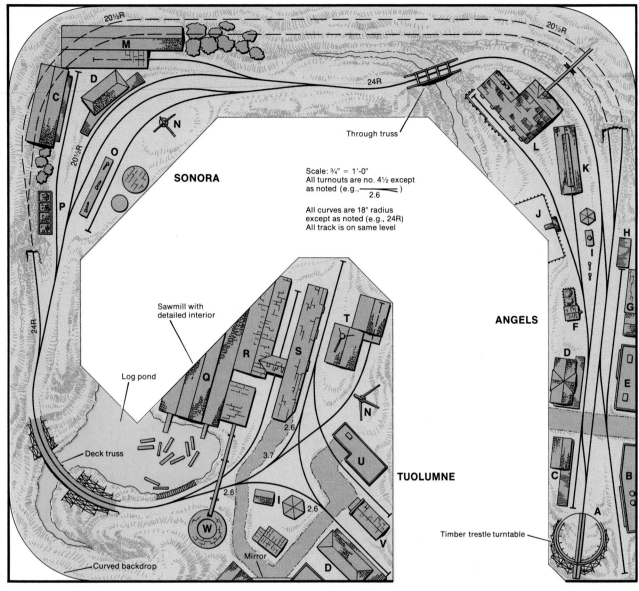

20½R

M

D

C

N

O

20½R

P

SONORA

24R

24R

Through truss

Scale: ¾" = 1'-0"
All turnouts are no. 4½ except
as noted (e.g., ————)
2.6

All curves are 18" radius
except as noted (e.g., 24R)
All track is on same level

L

K

J

H

ANGELS

G

F

D

E

C

B

A

Sawmill with
detailed interior

T

R S

N

Log pond

Q

2.6

3.7

U

TUOLUMNE

Deck truss

2.6

I

2.6

V

W

Mirror

D

Curved backdrop

Timber trestle turntable

STRUCTURES

A Trestlework turntable
B Foundry
C Freight house
D Depot
E Produce warehouse
F Sand
G Lumber dealer
H Ramp
I Oil and water
J Cattle pen
K Enginehouse
L Ore concentrator with
   aerial tramway
M Planing mill
N Crane
O Oil dealer
P Limestone
Q Sawmill
R Green sorter
S Storage shed and kiln
T Box factory
U Transfer warehouse
V General store
W Sawdust burner

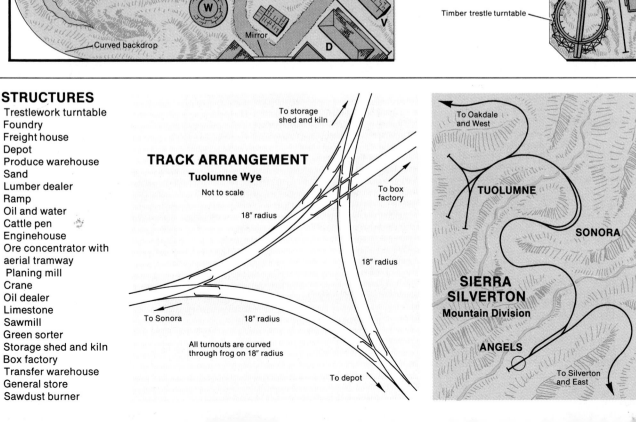

To storage
shed and kiln

TRACK ARRANGEMENT
Tuolumne Wye
Not to scale

To box
factory

18" radius

18" radius

To Sonora   18" radius

All turnouts are curved
through frog on 18" radius

To depot

To Oakdale
and West

TUOLUMNE

SONORA

SIERRA
SILVERTON
Mountain Division

ANGELS

To Silverton
and East

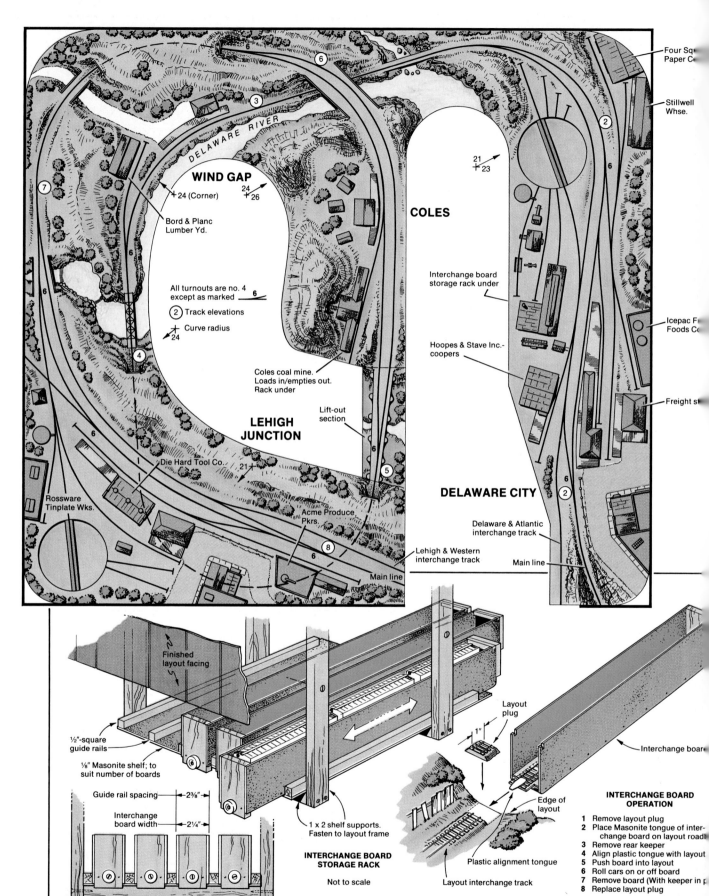

WIND GAP

+24 (Corner)

24
+26

Bord & Planc
Lumber Yd.

All turnouts are no. 4
except as marked   6

② Track elevations

+ Curve radius
24

Coles coal mine.
Loads in/empties out.
Rack under

Lift-out
section

**LEHIGH
JUNCTION**

Die Hard Tool Co.

21

Rossware
Tinplate Wks.

Acme Produce
Pkrs.

6

8

Main line

COLES

21
+23

Interchange board
storage rack under

Hoopes & Stave Inc.-
coopers

DELAWARE CITY

Delaware & Atlantic
interchange track

Lehigh & Western
interchange track

Main line

Four Sq
Paper C

Stillwell
Whse.

2

6

Icepac F
Foods C

Freight s

6
2

DELAWARE RIVER

Finished
layout facing

½"-square
guide rails

⅛" Masonite shelf; to
suit number of boards

Guide rail spacing ── 2⅜"

Interchange
board width ── 2¼"

1 x 2 shelf supports.
Fasten to layout frame

**INTERCHANGE BOARD
STORAGE RACK**

Not to scale

Layout
plug

1"

Interchange boar

Edge of
layout

Plastic alignment tongue

Layout interchange track

**INTERCHANGE BOARD
OPERATION**

1 Remove layout plug
2 Place Masonite tongue of interchange board on layout road
3 Remove rear keeper
4 Align plastic tongue with layout
5 Push board into layout
6 Roll cars on or off board
7 Remove board (With keeper in p
8 Replace layout plug

The Delaware & Lehigh RR

An HO line with working interchanges

BY BOB LUTZ

THE Delaware & Lehigh RR is a small point-to-point system carrying a light but steady bridge traffic. It demonstrates a practical method for actually moving cars off the railroad, rather than just simulating interchange. I've imagined that the prototype D&L was built to carry traffic from the Delaware & Atlantic RR over the hills to the Lehigh Western Ry. These connections, each as fictitious as the D&L itself, are heavy trunk lines.

The locale is the Delaware River Valley between New Jersey and Pennsylvania, and though I've taken considerable license with geography and place names, it captures the spirit of the area. The D&A corresponds to the real Pennsy at Trenton, N. J., and the LW Ry. to the Lehigh Valley at Easton, Penn. These prototypes are very large and the Delaware River is quite wide, hence the fictional license to fit them all into a small space.

I chose a point-to-point schematic as most representative of the D&L's purpose. It also requires a lot of switching at the terminals, which compensates for the short runs over the 46-foot main line. All the turnouts are well within arm's reach and can be manually operated. The two 12″ turntables could also be manual, geared to small cranks in the layout face. I decided that I could tolerate the narrow aisles and the liftout section to achieve the many operational features this little hill country railroad has to offer.

As in the real Delaware River Valley, the scenery would be mainly trees on rolling green hills. I would set the 0″ base elevation — water level — at 48″ above the floor to provide a better side view of the trains. Some structures could be stock kits, but most would have to be kitbashed or scratchbuilt as they are only false fronts (and backs) against the backdrop.

The time is late 1950s/early 1960s, with the little D&L still using steam power and earning a modest profit. The road buys used engines and cars and shops them itself, as new equipment would break the budget. The Bachmann Reading 2-8-0 with its wide Wooten firebox would be a good freight engine for a touch of local color.

The company-owned Coles Coal Mine is the D&L's major revenue source, but there are nine other small industries. All of these receive or ship via the two interchanges. Through or "bridge" traffic, interchange to interchange, is also important.

The industry sidings and the two interchange tracks have a total capacity of 28 40-foot cars. Still, I'd operate the D&L with no more than 18 cars on line at a time. This would leave room to maneuver, and after all, industry sidings on the prototype are never all full at the same time.

INTERCHANGE BOARDS

Interchange becomes a reality at Delaware City and Lehigh Jct. with the use of a simple gadget which I call an "interchange board." This idea can be used in any scale, wherever an interchange track runs to the edge of the layout. The drawing shows how I'd make the interchange board. Various materials could be used, and though it could be longer, as shown it holds three 50-foot cars. Don't make it too long — you might drop an armful of cars!

To use it, plug the interchange board into the layout as in the application drawing. Hold the board with one hand while you roll cars onto the board with the other. Remove the board to a storage shelf and interchange is a reality. Next time pick another board and the inbound cars won't be the same ones that went out.

The interchange board is a fiddle yard without turnouts or multiple tracks, and it gives you a way to use a lot of rolling stock without having too many cars on the track at one time. Make as many boards as you need, but always keep at least two empty.

The mine uses interchange boards too, for loads-out/empties-in operation. There could be 12 hoppers, 6 always loaded and 6 identical cars always empty. Four 3-car boards would let you rotate the loaded and empty hoppers on and off the layout.

All coal would be shipped off line, and after the D&L delivers loaded hoppers from mine to interchange, you'd roll the loads onto the board. Empty hoppers would be moved in reverse order: board to interchange, road freight to mine, and mine to board.

While freight is the D&L's lifeblood, I like to think that a railroad represents people going places. D&L operations can include a modest but frequent scheduled passenger service, with a combine-and-coach local and a gas-electric mail and express run. All in all, there's a fair amount of traffic to keep this small railroad busy. ♢

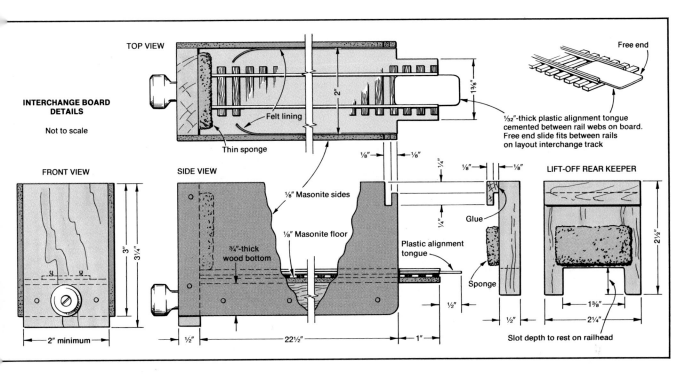

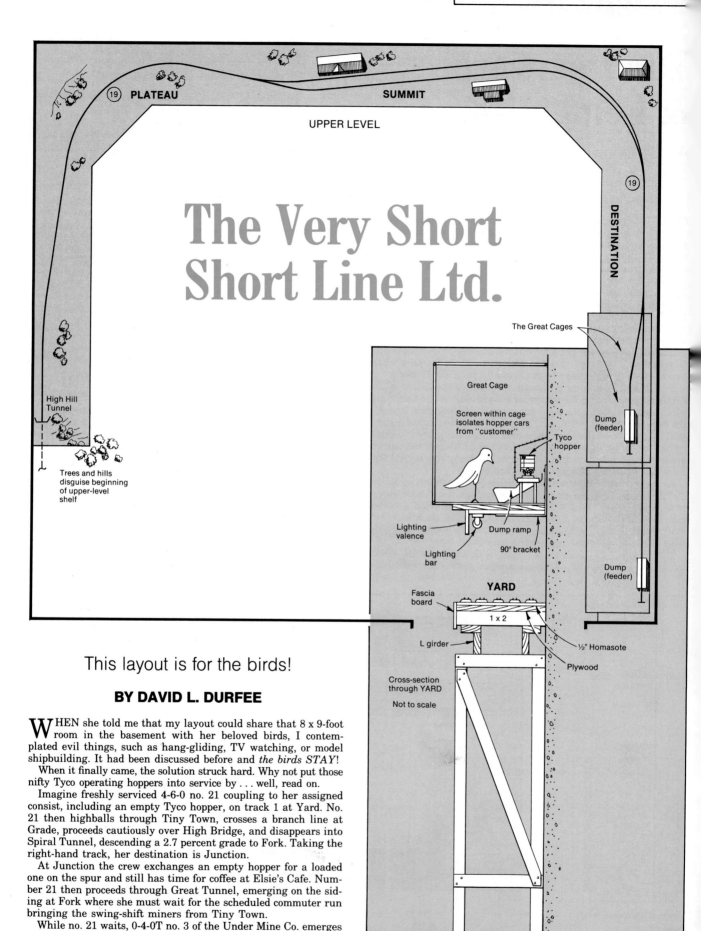

The Very Short
Short Line Ltd.

This layout is for the birds!

BY DAVID L. DURFEE

WHEN she told me that my layout could share that 8 x 9-foot room in the basement with her beloved birds, I contemplated evil things, such as hang-gliding, TV watching, or model shipbuilding. It had been discussed before and *the birds STAY*!

When it finally came, the solution struck hard. Why not put those nifty Tyco operating hoppers into service by . . . well, read on.

Imagine freshly serviced 4-6-0 no. 21 coupling to her assigned consist, including an empty Tyco hopper, on track 1 at Yard. No. 21 then highballs through Tiny Town, crosses a branch line at Grade, proceeds cautiously over High Bridge, and disappears into Spiral Tunnel, descending a 2.7 percent grade to Fork. Taking the right-hand track, her destination is Junction.

At Junction the crew exchanges an empty hopper for a loaded one on the spur and still has time for coffee at Elsie's Cafe. Number 21 then proceeds through Great Tunnel, emerging on the siding at Fork where she must wait for the scheduled commuter run bringing the swing-shift miners from Tiny Town.

While no. 21 waits, 0-4-0T no. 3 of the Under Mine Co. emerges

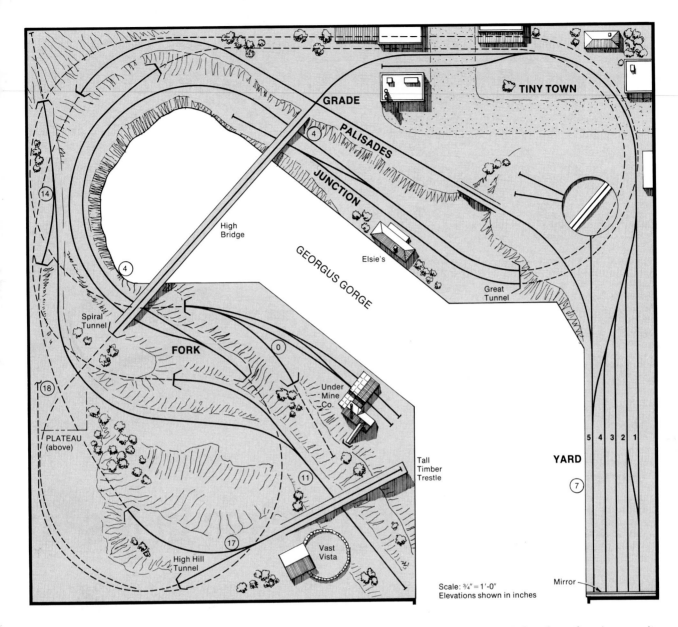

from Great Tunnel on the outside track, pushing a loaded hopper and pulling a short, dumpy coach for the arriving miners. After the commuter stops in Junction it pulls into Great Tunnel to hold out of sight, leaving the main line available for switching chores. Soon no. 3 is backing away with the empty hopper and loaded combine. Inside the tunnel they descend the 2.5 percent grade to Under Mine's tipple.

Meanwhile, ol' no. 21 arrives back at Yard, leaving her train for the switcher to sort while she escapes on track 2 to the round-house. There's priority freight in the yard now, and the goat promptly spots the loaded hopper ahead of a combine on track 5. This short train is now ready for Heisler no. 9, the power for the Birdland Branch.

Track 5 is exactly equal to the length of the branch's switchback leads so that train lengths do not exceed track capacities in the mountains. The geared locomotive couples on boiler-end-to, then pulls cab-forward out of Yard, past the turntable and along the Palisades, headed for the crossing at Grade and the hills beyond.

The 4 percent grades are tough, but no problem for the power-ful Heisler. Number 9 pulls, pushes, tugs, and shoves her consist ever higher through the switchbacks. The mountains border on the surrealistic since they follow no known geographical proto-type on this planet.

A scheduled stop with the engine precariously perched at the

end of Tall Timber Trestle, some 95 feet above the mine, permits tourists riding in the combine to visit Vast Vista Lookout and photograph the GIANT OPERATORS wallowing and wheezing in Georgus Gorge. The gawkers are horrified to see one of the giants grab ol' no. 9, turn it over, and poke at its wheels, much to the glee of the other. He then carefully returns it to the trestle.

Excitement over, no. 9 resumes pushing the train up into High Hill Tunnel and onward to Plateau, which is an entirely different world. Devoid of rugged terrain, Plateau is flat with a few trees and shrubs along the way to Summit. All model railroads have a Summit somewhere, and this is where the combine is sidelined while the loaded hopper is pushed on to Destination, site of the Great Cages.

Loaded hoppers must be brought to the Cages daily. There they are spotted over cam tracks which cause the hopper doors to open and dump payloads of, you guessed it, birdseed into the feeder troughs. This is much to the liking of Tweetsie and Parry Keet, who have been watching the railroad's operations with intense interest.

Although tiny, the Very Short Short Line Ltd., features out-and-back mainline operation from a busy terminus, while the two branch lines are mutually dependent on the main for traffic. And of course, there is a realistic sense of purpose to this road's oper-ations. The twittering of hungry birds demands daily train ser-vice, to the delight of the model railroader. ✿

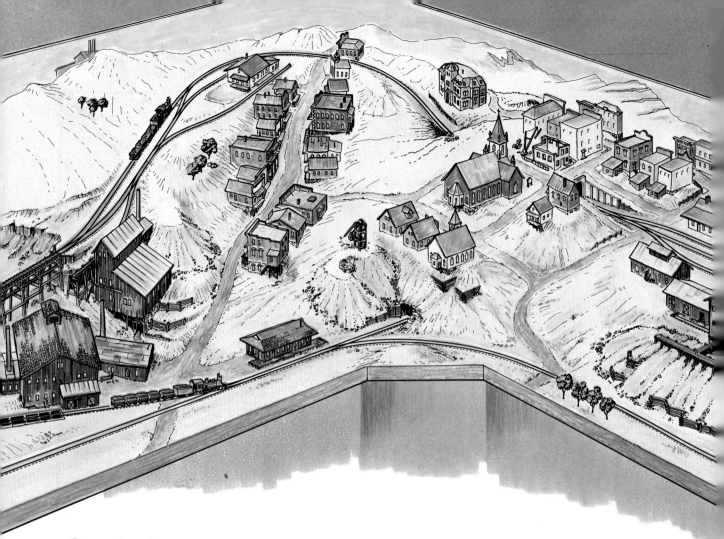

Our winning layout plan

The Virginia & Truckee in N scale

An N scale layout set in 1876
and the days of the Comstock Lode

BY STEVE RIDDLEBAUGH

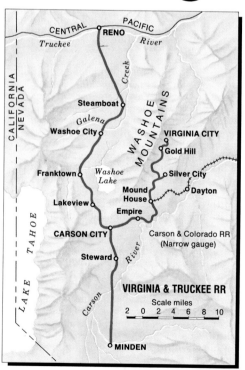

ONE of the richest strikes of all time was the Comstock Lode, discovered in 1859 by a group of ex-Forty-niners panning for booze money. They were so intent on finding gold that they ignored the "damned blue sand" that kept clogging their rockers. Finally some suspicious visitors had the blue sand assayed. It tested out at 3000 ounces of silver and 60 ounces of gold per ton!

The original discoverers sold out for the proverbial song. One was Henry Comstock, for whom the Lode was named, and another was his drinking buddy, James "Old Virginia" Finney, who lent his nickname to the mining camp that rose on the northern end of the Lode, Virginia City.

The logistics of supplying the mines and people that were soon working the Comstock Lode added up to a titanic transportation problem. The two Comstock Lode towns of Gold Hill and Virginia City had a population total of about 25,000 in the 1870s, making them one of the major urban centers west of the Mississippi River.

The Comstock was rich, but very expensive to work, with the result that the mines were actually rather risky ventures. By the late 1860s The Bank of California had invested in and foreclosed on enough mines and mills to control the Comstock. Three of the bank's wheels, William Sharon, Darius Ogden Mills, and William Ralston, decided to do something about the transportation problem choking the mining district. That something was the Virginia & Truckee RR.

During the Comstock's heyday, the V&T's three main cargoes were timber

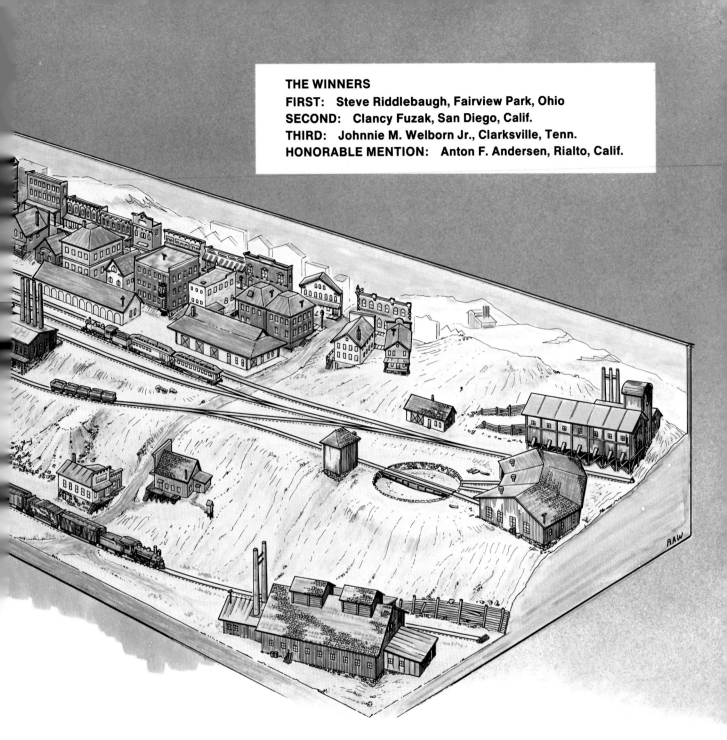

and cordwood in, ore out. The wood was cut along the eastern front of the Sierra Nevada and floated to the vicinity of Carson City and Washoe Lake in flumes. It was an easy way to ship lumber, but they couldn't get the water to flow uphill from Carson to Virginia, so the last leg of the trip had to be completed by train.

THE LAYOUT PLAN

I'm hardly the first person to suggest that the Virginia & Truckee is an ideal prototype for a model railroad, but I may be the first to propose an N scale version set in 1876. But why not? Bachmann has done a nice job of solving the motive power and rolling stock problem, and there are sufficient scratchbuilding supplies on the market to make the biggest problem one of finding sufficient time.

MEET OUR WINNER

STEVE RIDDLEBAUGH's HO home layout is an East Broad Top triple-decker. A photo appeared in Trackside Photos in the April 1981 issue.

Steve is 38, an aerospace engineer, and works for NASA. He and his wife Mary Jane have two children, John, age 4, and Susan, age 1. His interests include bicycling, music, player pianos, tinplate, Erector sets, and science fiction.

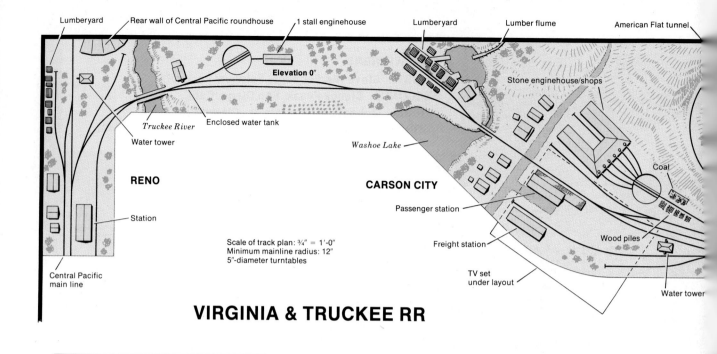

Lumberyard — Rear wall of Central Pacific roundhouse — 1 stall enginehouse — Lumberyard — Lumber flume — American Flat tunnel

Elevation 0"

Truckee River — Enclosed water tank

Water tower

Stone enginehouse/shops

Washoe Lake

RENO

Coal

Station

CARSON CITY

Scale of track plan: ¾" = 1'-0"
Minimum mainline radius: 12"
5"-diameter turntables

Passenger station

Central Pacific
main line

Freight station

Wood piles

TV set
under layout

Water tower

VIRGINIA & TRUCKEE RR

JUDGES' COMMENTARY

OUR FIRST PLACE railroad shows a strong sense of purpose, of trains progressing from one place to another. The layout is attractive from all viewing angles, with a good variety of interesting scenes. The amount of track is not excessive. The period setting and mining theme give the layout an interesting and somewhat unusual character. This should be an interesting layout to operate with plenty of switching as well as through-freights to run.

The layout's flowing, irregular shape fits well into the room and poses no barriers to other family activities. The layout would be easy to build, and construction would not put the room out of commission for other activities. Trains could be running in a short time, but the structures and other details might easily occupy the builder for years.

The five towns included on the layout plan were easily the most important points on the early V&T. Reno was the tie-in with the transcontinental railroad. Carson City was the headquarters city and home to the main shops, the head office, and the mint. Empire, which was just east of Carson City, was the site of many of the early ore-reduction mills. And Gold Hill and Virginia City sat atop the Lode. Most traffic was between Carson City and Virginia City, with relatively little out to Reno. Except for Empire, all of the trackage I show in these towns is condensed from what was actually there.

Much has been written about the Comstock Lode and the V&T, and photos of most of the buildings identified on the plan are included in readily obtainable sources. Many of the old buildings are still standing. *Silver Short Line* by Ted Wurm and Harre Demoro (Trans-Anglo Books, 1983) is the most comprehensive single source. *Steamcars to the Comstock* (Howell-North, 1957) is another good source, but Beebe and Clegg never did let the facts get in the way of a good yarn, so this book has to be carefully interpreted. *The Miners* volume from the Time-Life series on the old west is also a good reference. The *Narrow Gauge and Shortline Gazette* has published a lot of V&T data in recent months.

Model 4-4-0s are notoriously poor in tractive effort, so I made the railroad dead level, except for the stretch between Empire station and the Crown Point trestle. Here the grade is 3 percent, the gentlest I could find in the area and still gain sufficient altitude for the Virginia City area to look reasonably mountainous. A single-loop helix is hidden under the hill.

Most model railroads attempt to separate their towns with scenic barriers; this plan runs Empire, Gold Hill, and Virginia City together into one single scene. Gold Hill and Virginia City *did* run together in real life. Visually, Empire represents some lower-level trackage that did exist at Virginia; operationally, it's many miles away. The late great John Allen did the same thing in the Port/Great Divide area of his fabled Gorre & Daphetid.

All I did to condense the Gold Hill/Virginia City trackage was eliminate the mile or so of prototype trackage between tunnel no. 3 in Gold Hill and tunnel no. 6 in Virginia City (also known as the E Street Tunnel). Unfortunately, the Virginia City roundhouse and turntable were located in the eliminated section, so I relocated them next to the Virginia City freight house. This plan is for a true point-to-point layout, and those cowcatcher pilots make turntables an absolute necessity.

The buildings in Virginia City were jammed together like sampans in Hong Kong harbor. Malcolm Furlow's town of Sheridan, described in the July 1981 MR, would be a good guide to follow, but remember the railroad and the towns were brand spanking new and very prosperous in 1876. Weathering and decrepitude à la Furlow might be quaintly attractive, but it would be historically incorrect.

EQUIPMENT

You could cut two of Bachmann's old-time combines apart and rejoin the halves to make a full baggage and a coach. Rapido also makes a suitable combine and coach. The early V&T hauled ore in small four-wheel jimmies. They resembled a box atop a Bachmann passenger truck, and that's how I'd build them in permanently coupled blocks of ten.

Another source of freight cars should be the Nn3 cars announced by Kadee. Fitted with standard gauge trucks, they should scale out close to the standard gauge dimensions of a century ago. For closer-to-scale appearance I would equip the rolling stock with Kadee Z scale or Nn3 couplers, even though 1876 actually puts us in the link-and-pin era.

Some details remain to be worked out — that's part of the fun of building a layout — but I think this plan provides a good start for anyone interested in recreating a colorful chapter in American railroading and western history. ✿

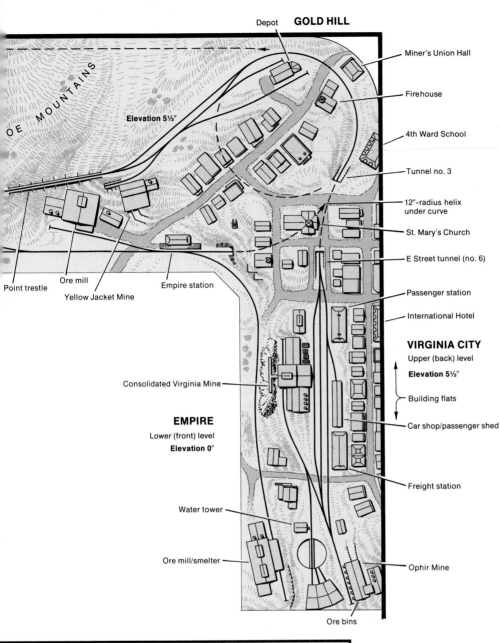

GOLD HILL

Depot

Miner's Union Hall

Firehouse

4th Ward School

Tunnel no. 3

12"-radius helix
under curve

St. Mary's Church

E Street tunnel (no. 6)

Passenger station

International Hotel

VIRGINIA CITY
Upper (back) level
Elevation 5½"

Building flats

Car shop/passenger shed

Freight station

Ophir Mine

TAHOE MOUNTAINS

Elevation 5½"

Point trestle

Ore mill

Yellow Jacket Mine

Empire station

Consolidated Virginia Mine

EMPIRE
Lower (front) level
Elevation 0"

Water tower

Ore mill/smelter

Ore bins

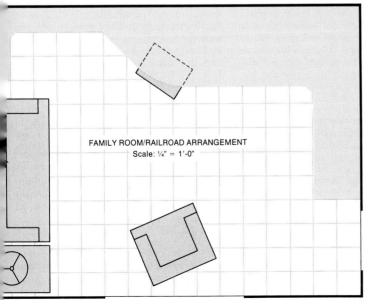

FAMILY ROOM/RAILROAD ARRANGEMENT
Scale: ¼" = 1'-0"

The Santa Fe Silsb

This buildable layout won thirc
prize and $150 for a teenager in ou
1983 layout planning contes

BY JOHNNIE M. WELBORN JR.

READY for today's trivia question? Where can you (or could you at one time) find the Santa Fe, Southern Pacific, Missouri Pacific/Burlington Northern, Kansas City Southern, and Rock Island all within the same general region? The answer is southeast Texas in and around the Beaumont area.

On my N scale layout plan I have attempted to portray this area of southeast Texas, which is basically a flat coastal plain. When you travel northward from Beaumont, the land begins to rise, but on the layout the rise will be minimal.

The layout should be built approximately chest high to allow the best viewing and the most practical use of the space under the layout. This should allow plenty of room for the portable television underneath it. Since the layout is no more than a couple of feet deep in most places (excluding Beaumont), there shouldn't be a problem with reaching the back edge.

To cope with the problem of access to the hidden tracks behind Beaumont, an opening should be left in the backdrop, and there should also be an opening in the rear base of the backdrop next to the hidden tracks.

Some of the major design criteria for the Silsbee District were:

• A scenically pure long main line (each scene being separated from all other scenes so that trains do not recross the same area).

• Realistic operation.

• Plenty of switching possibilities.

• A fairly accurate depiction of the area around my birthplace in Beaumont; in other words, I wanted to re-create what I remember as being distinct about the area.

I believe these criteria have been sufficiently met in my layout plan. There would be plenty of switching activity around the Beaumont yard and your basic run-of-the-mill way-freight switching in the various towns along the line. The layout allows for the possibility of expansion (most likely at Silsbee or from past the Espee crossing in Beaumont).

You're probably asking yourself "What in the world is the time period?" Since the earliest I can remember any equipment from is the early 1970s, I would model the modern to present era. Footboards and roofwalks would be gone, and if you're a careful observer you might see a CF7 or two (F7s converted into hood units).

The layout is basically point-to-point and would be operated accordingly. Turning facilities weren't provided at Silsbee because the majority of the trains would be double-headed. If the width of the layout were expanded a few inches, a turntable could be added for the purpose of turning single locomotives.

Most of the layout is pretty much freelanced. Beaumont has become the southern end point of the district instead of Seabreeze. Also, the Southern Pacific crossing has been moved from Kountze to Silsbee, and Voth (and several other points) has not been modeled. The industries may or may not match those that are in the towns modeled.

Now you should be ready to drag out the tools and wood to start construction of the Silsbee District of the AT&SF. ☼

KCS-SP interchange
tracks

Passenger yard

Backdrop

Office

Station

SP

Tower 38 (SP)

Crane

Concrete wharf

PORT OF
BEAUMONT

Waycars

Locomotive service

Rock and
gravel supplier

Shanties

strict in N scale

BEAUMONT

Electronics plant

Feed mill

Portable TV
under layout

SP interchange
25° crossing

SANTA FE JCT.

SP

VOTH

Oil pump

LOEB JCT.

Oil pump

Village Creek

Southern Pacific

LUMBERTON

Bulk oil loading

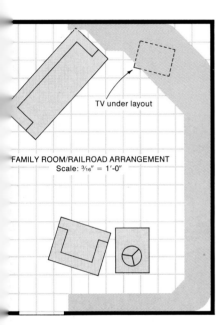

TV under layout

FAMILY ROOM/RAILROAD ARRANGEMENT
Scale: ³⁄₁₆″ = 1′-0″

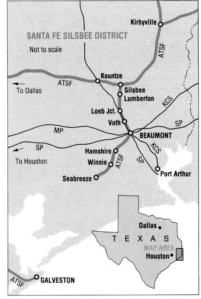

Turntable could go here

Team dock

SILSBEE

Logging camp
(loads in - empties out)

SP interchange

Highway

Station

Backdrop

SANTA FE SILSBEE DISTRICT

Scale of track plan: ½″ = 1′-0″
Minimum radius, visible track: 18″
Minimum radius, hidden track: 14″
All turnouts are no. 6

The Western Pacific in N scale

The Feather River Canyon is featured
on this Honorable Mention layout planning contest winner

BY ANTON F. ANDERSEN

MENTION the Western Pacific and most people think of Keddie Wye and the Feather River Canyon. Few people realize the line also has Williams Loop, where the railroad crosses over itself, and that Keddie Yard is one of the most suitable yards anywhere for model railroad purposes. My goal was to include all of these features in a mixed period (1940s to 1960s) N scale railroad.

The layout, as you can see, is planned for three levels. The upper level would be at eye level for a person my height — 6'-3". You could lower the railroad, but I recommend using one or two rollaround kitchen steps instead.

The lower level of the layout represents the Feather River Canyon. I thought it important to include the three river crossings. Intake Bridge, the newest bridge, was built in the 1960s when the line was shifted to higher ground above the reservoir to be created behind the Oroville Dam. The intake near the bridge served a powerhouse now underwater.

The Poe powerhouse is representative of those in the canyon. The water for the turbines is diverted several miles upstream and arrives by tunnel.

Don Kaplan photo

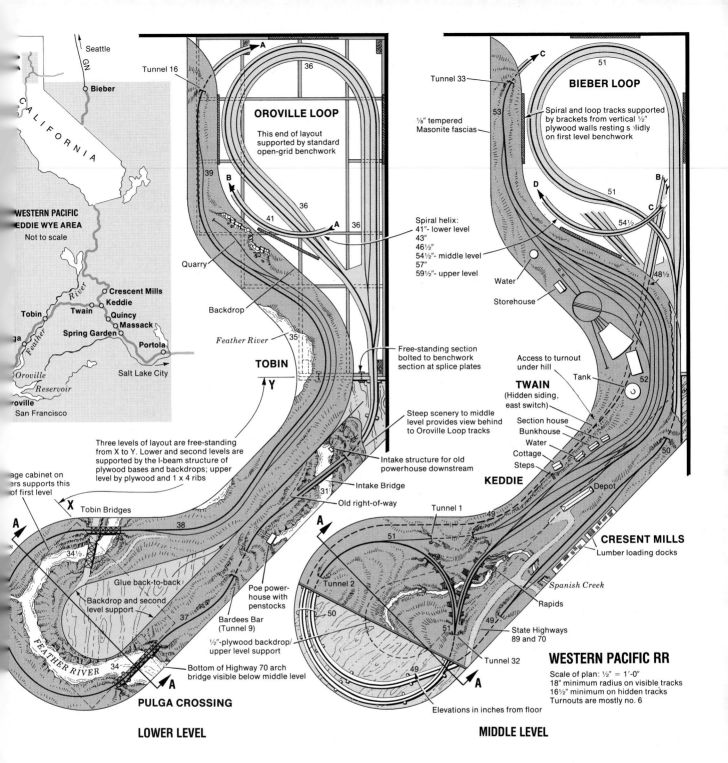

WESTERN PACIFIC
KEDDIE WYE AREA
Not to scale

California map showing: Seattle, Bieber, Crescent Mills, Keddie, Tobin, Twain, Quincy, Massack, Spring Garden, Portola, Salt Lake City, San Francisco, Oroville Reservoir, Feather River

Tunnel 16

OROVILLE LOOP

This end of layout supported by standard open-grid benchwork

36

39
B
36
41
36
A
36

Quarry

Backdrop

Feather River

35

TOBIN

Y

Free-standing section bolted to benchwork section at splice plates

Steep scenery to middle level provides view behind to Oroville Loop tracks

Intake structure for old powerhouse downstream

Intake Bridge

31 Old right-of-way

Three levels of layout are free-standing from X to Y. Lower and second levels are supported by the I-beam structure of plywood bases and backdrops; upper level by plywood and 1 x 4 ribs

cabinet on
rs supports this
of first level

X

Tobin Bridges

A

34½

Glue back-to-back

Backdrop and second level support

38

37

Poe power-house with penstocks

Bardees Bar (Tunnel 9)

½"-plywood backdrop/ upper level support

FEATHER RIVER 34

Bottom of Highway 70 arch bridge visible below middle level

A

PULGA CROSSING

LOWER LEVEL

Tunnel 33

⅛" tempered Masonite fascias

BIEBER LOOP

51

53

Spiral and loop tracks supported by brackets from vertical ½" plywood walls resting solidly on first level benchwork

C
D
51
B
Y
C
54½
48½

Spiral helix:
41"- lower level
43"
46½"- middle level
57"
59½"- upper level

Water

Storehouse

Access to turnout under hill

Tank

52

TWAIN
(Hidden siding, east switch)

Section house
Bunkhouse
Water
Cottage
Steps

50

KEDDIE

Depot

49

Tunnel 1

51

CRESENT MILLS

Lumber loading docks

Spanish Creek

Tunnel 2

50

Rapids

49

State Highways 89 and 70

51

49

Tunnel 32

49

A

Elevations in inches from floor

MIDDLE LEVEL

WESTERN PACIFIC RR

Scale of plan: ½" = 1'-0"
18" minimum radius on visible tracks
16½" minimum on hidden tracks
Turnouts are mostly no. 6

Pulga Crossing has the State Highway 70 bridge crossing high over the railroad truss bridges.

Diving into tunnel no. 16 we start up the helix to the middle level. Trains can lay over on the hidden siding to mark time and create the illusion of traveling a great distance.

The middle level starts with the track emerging from tunnel no. 32 and going out onto the Keddie Wye trestle. This scene is possible because the canyon can dip down into the hole created by the lower-level backdrop. (See the cross-section drawing.)

The main line takes the wye's right leg to Keddie, enters tunnel no. 33, and climbs to the upper level. As before, a hidden layover siding is provided.

Trains taking the left leg of the wye end up on the Bieber line and proceed past the two sawmills at Crescent Mills before reaching a hidden two-track reverse loop.

Trains first appear on the upper level at the high steel trestle, a scene made possible by using the space behind the Keddie Wye backdrop to gain the depth for a canyon. The line proceeds

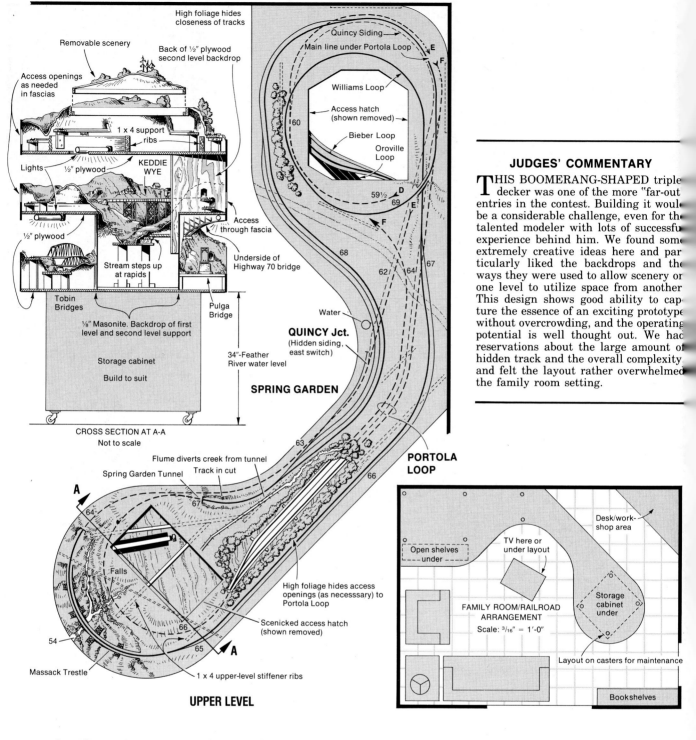

CROSS SECTION AT A-A
Not to scale

UPPER LEVEL

THIS BOOMERANG-SHAPED triple decker was one of the more "far-out" entries in the contest. Building it would be a considerable challenge, even for the talented modeler with lots of successful experience behind him. We found some extremely creative ideas here and particularly liked the backdrops and the ways they were used to allow scenery on one level to utilize space from another. This design shows good ability to capture the essence of an exciting prototype without overcrowding, and the operating potential is well thought out. We had reservations about the large amount of hidden track and the overall complexity, and felt the layout rather overwhelmed the family room setting.

past the siding at Massack, around Williams Loop, and into Spring Garden.

At Spring Garden the line leaves the watershed of the North Fork of the Feather River and passes through 1½-mile-long Spring Garden tunnel to the Middle Fork. The tunnel entrance at Spring Garden is protected from a creek by a flume that diverts the water away. The line ends at the Portola loop. The lead to the loop is accessible through an opening in the scenery hidden by thick trees and shrubs.

OPERATION

The railroad, when stretched out, is a single-track line with six sidings. (The first yard track at Keddie is a controlled siding.) The sidings are 10 feet long, providing for 25- to 30-car trains pulled by 3 or 4 engines.

You'd need the following trains for full operation:
- 1 *Zephyr*: 3 or 4 engines, 10 to 12 passenger cars.
- 1 *Zephyrette*: single RDC combine.

- 3 or 4 freights: 25 to 30 cars, one to be a solid reefer block.
- 1 Bieber pool through-freight: mixed WP; Great Northern; or Spokane, Portland & Seattle locomotives, 25 cars.
- 1 Bieber mixed local: 2 units, 10 cars, rider coach or drover-style caboose.
- 1 mainline local: 2 units, 10 cars.

Mainline freights would set out blocks of cars at Spring Garden, Keddie, or Tobin to be worked by the locals or picked up by other freights. The Bieber pool works Oroville to Bieber, occasionally setting out or picking up at Keddie. A helper at Keddie is required to protect the Bieber Line.

Motive power would be primarily F units and Geeps with m.u.'ed switch engines for the locals. Steam power used would be 2-8-0s or 2-8-2s for the locals with 2-8-8-2s for some freights or the Bieber pool. Any of the three could protect the helper pool.

By now you've probably gotten the message — lots and lots of railroading in a small space! ☼

The Northwestern Pacific in N scale

This triple-decker won second place and $300
in our 1983 layout planning contest

BY CLANCY FUZAK

A N N SCALE LAYOUT for the family room — now there was an intriguing challenge, and the 50-square-foot maximum was close to something I might actually be able to negotiate someday. But N scale? That means contemporary railroading doesn't it? My personal favorite, the 3-foot-gauge North Pacific Coast at the turn-of-the-century seemed out of the question. But what about the railroad the NPC eventually became part of — the Northwestern Pacific?

Northern California railroading was considerably consolidated with the formation of the Northwestern Pacific in 1907 under joint Southern Pacific and Santa Fe ownership. By that time my favorite North Pacific Coast had already become the North Shore, introducing efficient out-side third rail (actually fourth rail, since the line was dual gauge) electric commuting to Marin County. The North Shore in turn became part of the NWP.

On the three levels of my layout plan I've included three distinctive areas of the NWP as they were in 1919. These areas are indicated on the prototype map. I had my reasons for the choice of date. Prohibition wouldn't go into effect until January 1920, and I wanted to generate traffic from the Korbel Winery and a typical hop kiln. A major fire in September of 1923 virtually eliminated the Russian River lumber industry, which I also wanted to include.

World War I was over and normal traffic was the order of the day. Finally, and most important, I wanted to model the steam era and also represent the massive commuter traffic as it was in the days before the Golden Gate Bridge.

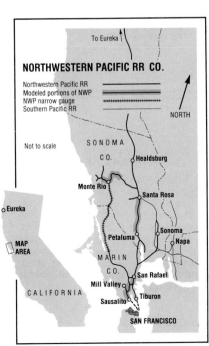

NORTHWESTERN PACIFIC RR CO.

Northwestern Pacific RR
Modeled portions of NWP
NWP narrow gauge
Southern Pacific RR

NORTH

Not to scale

To Eureka

SONOMA CO.

Healdsburg

Monte Rio

Santa Rosa

Eureka

Sonoma

Petaluma

Napa

MAP AREA

MARIN CO.

CALIFORNIA

San Rafael

Mill Valley

Sausalito

Tiburon

SAN FRANCISCO

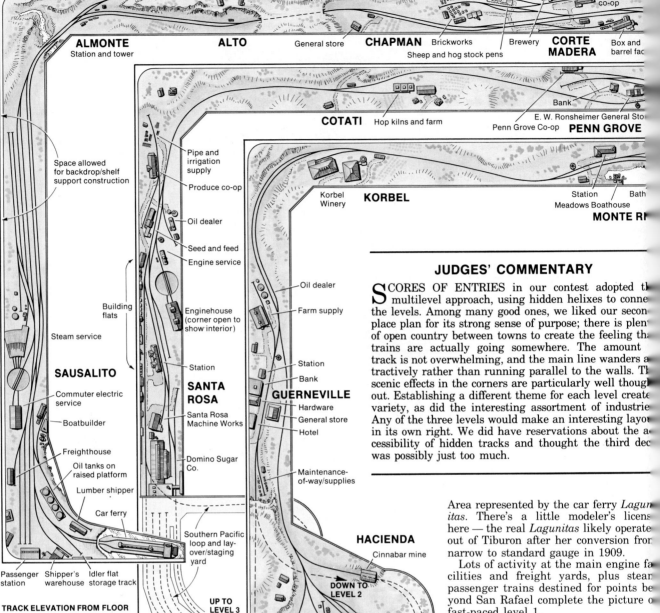

ALMONTE Station and tower

ALTO

General store

CHAPMAN Brickworks

Sheep and hog stock pens

Brewery

CORTE MADERA

Produce co-op

Box and barrel fac

COTATI Hop kilns and farm

Bank

E. W. Ronsheimer General Stor

Penn Grove Co-op

PENN GROVE

Space allowed for backdrop/shelf support construction

Pipe and irrigation supply

Produce co-op

Oil dealer

Seed and feed

Engine service

KORBEL Korbel Winery

Oil dealer

Farm supply

Station

Meadows Boathouse

MONTE RI

Building flats

Steam service

Enginehouse (corner open to show interior)

Station

SAUSALITO

Commuter electric service

Boatbuilder

Freighthouse

Oil tanks on raised platform

Lumber shipper

Car ferry

Passenger station

Shipper's warehouse

Idler flat storage track

SANTA ROSA

Santa Rosa Machine Works

Domino Sugar Co.

Station

Bank

GUERNEVILLE

Hardware

General store

Hotel

Maintenance-of-way/supplies

Southern Pacific loop and lay-over/staging yard

UP TO LEVEL 3

HACIENDA

Cinnabar mine

DOWN TO LEVEL 2

Oil

Station

Reduction works

TRACK ELEVATION FROM FLOOR
FIRST LEVEL: 38"
SECOND LEVEL: 52½"
THIRD LEVEL: 70"

NORTHWESTERN PACIFIC RR

Scale of track plan: ½" = 1'-0"
Minimum main line radius: 16"
Turnouts are no. 4 or 5

JUDGES' COMMENTARY

SCORES OF ENTRIES in our contest adopted th multilevel approach, using hidden helixes to conne the levels. Among many good ones, we liked our secon place plan for its strong sense of purpose; there is plen of open country between towns to create the feeling tha trains are actually going somewhere. The amount track is not overwhelming, and the main line wanders a tractively rather than running parallel to the walls. Th scenic effects in the corners are particularly well thoug out. Establishing a different theme for each level creat variety, as did the interesting assortment of industrie Any of the three levels would make an interesting layo in its own right. We did have reservations about the a cessibility of hidden tracks and thought the third dec was possibly just too much.

Area represented by the car ferry *Lagun itas*. There's a little modeler's licens here — the real *Lagunitas* likely operate out of Tiburon after her conversion fror narrow to standard gauge in 1909.

Lots of activity at the main engine fa cilities and freight yards, plus stear passenger trains destined for points be yond San Rafael complete the picture o fast-paced level 1.

LEVEL 2

Level 2 features the NWP main lin between Petaluma and Santa Rosa. The electrics have been left behind, and oil burning Americans and Ten-Wheeler handle the traffic. Passenger traffic i still important, but local farming anc ranching keep way freights busy as wel Interchange with the SP is included a Santa Rosa.

This interchange is no dummy. Espec mixed trains actually would roll in from the hidden staging area and exchange both freight and passengers with the NWP. The SP would use NWP facilitie to turn, water, and fuel its engines.

The Domino Sugar complex at Santa Rosa is an artifice to conceal the end of the SP loop and hide the holes where both railroads penetrate the backdrop. I've laid out the trees, buildings, and track arrangements so as to block casual views of these penetrations. Obviously the Domino siding isn't intended for re ceiving trainloads of sugar beets, but it

THE LAYOUT ROOM

I chose a bookshelf-style layout to allow maximum floor space in the room for other activities. The space under the lay-out on each end wall could be used for storage. A secretary-type chair should be available for the Sausalito operator, as the lower deck is too low to operate com-fortably while standing. Four single-step platforms should also be available for the third-level operators.

LEVEL 1

Each of the levels of the NWP empha-sizes a different type of operation. The

lowest level features commuter service. San Francisco, as it still is today, was the focus of the Bay Area's economy.

Level 1 would feature one- to four-car electrics making runs to the Sausalito ferry landing over several routes. The passenger ferry boats are waiting just beyond the passenger station and off the layout. Fast-clock, timetable operation would keep the crews hopping during the morning and evening rushes. Half-hour headways were the norm, 20 min-utes not uncommon.

There'd be plenty of freight operation too, with the main freight connection to San Francisco and the rest of the Bay

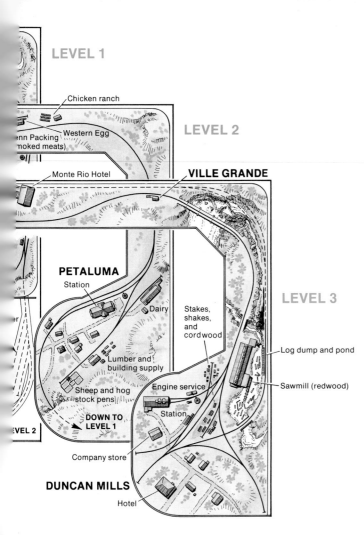

LEVEL 1

Chicken ranch

Western Egg

nn Packing
noked meats)

Monte Rio Hotel

LEVEL 2

VILLE GRANDE

PETALUMA

Station

Dairy

Stakes,
shakes,
and
cordwood

LEVEL 3

Log dump and pond

Sawmill (redwood)

Lumber and
building supply

Sheep and hog
stock pens

Engine service

Station

EVEL 2

DOWN TO
LEVEL 1

Company store

DUNCAN MILLS

Hotel

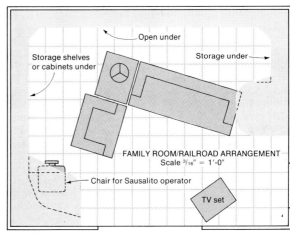

Open under

Storage shelves
or cabinets under

Storage under

FAMILY ROOM/RAILROAD ARRANGEMENT
Scale 3/16" = 1'-0"

Chair for Sausalito operator

TV set

uld receive supplies or ship boxcar
ads of sugar.

LEVEL 3

Level 3 depicts the Guerneville Branch
long the Russian River between Korbel
elocated on the track plan west of
uerneville) and Duncan Mills. Here
e magnificent redwood country draws
ordes of summer tourists, keeping the
assenger runs full.

Freight revenues are high too — on
he model NWP there's still plenty of
edwood for the Duncan Mills Land &
umber Co. Right now they're cutting
outh of Monte Rio, down on the branch
hich in reality was 3-foot gauge and
riginally built by the North Pacific
oast. Loaded log cars from the branch
ome on stage through the tunnel under
he Monte Rio hotel, and they're really
he same loaded cars that were earlier
elivered to Duncan Mills for dumping
nto the log pond. The hidden connecting
racks give us loads-in, empties-out op-
ration at the lumber mill and the oppo-
ite at the Monte Rio siding.

Three-hundred-foot redwoods are a bit
versized for a model railroad, but the
ookshelf concept can help. At least one
r two large trees on the grounds of the
Monte Rio Hotel might have survived
he loggers' axes. Because you'd be look-
ng up at it, a forced-perspective redwood would look pretty convincing on
level 3.

The level 3 cinnabar (mercury ore)
mine and reduction works at Hacienda
are borrowed from the real New Almaden
complex of the South Pacific Coast Ry.
The justification is simple: I like mining!

The mine and reduction works are connected by hidden tracks to make another
loads-in, empties-out operation. Eight-car
trains of empties enter the mine and proceed around on the hidden loop to Guerneville. From there they supposedly will
head east to another mine, but in fact
they turn up at Hacienda again. Loads
are delivered to the reduction works, and
empties are picked up there. Since mercury is shipped in compact (but heavy)
flasks in baggage cars, the daily mixed
train readily handles the plant's output.

STRUCTURES AND ROLLING STOCK

Any attempt to model a specific prototype and period requires lots of scratchin'
and bashin'. The more authentic you
want to be, the more effort it'll take. A
few key structures would set the scene
for the NWP, but beyond that it's up to
individual taste. I've largely free-lanced
both the track plan and the industries.

The key NWP structures are the car
ferry *Lagunitas*, the Sausalito passenger
terminal, and the Korbel Winery on
level 1, the Petaluma and Santa Rosa
stations and a typical hop kiln on level
2, and the Monte Rio Hotel on level 3.
These would have to be scratchbuilt,
since appropriate kits aren't available.

Motive power is perhaps the biggest
problem to be overcome. An 0-6-0 for the
Sausalito yard is easy enough, but suitable Americans and Ten-Wheelers aren't
available. A bit of bashing could come
close enough, though. Since many of the
electrics were converted passenger cars,
this is the route to follow. The Joe
Works Shay could be put to work hauling cinnabar or redwood logs.

Finding prototype information will call
for some research, and I've included a list
of references with the plan. I think those
who give it a try will find that learning
about a favorite railroad can be just as
much fun as modeling it. ◊

References:
● *The Northwestern Pacific Railroad*
by Fred A. Stindt and Guy L. Dunscomb
(1964), published by the authors
● *Interurban Railways of the Bay Area*
by Paul C. Trimble (1977), Valley
Publishers
● *South Pacific Coast* by Bruce A. Mac-
Gregor (1968), Howell-North, (for infor-
mation on Hacienda reduction works)
● *NMRA Bulletin* articles on NWP
motive power by Amos R. Tinkey
● *Electric Railway Pioneer* by Harre
W. Demoro (1983), Interurban Press
● *Narrow Gauge to the Redwoods* by
A. Bray Dickinson (1967), Trans-Anglo
Books
● *Redwood Railways* by Gilbert H.
Kneiss (1956), Howell-North

Index